A SKETCH MAP HISTORY OF EAST AFRICA

New enlarged edition

by
J. C. SSEKAMWA, M.A., Dip. Ed. (E.A.)
Senior Lecturer in Education, Makerere University

HULTON EDUCATIONAL PUBLICATIONS LTD

© J. C. SSEKAMWA 1971

ISBN 0 7175 0757 2

First published 1971 by Hulton Educational Publications Ltd,
Raans Road, Amersham, Bucks.

Reprinted 1973

Reprinted 1974

Reprinted 1976

Printed in Great Britain by
Biddles Ltd, Guildford, Surrey

Preface

Historians can only give the most important facts in any period and they are bound to leave aside many lesser events that helped to bring about changes. In the same way they can only mention a handful of the leaders and those nearest to them. They say nothing of the millions of ordinary men and women who gave their work and loyalty. I therefore dedicate this book to those unnamed people who contributed so greatly to East Africa's history.

My sincere gratitude goes to Dr. J. B. Webster, late Professor of History, Department of History, Makerere University who encouraged me to write this text book and patiently and assiduously read my manuscript.

J. C. Ssekamwa

Acknowlegements
The author wishes to thank the following for their assistance:
Maurice I. Makatiani, B.Ed. Hons., Academic Dip. Ed. (London) and Sam Jombwe for research and origination of maps and diagrams; also E. W. J. Bateman and Cartographic Enterprises; Dr. Muhammad Iqbal, M.Sc., M. Phil. for additional material on Islam in East Africa; S. M. E. Lugumba, M.A., Dip.Ed. for information on East African railways.

Contents

1 Geography and its Influence on East African History

East Africa covers 1 670 000 square kilometres. The Indian Ocean on its eastern side forms a natural boundary; to the west it borders on Congo Kinshasa (Zaire), Rwanda and Burundi, and to the north on the Somali Republic, the Sudan Republic and Ethiopia. In the south Zambia, Malawi and Mozambique are its boundaries.

The region is broadly divided into three main climatic and vegetation zones. The first zone includes two areas, the Coastal Strip along the shores of the Indian Ocean and the Lake Victoria region where the climate is semi-tropical and humid, with plenty of rain. Because of the climate, the forests and good soil, the people have tended to live in settled farming communities.

The second zone is called the Central Plateau. It stretches across central Uganda, and covers the central region of Tanzania and Kenya. This zone is dry and in the old days it hindered human travel because it was difficult to cross. It later became inhabited by pastoral people who kept on moving in search of water and grass.

The third natural zone is the semi-temperate mountain region where the climate is cooler and healthier. It includes the highlands of Kenya and Tanganyika. In Uganda, the highlands are in Kigezi, on the slopes of Mt Ruwenzori and the western slopes of Mt Elgon. Generally, the mountain regions are heavily populated.

East Africa is a region of large lakes. With the exception of Lake Victoria, the largest in East Africa lie in two long chains, one in the Eastern Rift Valley and the other in the Western Rift Valley. Those in the Western Rift Valley are Lake Albert, Lake Edward, Lake Kivu and Lake Tanganyika; those in the Eastern Rift Valley are Lake Rudolf, Lake Baringo, Lake Natron, Lake Eyasi, Lake Manyara, Lake Rukwa and Lake Naivasha. The area between Lakes Kyoga, Albert, Edward, Victoria and Tanganyika is known as the interlacustrine region, meaning the area among the lakes. Because of the special political development which took place in this area,

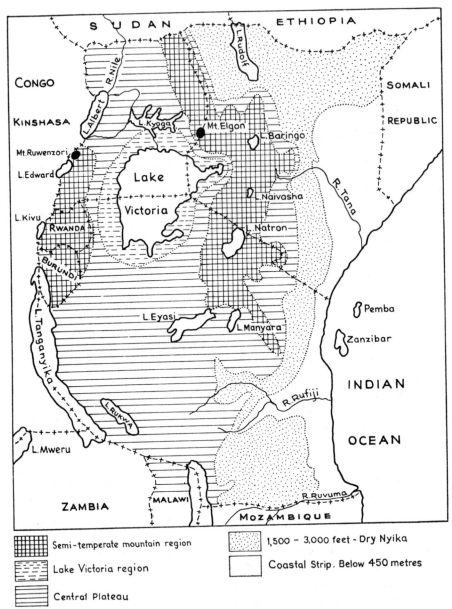

Climatic and vegetation zones

Note : *Lake Albert became Lake Mobutu in 1974*
Lake Edward is now Lake Idi Amin Dada

the interlacustrine region forms an important historical sub-region of East Africa.

The Uganda area of East Africa is drained by the Nile which originates in Lake Victoria, flows north to Lake Kyoga, west to Lake Albert and again north towards the Sudan and Egypt. Most of the rivers of Kenya and Tanzania – the Lukonya, Pangani, Ruvuma, Rufiji and the Tana – flow eastward into the Indian Ocean. Although the rivers and lakes did provide a means of internal communication, they were more limited than usual in this regard. Few of the rivers were navigable for long distances and then only in the wet season. They could not be relied upon as highways between the interior and the coast.

In ancient times East Africa produced valuable materials for trade, such as tortoiseshell, gum copal, ivory and for a long time the gold from Zimbabwe (Rhodesia) was exported from the East African coast. These commodities attracted Greek, Roman, Arab and Persian traders to the coast. From the seventh century Arabs from both Oman and Shiraz on the Persian Gulf settled on the East African coast where they built cities and introduced the Islamic religion and customs.

However, the penetration of the interior from the coast was not made until the nineteenth century. Nor did many people from the interior make the journey to the coast before the eighteenth century. Goods arrived at the coast by a system of barter from one person to another. The absence of direct contact between the east coast and the interior was due to several isolating factors, including the dry infertile region immediately behind the coastal strip, the steep escarpments of the eastern and western valleys, the lack of navigable rivers and diseases such as sleeping sickness from the tsetse fly and malarial fever from the mosquito.

2 The Peoples of East Africa

The broad division of the peoples of East Africa into ethnic groups is based on 'language families'. Within each of these, however, there may be numerous linguistic differences found among groups classified as 'tribes' for want of a more suitable term. Different customs may also exist. Larger ethnic groups may number between one and three million and the smaller consist of only a few thousands. Undoubtedly the Bantu is the largest of the five main ethnic groups. The present distribution of the groups has resulted from a series of migrations dating back many hundreds of years.

The Bantu Family of Languages

The Bantu peoples live in a large area of East, Central and South Africa. They speak languages which are related in grammar and in vocabulary but which are not necessarily understandable between one group and another. Thus there are numerous languages within the Bantu language family. In the interlacustrine region from the Bahaya in northern Tanzania to the Basoga in eastern Uganda, people speak what might be called various dialects of one language since they can all understand each other, sometimes with ease, sometimes with difficulty. The Baganda and the Banyarwanda are the two largest groups in this interlacustrine area, which also includes the Banyoro, the Banyankole, the Bakiga and other smaller groups. Three examples of Bantu-speaking peoples in Tanzania are the Nyamwezi, the Sukuma and Chagga, and in Kenya, the Kikuyu, Wakamba and Baluya, each of these speaking distinct languages.

The Nilotic Family of Languages

The Nilotic family of languages is often divided into three sections:

10

the Kalenjin section among people of the Kenyan highlands; the Nilotics represented by the Masai of Central Kenya and Tanzania, and the Karamojong, and Iteso of North-Eastern Uganda and North-Western Kenya. The third section is represented by the Luo-speaking peoples, the Acholi and Langi of Northern Uganda and the Luo of Western Kenya. The Iteso and Karamojong can understand each other's languages and the Luo-speakers are also able to understand each other with varying degrees of difficulty.

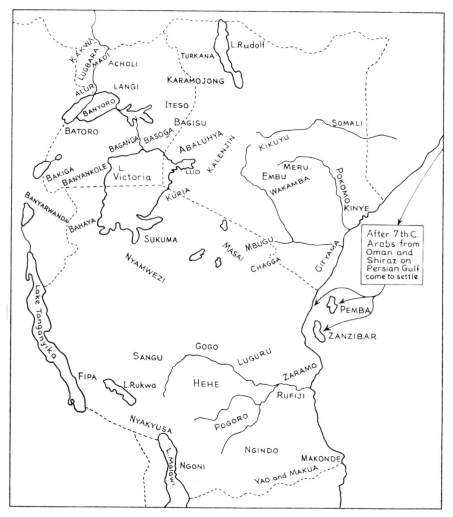

The Peoples of East Africa

The Cushitic Family of Languages

People speaking these languages are found in North-Eastern Kenya – the Somalis and the Turkana in the north, the Mbugu in Usambara, the Kinye of the Lower Tana and the Iraqw in North Central Tanzania.

The Arabic and Kiswahili Languages

As long ago as the first century A.D., traders from Arabia and Persia were in contact with the East African Coast. Some of them settled permanently on the coast, either because they wanted to start new homes or because they were unhappy with the political situation at home. From the seventh century more Arabs from Oman and Shiraz on the Persian Gulf came to settle on the coast to avoid further troubles resulting from religious and political disagreements. The Arabs retained the Arabic language and formed large communities in the coastal towns where many of them intermarried with the Africans. In the nineteenth century, there was an influx of Omani Arabs, due to Sultan Seyyid Said's settling in Zanzibar from 1840, because he came with many of his supporters; and there were other Omani Arabs who looked on Zanzibar as a new place with plenty of opportunities for becoming rich.

As a result of intermarriage between Arabs and the Africans there came into being a people called Swahilis or Afro-Arabs. However, those coastal Africans who spoke Kiswahili and professed Islam were referred to as Swahilis, even though they did not have mixed blood. This fusion created a new culture and a new language, called Kiswahili, which combined the grammatical structure of Bantu with many Arabic words. Kiswahili is an African and not an Asian language and spread widely in East Africa and parts of Central Africa, where it is used as a language of long distance trade and a means of communication among people of varied vernaculars. Kiswahili ultimately became the national language of Tanzania, and Kenya and Uganda have adopted it as such.

Asian Languages; Gujarati and Hindu

Asians migrated from Asia to East Africa in the nineteenth century, coming as financiers to Sultan Seyyid Said. Immigration increased tremendously during the colonial period. Asians were first brought in by the British Government as labourers to help build the railway from Mombasa to Kampala when construction began in 1896. When the railway reached Kisumu in 1901 the building stopped for a time. It was resumed later and the line reached Kampala in 1931. Most of the Asians who had come from India as workers on the construction of the railway did not return to India; instead they took to establishing trading stores along the railway and in the countryside of East Africa. Meanwhile other Asians interested in trade and not connected with the building of the railway were coming in mostly from India. They began to set up business stores in all parts of East Africa. The policy of the British Government from 1900 was to encourage Asians to trade while the Africans grew crops which they sold to the Asians. As a result of this policy many Asians migrated to East Africa throughout the colonial period and, owing to their propensity for having large families, there was also a tremendous increase in their numbers.

European Languages

The British migrated from Europe towards the end of the nineteenth century. Some came as traders and farmers, others as missionaries and the rest as political administrators. To the above group were added British settlers mostly in Kenya, starting from 1903. But their number up to the period of independence in 1960 did not increase as much as that of the Asians, being at that time about 50 000. Those British people engaged in trade were few in number as commerce was, on the whole, concentrated in the hands of the Asians.

The English language became widespread all over East Africa and is now used as a medium of instruction especially in secondary schools.

Other European languages that have found their place in East Africa as a result of European connections with this area are Portuguese, French and German. Portuguese was never spoken by the people when the Portuguese came to East Africa from 1498 until 1688 as there was no attempt to teach it. Many French and French Canadian missionaries came to teach during the colonial period, but they had to use the English language and spoke French only among themselves. It is only during the independence period that attempts have been made to teach French in schools with the long-term aim of having easy communication with African French speakers.

The German language might have had an influence almost as great as English if history had not decided otherwise. The Germans came to Tanganyika from 1886 and extended their sphere of influence over Rwanda and Burundi and all this area formed what was called up to 1918 German East Africa. From the very beginning the Germans took an active part in giving education to the people within this area and they taught them both Kiswahili and the German language. But their influence stopped with the end of the First World War; Tanganyika was given to Britain for supervision and Rwanda and Burundi to Belgium by the League of Nations which later became the United Nations Organization. As a result, English was taught in Tanganyika and French in the rest of the former German East Africa.

3 The Kingdoms of Lake Victoria (or the Interlacustrine Kingdoms) 1250-1650

The Lake Victoria or Interlacustrine Kingdoms flourished in Southern Uganda and Western Tanzania. Their origins are wrapped in mystery and their founders are now represented as gods or demi-gods. The early period of their history is often referred to as the rule of the gods or the period of mythology.

Bunyoro-Kitara

The earliest of these kingdoms was Bunyoro-Kitara, possibly founded towards the end of the thirteenth century.

The period of mythology in this kingdom is called the reign of the Batembuzi. This period lasted for about five reigns roughly from 1250 to 1325 and it was succeeded by the rule of the Bachwezi under Ndahura. The Bachwezi evolved a centralized monarchy which had representatives in different districts and provinces. As a result of this system they administered a large empire which included Buganda, Karagwe, Toro, Ankole, and Busoga. Their rule lasted from about 1350 to 1500.

At the beginning of the sixteenth century, the Luo under Isingoma Mpuga Rukidi superseded the Bachwezi and founded the Babito dynasty. They were initiated into the monarchical ceremonies by the Banyoro people who were connected with the kingly ceremonies of the Bachwezi.

Owing to this Luo migration, the empire of Bunyoro-Kitara broke up. Independent states emerged, the most significant of which were Bunyoro under the Luo Babito, Ankole under the Bagabe, Buganda under the Bakabaka and a number of Busoga chiefdoms.

The Luo immigrants set up several related dynasties and sub-dynasties. Of these, the dynasty of the Babito of Bunyoro was the most important. Other dynasties were in Bukoli, Bugwere, Bulamogi and Bugabula in the western part of the present Eastern

Region of Uganda. These dynasties had similar political institutions and royal regalia to the Babito of Bunyoro, but were not under the effective political control of Bunyoro.

Up to the end of the seventeenth century Bunyoro still exercised influence, if not control, over Buganda, Ankole, Rwanda and Karagwe, but, from then onwards, the secondary states gradually gained complete independence.

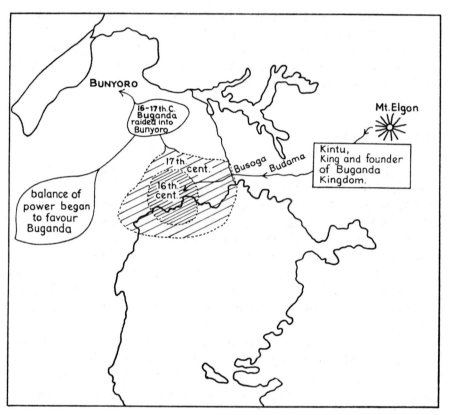

The Kingdom of Buganda

The Kingdom of Buganda

The Kingdom of Buganda lay to the east of Bunyoro. It originally belonged to the very large empire of the Bachwezi of Bunyoro – Kitara. At first it was quite small. It was divided into three countries which bear the same names today: Busiro, Kyaddondo and Mawokota, though the area of these countries is now much larger.

The period of mythology in Buganda began with Kintu, the king and founder of the kingdom, who came from the direction of Mount Elgon through Budama and Busoga.

From the sixteenth century to the second half of the seventeenth century, the Baganda raided Bunyoro seeking more land for expansion.

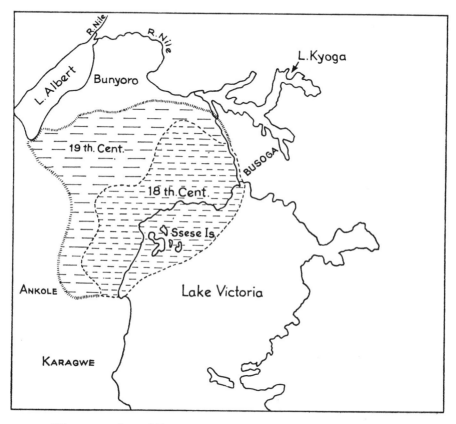

The expansion of Buganda in the 18th and 19th Centuries
Note: Lake Albert became Lake Mobutu in 1974

Bunyoro, however, was still strong and it held its own against the Baganda. At one time during the reign of King Nakibinge, in mid sixteenth century, Buganda was temporarily overrun by Banyoro

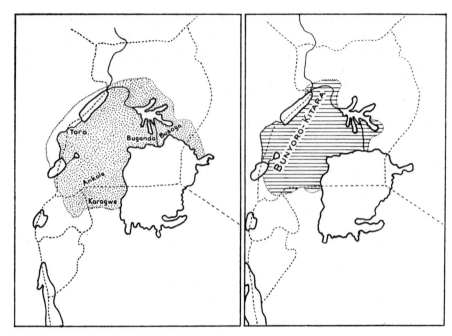

The kingdom of Bachwezi under Ndahura during the early 15th Century

The kingdom of Bunyoro-Kitara during the late 15th Century

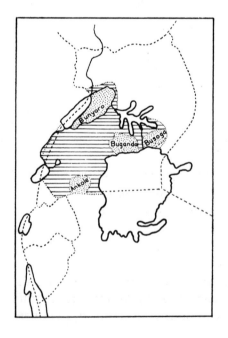

The empire of Bunyoro-Kitara broke up and independent states emerged in the 16th Century

warriors. From the second half of the seventeenth century, however, the balance of power began to change in favour of Buganda.

The Kingdom of Ankole

When the Luo dynasty of the Babito superseded the Bachwezi dynasty of Bunyoro in the sixteenth century, we saw that the empire of Bunyoro-Kitara broke up into several kingdoms, each one going its own way.

While the Chwezi dynasty was driven out of Bunyoro-Kitara, it survived in Ankole. Ruhinda, the son of Wamara the former Muchwezi of Bunyoro, started to rule in Ankole around 1650. He established the Hinda dynasty which reigned until 1967, when all kingdoms were abolished in Uganda. Ruhinda consolidated the kingdom of Ankole, which was at first often subjected to raids from Bunyoro. The kingdom was characterized by an aristocracy of pastoralists and a lower class of agriculturists.

Having consolidated his position in Ankole, Ruhinda extended his power to the south. Towards the end of the sixteenth century, he left Ankole with a group of his followers to conquer Buhaya to the west of Lake Victoria. He deposed the local ruler in Buhaya and established a new dynasty of the Hinda. Later he sent out his sons, each with a set of royal drums, to found Hinda sub-dynasties in the Bukoba region. In these interlacustrine kingdoms the drum was part of the royal regalia and it signified possession of power by a ruler or king within each kingdom.

The Hinda brought a centralized monarchy to the Bukoba area and they reorganized the existing clans into larger administrative units, setting up eight chiefdoms, headed by Hinda chiefs. These chiefdoms were Kianja, Bakara, Kyamtwara, Kiziba, Bugabo, Ihangiro, Misenyi and Karagwe. After the initial period and especially after Ruhinda's death, the chiefdoms became independent kingdoms.

The subsequent history of the Interlacustrine Kingdoms is given in Chapter 9.

4 The West Nile

There are six major language groups in West Nile: Lugbara, Alur, Kakwa, Madi, Kebu and Lendu. The Alur and the Lugbara form three-quarters of the population in this area, through assimilation of people from other ethnic groups and a high birth rate.

The Lugbara

The Lugbara are Bari speakers and are members of the Moru-Madi sub-group of the eastern Sudan or Nilotic group. They are related to the Madi and their languages are mutually intelligible. Their culture is also similar. In addition, many of the Lugbara are connected to the Kakwa by common ancestry. These two elements have fused to form one Lugbara people.

The Lugbara live in the plateau which is bounded by the Nile and Mounts Liru, Wati and Witu. They started to come in 1600 from the Juba region of the southern Sudan (where they were already living by A.D. 1000).

The Migration of the Lugbara

Between A.D. 1000 and 1500 the Bari and the Latuke from the eastern part of the Sudan began a regular invasion of the Juba region, forcing out the Moru-Madi groups. Then, a few families at a time, the Moru-Madi began to migrate from the Juba region, reaching Uganda between 1600 and 1650 and called 'Madi'. But when in 1888 the Arabs penetrated this territory seeking slaves they found south-east of today's Kakwa area a clan known as Lugbari which spoke both Kakwa and Lugbara. They applied the name of Lugbara to all the Madi people south-east of Kakwaland. The name was subsequently adopted by the British who applied it to all the Madi in this area.

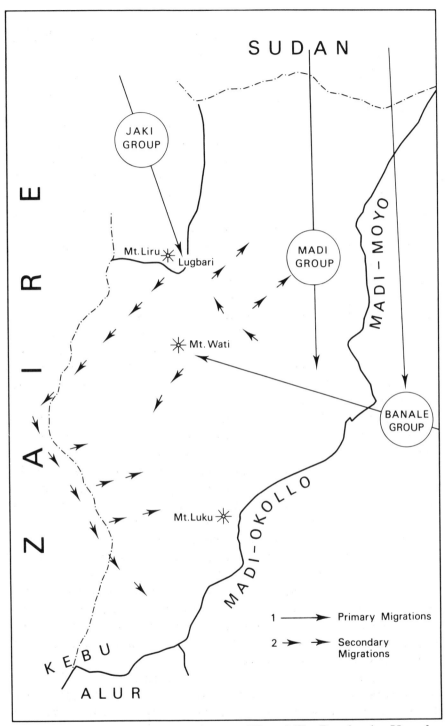

Migrations and settlements of some West Nile Peoples in Uganda

The Lugbari clan also belonged to the Madi, but their different pattern of movement and their isolation from the main group resulted in their developing a separate dialect. The existence of the three groups of Lugbara is due to the different ways in which they migrated from the Juba region.

The first group came straight from Moru in the Juba region and made its home south-east of Mount Liru. They increased and continued to expand in the area between the Nile and Mount Liru.

The second group, the Banale, was led by Utere from the Juba region and first settled in present-day west Acholi before the Luos reached it. After the death of Utere, his son Banale led the whole group across the Nile and settled near Mount Wati. Here Banale married and had a son called Anguduru. He in turn had seven sons who founded the Banale clans in this area. Banale lived to a great age and was buried near Mount Wati.

The third group trace their ancestry to Jaki. They first settled around Mount Witu where Jaki died. According to the Kakwa, Yeki their ancestor was a brother of Jaki and the present differences between them and the Lugbara result from the fact that their ancestor's sons left the Sudan at different times, mixed with different ethnic groups and settled in different areas in the West Nile. Consequently the Jaki group spoke a dialect of the Lugbara or Madi language. Some Lugbara of the Jaki group went to Zaire. Others returned to Vurra. From 1600 to 1650 there was contact and intermarriage between the three groups so that they developed as one society.

In their wanderings from the Sudan, and before finally settling in Lugbaraland, the Banale and Jaki groups had developed different dialects from the original language. But after contact with the group that had come straight from Moru, they adopted their own language, a form of Moru-Madi which the Lugbara developed.

Between 1630 and 1680 the three Lugbara groups consolidated their position in the area. From 1680 they began to spread all over what is Lugbaraland today, moving in small groups of a few families, some going west and others south of Mount Wati and Mount Liru. Within this expansion the Lugbara also assimilated other ethnic groups such as the Kebu who were already in the region, although the majority of the Kebu had already moved to Zaire.

The Kebu were very important to the Lugbara, for they were metal-workers and could produce iron tools. The Lugbara made friends with those who were unwilling to migrate so that the Kebu would stay among them and continue their valuable craft.

In their movements between 1790 and 1850 the Lugbara met the Kakwa in Aringa. The Kakwa intermarried and adopted the Lugbara language and other aspects of the culture. The Kakwa clans concerned were the Lormoju, Leiko, Morobu, Le'ba, Riaka, Kerikula, Reli, Tomario, Nyamara and Ingili. The Lugbara likewise absorbed some of the Madi and Alur.

Political Organization

Though the Lugbara clans spoke one language and had a common culture they were always politically independent. They had no paramount chief who ruled all the clans, so were decentralized. The clan was the largest political unit, headed by a chief called 'opi'. He made political and military decisions for the clan and settled all disputes, whether internal or with other clans. Cases were tried by a council of elders presided over by the opi.

Each clan also had its 'ojoo', a medicine man, soothsayer and diviner. The opi sought wise counsel from him in time of war, famine and epidemics. Among some clans, for instance in Aringa, it was obligatory for all opii to be rainmakers. This applied to all the Kakwa.

The Lugbara clans of Tereo – the Katini, Ayivu, Beliafe, Ombaci and Ewadri – had begun a system of centralization before the coming of the British. They all recognized one overall opi, provided by the ruling family in the Beliafe clan.

Economy

The economy of the Lugbara was based mainly on cattle-rearing and farming. Their first tools were wooden hoes. Later, when the Lugbara moved into Kebuland, they changed to iron hoes and implements such as arrow points, spearheads, knives, bracelets, bangles and rings. The Kebu were displaced as the Lugbara increased and the majority of the Kebu moved south. As we have already seen, the Lugbara absorbed some Kebu into their midst as blacksmiths. But since the majority of the Kebu had moved further south, the Lugbara obtained most of their iron weapons through long-distance trade. They bartered livestock and foodstuffs or rendered services in exchange.

Military Strength

The Lugbara had no standing army. When war came, all able-bodied men in a clan were called on to fight. Usually, since the Lugbara clans had no paramount chief to unite them, each clan waged its own wars, against another clan or a different ethnic group living nearby. In the latter case, several clans would unite to fight after their opii had arranged an alliance. Each clan had a military commander or captain called 'keigo' or 'ambo'. He was skilled in war tactics, but had no power to declare war or to end it. Those were matters for the opi.

Relations between the Lugbara and the Alur

When the Lugbara moved in to southern Lugbaraland, they met the Kebu, Madi and Alur. While in the rest of Lugbaraland clans were led by political leaders, here in the south they had warrior leaders called 'aju drile' who helped them occupy and retain territory. In this area the Ocoo clans developed cow-hide armour known as 'gombere'. It was effective against arrows and spears and gave added power to the warriors. Other Lugbara clans − for example the Vurra and Ayivu − also wore it, after suffering many defeats from the Ocoo. The armour gave the southern Lugbara superiority over the Kebu. The majority of the Kebu fled to Zaire and the remainder were absorbed by Lugbara, including the Tuli, Paanza, Ozoo, Okavu and Ayavu. Some of the Madi fled to the present-day Madi county of the West Nile and are known as Madi Okollo, to differentiate them from the Madi-Moyo in Madi district. Those who remained, especially in Bondo and Arivu, were absorbed by the Lugbara.

The Lugbara engaged in a long and fierce clash with the Alur, quite different in character from their fighting with the Madi and Kebu. This was between the Ayivu clan in southern Lugbara and the Alur clans around Warr.

The Alur of the Okoro chiefdom were expanding northwards from Pakwach while the Lugbara of the Ayivu clans were expanding southwards towards Pakwach. Both groups met in the mid-eighteenth century at the river Odrua. The river was agreed as the boundary between the Alur and the Ayivu Lugbara. Hostilities arose because each group raided the cattle of the other and eventually wanted to take land across the river. Three major battles were fought by the two groups before the arrival of the Europeans. One was at Anguza another at Awere and the third at Aduamin.

After these battles relations, especially by the beginning of the nineteenth century, became more stable. Each group recognized the strength of the other and realized that prosperity lay in co-operation and trade rather than in cattle-stealing and land-grabbing. Peaceful trade began between the southern Lugbara and the Alur. One of the most famous markets was established by an Alur chief at Anyavu in southern Lugbara. The Alur, who had more cattle than the Lugbara, brought beasts to the market for slaughter to provide meat for the Lugbara. They also brought salt from the Nile, millet, simsim and other foodstuffs. The Lugbara learnt the Alur language and trade was harmonious.

From this period the southern Lugbara came under Alur influence. The Alur controlled trade and their language was commonly used for business dealings. By the 1870's the Alur also began to influence Lugbara political affairs. For example, the position of opi, the highest Lugbara office, had been hereditary. By the 1870's, owing to Alur influence, it was no longer so. Clan chiefs in Okoro would fill these positions with Lugbara chosen for their political influence and sympathy to the Alur cause. The opii so appointed were generally agents of Alur chiefs and served their interests. The Lugbara chiefs or opii collected tribute twice a year in the form of foodstuffs for the Alur chiefs. Religion was another factor in the ascendancy of the Alur. They had greater powers of making rain and curing mental and physical disabilities through medicine-men and women. The Alur readily absorbed the Kebu and the Lendu also.

Economic Co-operation

In the whole West Nile area trade brought different ethnic groups into even greater contact with one another.

Kebuland was rich in iron ore and the Kebu produced iron goods for the entire West Nile. Centres of manufacture in Kebuland before the coming of the white men were Zeu, Awang and Kalanza.

The Lugbara and Alur were farmers and cattle-rearers. The Lendu were potters. The Lendu, Lugbara, Madi and Alur had no iron ore and so they traded cattle and foodstuffs for iron goods from Kebuland. But the Nyangilia clan of the Kakwa was skilled in the use of metal. The ore came from Omi, now in Zaire. All the Kakwa people and a section of the northern Lugbara obtained iron tools from this clan. The Nyangilia received livestock and foodstuffs in exchange.

The Parombo mainly controlled this trade. These people, belonging to the Luo group and speaking their language, came from Palwo near the banks of the Somerset Nile or Chope. About 1735 they crossed the Nile and settled in Kero in modern Padyere. The Parombo travelled also into Bantu and Lendu areas and there was considerable intermingling of the different groups.

From Padyere the Parombo directed trade in neighbouring Paidha, Atyak and Kebuland, Panyimur on Lake Sese Seko Mobutu, around Wadelai and Pakwach and in present-day eastern Zaire. Salt extracted from Kibiro by the Banyoro and dried fish were imported from Panyimur into Paromboland and sold to Alur, Kebu and Lugbara.

From the Alur and Kebu the Parombo obtained iron articles, livestock and foodstuffs which they took to Panyimur. Bark cloths from the Banyoro and Baganda were also traded. By the mid-nineteenth century Arabs from Zanzibar were already in Bunyoro and their goods – cloth, glass beads, bracelets and firearms – were being shipped across the lake to Panyimur.

5   City States on the East African Coast up to 1497

The east coast of Africa has been inhabited by Africans for centuries, although the origins of the earliest people are unknown. They lived under a tribal system, each settlement having its own chief. Later, from the first century A.D., the coast was occupied by people of the Bantu group in their migration from south and central Africa. It is they who have given a lasting character to the coast. By the sixth century the Bantu had spread from Sofala to Somalia. They established well-organized communities ruled by elected kings, with effective armies and an influential priesthood.

Early Traders and Settlers

East Africa's coast has long been in contact with the outside world, unlike the interior which was not effectively penetrated by foreigners until the nineteenth century. The Greeks, Phoenicians and Egyptians used to land on the coast, calling it Azania. Arabs and Persians too would frequently visit it. To them it was 'the land of the Zenj' – the black men's land. In the sixth century Indians also came in search of merchandise. It was they who introduced the coconut palm, now a familiar plant there. The Indians, Persians and Arabs found little difficulty in reaching the coast, owing to the monsoon winds which blow in a south-westerly direction towards East Africa from December to March and in a north-easterly direction from April to September.

Arabs from Oman and Persians from the Persian Gulf were the main traders, importing such goods as daggers, hatchets, lances, awls and glass beads. In return they exported ivory, rhinoceros horns, tortoiseshell, wood – and later gold – from Central Africa. In the course of trading, Arabs and Persians settled on the east coast about the third century. Up to 695 there was only a trickle of settlers, but thereafter numbers increased. Oman was then ruled by chiefs Suleiman and Said, with Caliph Abdul Malik as overlord. The chiefs attempted to rebel against him, but his superior forces routed Suleiman and Said, who fled with their followers to the east coast of Africa.

About 740 another large contingent of Arabs followed, members of a strict Islam sect known as the Zaidiyah which had broken away from the Shiite Islam group. Seeking to avoid persecution, they settled near Shungwaya.

About 920, more Arabs fleeing from political harassment settled in Mogadishu and Barawa. Another refugee was a son of the Sultan of Shiraz in Persia whose mother was a slave. Disowned by his half brothers, he and his six sons decided to make their home in East Africa. They settled in Mombasa, Pemba and Kilwa. But, as time went on, the Persian element became submerged by the African and Arab elements in these cities.

Arab immigration continued under the impetus of political and religious persecution in South Arabia and the desire to find better economic conditions. Persian and Arab immigrants settled in established African townships, though in separate communities. The Africans already had highly organized kingdoms there of which, unfortunately, we have very little knowledge. More reliable information dates from the ninth century when Arabs and Persians started mingling and intermarrying with East Africans.

City States

By 1400 there were thirty towns along the East African Coast between Southern Mozambique and the Horn of Africa. Each was a walled city state, completely autonomous and governed by a ruling dynasty. Its rulers and inhabitants dominated the surrounding countryside and controlled local trade routes. The more powerful tried to gain ascendancy over the weaker city states and there were constant struggles over trade routes.

As the towns grew in strength their culture became increasingly Swahili. It was based on Islam, a mixture of Arab and African customs and the Bantu language, with some Arabic additions. This culture was strengthened by the intermarriage of Africans and Arabs; Arab refugees commonly arrived in Africa without their womenfolk and therefore took African brides, who, on the whole, would retain their Bantu language and the Arabs tried to adopt it also. The wives became Muslims and adopted Arab customs. The children of such marriages were brought up in an atmosphere of Muslim religious practices,

Afro-Arabian customs and the Kiswahili language. Swahili culture was also adopted by some Africans. Thus a distinct group of Swahili arose and even evolved its own ruling dynasties.

Each settlement was deliberately sited on an island or peninsula to safeguard it from attacks. As time went on walls were built around many of them and they achieved the position of independent city states, ruling over the surrounding territory and the Africans living there. The inhabitants of the city states grew crops on the mainland. But they never ventured in great numbers far into the interior. With the coming of Arabs, there was often a shift of power. Sometimes Arabs overthrew an African dynasty and set up their own. Similarly the Swahilis might overthrow an existing African dynasty and rule in its place. By the tenth century some cities had Arab dynasties, some were under Swahili rule and others had African rulers. By the thirteenth century Mogadishu was the most famous city state on the Banadir coast north of Mozambique. Ruled by a council of Swahili elders, it grew rich on the Sofala gold trade.

Among the Persian immigrants was the Shirazi clan from the eastern side of the Persian Gulf. Other Shirazi settled at Bur Gao, now called Port Dunford. Here they mixed with the Africans and, though retaining elements of their former culture, became Swahili.

The Shirazi then moved southwards from the Banadir coast. By the middle of the twelfth century they had begun to settle on Shanga, Manda, Tanga, Pemba, Mafia, the Comoro and Kilwa. Then they seized power and set up the so-called Shirazi dynasties in all these islands. Their character was predominantly African, owing to Swahili influence.

All the coastal settlements consisted of prosperous towns with well-made narrow streets, stone houses with windows and flat roofs and beautifully carved doors. As the coast became converted to Islam, stone mosques were built.

The Arabs and Persians passed on some of their customs to their Swahili descendants. Feuds, therefore, a common feature of the Arab and Persian way of life, were also handed down and the towns were in a perpetual state of internal strife over succession or trading advantages. Constant wars developed between towns. Pate and Mombasa in particular held other towns in bondage, as did Mogadishu, Zanzibar, Pemba and Kilwa. Kilwa's pre-eminence lasted longer than that of the others. Even in 1498 the Portuguese found Kilwa in a position of supremacy. The feud between Mombasa and Malindi was of long duration and the fighting lasted for centuries. It was only resolved when Malindi made an alliance with the Portuguese and finally crushed Mombasa (see Chapter 10). The Portuguese abolished the Mombasa dynasty and appointed the sultan of Malindi ruler of Mombasa also.

Though trade in the towns was normally by barter, currency was gradually introduced, first cowry shells, then money from China and finally the cities issued their own. Money, though it supplemented the barter system, did not supplant it.

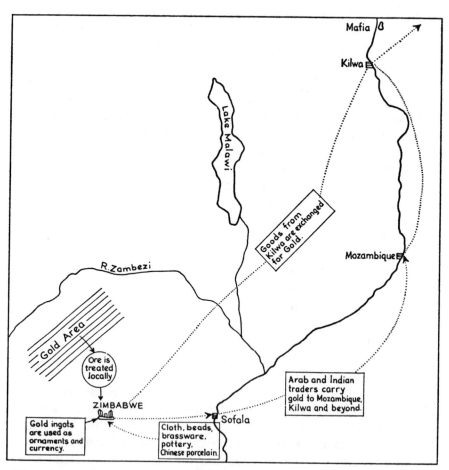

The mining of minerals, especially of gold, was an important occupation for people in Zimbabwe

Kilwa

Kilwa was foremost in promoting trade and currency. Established in the tenth century by rulers of pure African descent, its people traded with Arabs who visited the coast. It was later conquered by Swahilis of mixed African and Shirazi ancestry from Banadir. Though they still called themselves Shirazi, they were in fact mainly Swahili. Ali bin al-Hassan was their first Shirazi king. Under the Shirazi-Swahili rulers, Kilwa first rose to importance in the thirteenth century. Sofala and the south-eastern coast came under its domination, giving Kilwa a monopoly of the Zimbabwe gold and ivory trade.

Mining, especially of gold, was an important industry in Zimbabwe (modern Rhodesia), even before A.D. 1000. Most sites of gold and other mineral-bearing ores were found by Africans before the arrival of the Europeans, who discovered new mines in the second half of the nineteenth century. African miners had long been skilled in the techniques of mining and smelting. Gold ingots were used as ornaments and currency and passed on to the people on the east coast who in turn sold them to Arabs and Indians. In exchange the people in Central Africa received cloth, beads, brassware, pottery and Chinese porcelain. Kilwa's prosperity resulted in the building of the impressive palace known as Husuni Kubwa. Kilwa also increased its hold over Mafia, Zanzibar and Pemba.

From 1450, however, Kilwa was plagued with intrigues over succession and the wars that ensued within the island. Its trade declined and islands formerly under its sway now asserted their independence. The Portuguese on their arrival made Mombasa their headquarters and Kilwa thereafter became of little consequence.

Zanzibar and Pemba

As early as the fifth century, Africans from the mainland settled in Zanzibar and Pemba. Immigrants, fleeing from religious and political unrest in Persia, Arabia and India, made their home on these two islands from the seventh century onwards. An African dynasty developed. But by the tenth century the Omani Arabs deposed the African rulers. This new dynasty governed both the African people and the Arab settlers and both islands became more prosperous. However, by the fourteenth century they came under the control of Kilwa. Zanzibar resented this dominance and was particularly jealous of Kilwa's gold and ivory trade. When Kilwa's power began to wane in the fourteenth century Zanzibar reasserted its sovereignty and as a sign of independence issued its own currency.

Mombasa, Malindi and Pate

Mombasa and Malindi were twelfth-century African foundations. Mombasa flourished on the export of ivory and slaves from the hinterland and iron mined on the east coast. At this period iron was one of the most valued commodities and there were many mines producing ores of very high quality. Foreign traders came from Java and Sumatra every year to buy ore for sale in Indian markets. East coast Arabs and Africans had developed their own trading fleets for exporting to India.

Both Malindi and Mombasa's African dynasties were overthrown by the Shirazi-Swahili rulers in the thirteenth century. Under them Mombasa had by 1500 emerged as the leading town on the coast since the decline of Kilwa, and sought to dominate Malindi. The latter joined forces with the now enfeebled Kilwa against Mombasa in an attempt to preserve its independence. But this was not achieved, as we have seen, until the arrival of the Portuguese who allied themselves with the rulers of Malindi, subjugated Mombasa and appointed a Malindi prince as ruler. Pate was founded between the tenth and twelfth centuries. Its African rulers were, however, superseded in the thirteenth century by Omani who gradually merged with the African community and adopted the Swahili culture and the language. Pate rose to prominence under Sultan Omar, who ruled about 1350. He amassed wealth by trading with Asian countries across the Indian Ocean and a profitable trade developed with India also. Pate became supreme among the coastal city states.

All the city states naturally turned towards India, for their prosperity depended on dealings with Asian and Arab countries. They were outward-looking, sophisticated, receptive to new ideas and had a strongly developed commercial sense. They imported luxury goods such as stoneware from Siam and porcelain from China and in return sold ivory to the Chinese through Persian merchants. It is recorded that between 1417 and 1422 emissaries from China visited the coast. The citizens built strong stone houses and well-constructed roads. Geographical factors, however, cut them off from the African interior. Their only contact was the trade route from Central Africa through

Sofala, which gradually opened up and lost its terrors as more travellers made their way there.

Social Groups and Occupations

By the twelfth century, a hierarchy was established in the coastal settlements. The ruling classes in each city state were Swahilis of mixed Arab and African blood. Below them were other Swahilis – landowners, skilled artisans and merchants. Next in rank were the pure-blooded Africans who carried out menial tasks and cultivated the land. Then there were the pure Arabs, many of them recent arrivals or staying for a short time only on trading expeditions. Those who stayed would marry Swahili girls and the number of Swahili inhabitants therefore rose. Finally there were the African slaves. After selecting those suitable for soldiers or house servants, the Swahili

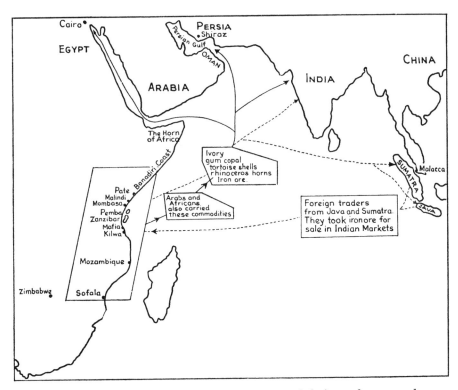

The City States of the East African coast and their trade across the Indian Ocean

and Arab merchants shipped the rest across the Indian Ocean and to Egypt to be sold.

Certain pure Africans, converts to Islam, were independent farmers or traders. Their African heritage became mixed with Arab elements and they were therefore culturally more akin to the Swahilis. They were quite distinct from the non-Muslim pure Africans of the interior.

Relations between the city states and the inhabitants of the interior were limited. Far inland African life continued in its original form. Tribes were warlike and sometimes attacked the coastal towns. The only real link between the city states and Africans inland was trade. Goods from the interior reached the coast by a system of barter from one tribe to the other. Swahilis and Arabs therefore had no need to penetrate the interior. Such spasmodic excursions as they made were in search of merchandise and there was no hint of missionizing zeal.

Generally speaking, the coastal people could obtain ample supplies of iron ore, gold, ivory, rhinoceros teeth, tortoiseshell, leopard skins, gum, copal and slaves near at hand. The interior was fairly inaccessible because there were no long rivers from it to provide a natural waterway. Immediately behind the coast lay desert. There were dangers from warlike tribes, malarial fever caused by mosquitoes and sleeping sickness spread by the tsetse fly. It was only in the mid-nineteenth century that a shortage of commodities and a desire for new supplies of slaves and ivory provided a motive for exploring the interior.

The people of the coast engaged in shipbuilding, navigation and agriculture, growing rice, millet, bananas, oranges, lemons, pomegranates and figs. They reared goats, sheep, cattle, hens and kept bees for honey. They wore cloth, mined and smelted copper, carved ivory and bones, made jewels and were expert stonemasons.

The Slave Trade

One strange and baffling phenomenon in African history is the way in which foreigners exploited Africans as slave labour while the Africans meekly acquiesced. Their own leaders would often sell those under them. When the slave trade was finally outlawed in East Africa, this part of the continent had, for two thousand years, been a human hunting ground raided by Asians, Arabs, Swahilis and Europeans. Records from Egyptian and Greek times mention the Africans' outstanding physique and stature. Their capacity to withstand rough weather and conditions made them suitable for all kinds of heavy work which their captors, the Arabs, Swahilis, Asians and later on the whites, could not do. Yet for all their physical superiority, the Africans succumbed to the degradation of slavery for centuries.

A possible explanation is that in African societies slavery existed as an institution. If one tribe defeated another the victors would take the defeated as slaves. The captives were not roughly treated and were usually assimilated into the conquering tribe by marriage. Some of them – or their children – would attain positions of responsibility within their new society and identify themselves completely with it. In this way, slaves in African societies were able to become free members of other groups. African proverbs are full of references to slaves: how they had to be treated kindly and how they were allowed to rise from servitude so that it did not become irrevocable.

The arrival of the Arabs and their desire for slaves stimulated deliberate attempts among the chiefs to capture peoples of other tribes, tempted by the prospect of merchandise offered in exchange.

Unfortunately the victims were not skilful in evading capture and were readily carried off into slavery, either to the coast or across the Indian Ocean. Once sold to the Arabs and Swahilis the slaves were shipped, fettered, starved and separated from others of their own tribe and language. Although they were all black, they were strangers and often divided by feuds, so that there was no possibility of organized resistance to their masters.

When they reached their destinations in Egypt, India and Arabia, however, they did unite effectively and even overthrew existing régimes. It is estimated that by the time the Portuguese reached the east coast of Africa, twelve million Africans had been shipped across the Indian Ocean. They went to Egypt, Turkey, Arabia, India and Persia and became a permanent element in the population of those countries. In Mesopotamia they revolted in 850, and in 869 the same thing happened in Persia. Between 1459 and 1474 there were 8000 of them in Bengal alone. They revolted, killed the king and ruled until 1493. When eventually defeated they were expelled from Bengal and dispersed throughout India. Such united action against their oppressors was, unfortunately, unknown in Africa itself.

The slave trade in Africa and in East Africa particularly was a main cause of decreasing population. Many died in the wars fought to capture slaves from other tribes and many of the captives died on the journey to slavery or soon after arrival.

This depletion of the population had serious effects on African societies. Its gravity can be estimated if one looks at it in terms not only of a hundred years but of two thousand years.

To put the African slave trade into historical perspective, it must be remembered that Africans were not alone in being subjected to such treatment. During the days of the Roman Empire, for example, many captured Africans, Europeans and Asians were treated as slaves. European and African tribes were in the habit of selling other tribesmen to the Romans as slaves. But the African slave trade persisted longest and was made worse by the intervention of non-Africans. The pernicious results of their activities can still be seen today.

6 The Eastern Bantu Peoples of Kenya and Tanzania

Kenya

The major groups of the Eastern Bantu peoples in Kenya are the Kikuyu, the Meru, the Embu, the Kamba, the Taita, the Chuka and the Pokomo. The Eastern Bantu peoples, like all other Bantu peoples, descended from an old Bantu nucleus in northern Katanga. From this area the forefathers of the present Eastern Bantu peoples moved in great numbers, starting roughly from the beginning of the first century A.D., and occupying the East African Coast between Lamu and the River Juba by the tenth century. They called this area Shungwaya, near Port Dunford Bay. Between the thirteenth and sixteenth centuries, they spread into the coastal region and into the interior. The Pokomo and the Chuka were the first to move, from about A.D. 1300; they were followed by the Embu around 1425 and then by the Kikuyu about 1545.

The settlement of areas by different groups of people who seemed ever to be on the move is most characteristic of early African history and one may imagine that there was a great sweep of peoples moving in very large numbers from one area to another, usually at the same time. But people of the same tribe moved in small family groups in search of better land and water and sometimes to avoid an unhealthy location, leaving some of their ethnic group behind. Having established themselves in a new settlement that looked ideal, they would either send for their relatives who had remained behind, or those who had remained behind would just start moving, tracing the footsteps of those who had gone before them without waiting to be called. So the movement of one group of people and settlement in a new land was usually gradual, unless the whole group had been driven away by a hostile and much stronger group of people.

There is another important question with regard to the number of people in each tribal group at this time of constant migrations. The number in one group would range between a few hundred and

37

a few thousand people. The groups named above were usually in the region of a few hundred each. On settling down, they increased in number and reached a few thousand each.

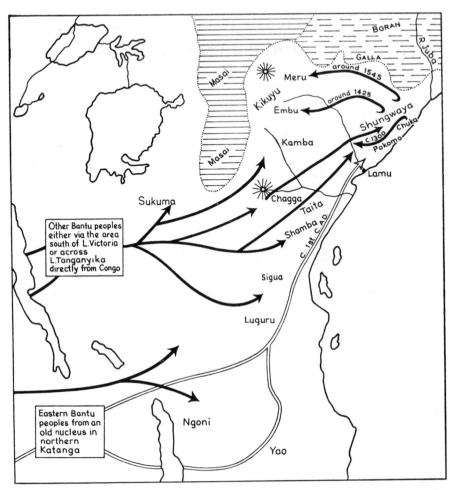

The migration movements of the Eastern Bantu peoples of Kenya and Tanzania

The Kikuyu lived for a long time in the forests because of the Masai raids which prevented them expanding northwards to the west of Mount Kenya. So they expanded southwards into Southern Kiambu District where they had arrived by 1800. They took over the land of the Laikipia Masai and they also displaced the Dorobo in this southward movement.

Tanzania

The Chagga, the Gweno, the Sukuma, the Shamba and other related groups belong to the original wave of Bantu immigrants from the Congo, but to settle in their present places, they dispersed from the Taita hills. Other Bantu people in this area came either via the area to the south of Lake Victoria or across Lake Tanganyika directly from the Congo.

Of all Eastern Bantu peoples in Kenya and Tanzania, only the Chagga and the Shamba had evolved a form of kingship by the beginning of the eighteenth century. The Chagga kingship in the Kilimanjaro region helped to bring a large area under one administration. By 1840 chief Horombo had put two-thirds of Chagga land under his administration and had built forts for security, especially against the Masai who were raiding from Northern Tanzania. His empire collapsed after he was assassinated by the Masai. By the 1870's, his successor, Rindi, also known as Mandara of Moshi, had extended his rule over a similar area which included the area between Tela and Mriti.

The Shamba of Usambara also evolved their kingship early in the eighteenth century. Due to Masai raids from Northern Tanzania, there was the necessity of organizing a centralized rule to defend the people more effectively. Hitherto there were several chiefs, each of whom led a group of people, but as far as defence was concerned there was a need for concerted action directed by one man. The king managed to keep a large area under control by appointing his own sons as local chiefs, who would not disobey him or try to depose him because they feared being cursed by their father.

7 Kalenjin Peoples

The Kalenjin peoples are occasionally called the Highland Nilotics. At one time they inhabited an area along the southern fringe of the Ethiopian highlands in the Lake Rudolf area which is now called the Kalenjin cradleland. Some time before A.D. 1000 the Kalenjin slowly began to spread in southern and central Kenya. They then numbered several thousand, but they later broke up into smaller groups, each group adapting its own way of life. By A.D. 1000 they had reached the area of Mount Kamalinga, from where they continued to move on gradually and, by the beginning of the seventeenth century, they had settled in the Mount Elgon area.

A second major dispersal of the Kalenjin took place from the area of Mount Elgon and a number of different peoples developed among them such as the Nandi, Kipsigis, Tugen, Kamasya, Elgeyo, Marakwet, Suk and the Elgon Kalenjin, each of these groups numbering a few hundred people with the exception of the Nandi who tended to be a few thousand strong. The Nandi settled around Adlai in the south while the Kipsigis extended into Sirikwa and Kisii.

The Nandi

After the dispersal from the Mount Elgon area, the Nandi emerged in the seventeenth century as the most numerous and strongest group of the Kalenjin peoples and they settled along the southern Nandi escarpment. From this area they started to expand northwards. They defeated the Uasin Gishu Masai in the 1870's and raided the people of Nyanza of Western Province of Kenya, the Karamojong of North Western Kenya, the inhabitants of Mount Elgon, the Suk, the Keyo and the Tugen. As a result they became the strongest power in Western Kenya and their expansion was only stopped by the coming of the British in the 1880's.

The Masai

The ancestors of the Masai and of the Kalenjin are generally considered as having been one community originally and they lived in the Lake Rudolf area of Kenya and Ethiopia. When the group left this area during the first thousand years A.D., the forefathers of the Kalenjin took a south-westerly route and eventually arrived in the area of Mount Elgon. Another group of the Kalenjin travelled southwards, arriving in the Uasin Gishu Plateau, and it is this group that constitutes the Masai. The Masai were primarily pastoralists; their characteristic was to keep on the move, herding cattle.

In A.D. 500 the Masai had not been really numerous and they were an obscure people. However, their expansion was rapid because of the aggressive warlike attitude which they adopted towards their neighbours and, by the 1750's, they had expanded as far south as Northern Tanzania and they had grown in numbers to more than ten thousand.

By the second half of the eighteenth century they had reached Northern Tanzania, where some of them still live. They settled in areas of the Rift Valley, the Trans Nzoia and the Uasin Gishu Plateau of Kenya. They had enormous herds of cattle, grazing them all over these areas and antagonizing their neighbours. Many battles were fought with those who would refuse them grazing rights, and the Masai would even organize cattle raids against their neighbours so as to increase their own herds. However, they were never ruled by one central authority; there were several leaders who led different groups.

By the middle of the nineteenth century Masai people were established in large areas of the Rift Valley and in the Uasin Gishu plateau in Kenya, where groups of the Kalenjin family had already settled. All this large area was not under their effective control however; they used it mainly for grazing and it cannot be regarded as a Masai empire.

The Masai were divided into two groups according to occupation, the pure pastoralists and those who combined agriculture with cattle herding, who were called the Kwavi and who were more warlike. Both groups absorbed Kalenjin culture, which they found in these areas; they added relatively few distinct elements of their own. Though they imposed their language on the Kalenjin in the process, they often used the ideas and institutions of the majority people.

The later history of the Masai from approximately the beginning

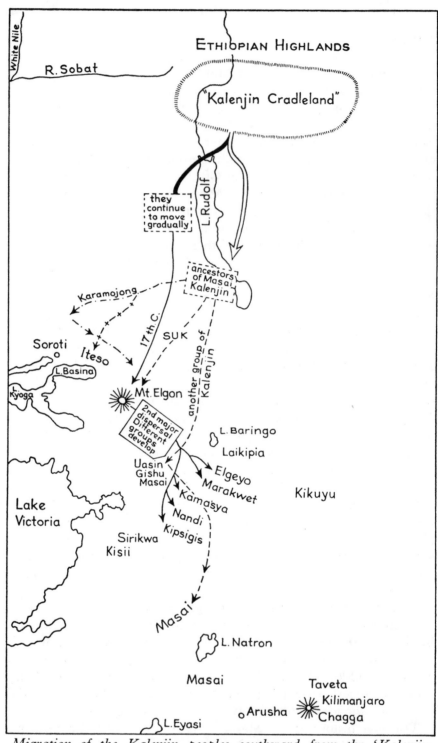

Migration of the Kalenjin peoples southward from the 'Kalenjin Cradleland'

of the nineteenth century consists of raids and counter-raids and civil wars between the two groups over land rights. The pastoral Masai particularly feared that the Kwavi (agricultural Masai) were taking too much land under cultivation and cattle. After fighting for a long time the pastoral Masai managed to defeat completely the agricultural Masai who lived in Uasin Gishu and Laikipia.This defeat greatly weakened the agricultural Masai, who at first had been aggressive and had fought with distant communities and successfully raided the pastoral Masai. After their defeat they were overshadowed by the pastoral Masai and later on by the Nandi, whose power was rising high. The remainder of the Kwavi Masai took refuge among the Kikuyu, the Chagga, and among the people around Taveta, the Kenya Coast and Arusha and they served under local rival leaders as mercenaries.

These Masai civil wars greatly diminished the population of the Masai of both groups and left their areas, such as the Laikipia plateau and the district east of Kilimanjaro, very much depopulated. Fighting did not stop with the defeat of the agricultural Masai, however, for there were conflicts and jealousies among the pastoral Masai also, because they lacked a centralized political structure. So each section, under its leader, attacked another and local 'laibons' played an important role. The laibons were religious experts who were highly respected within their community as foretellers of the future. They directed war campaigns and tried to predict the results of each war campaign.

By 1884, the Purko section of the pastoral Masai had won overall power from the rest of the pastoral Masai. The Purko were led by their laibon Mbatian, a son of Supet who was reckoned to be the greatest religious expert. Mbatian began to lead the Purko in 1866 and by his death in 1890 he was supreme ruler, not only of the Purko, but of all the pastoral Masai. On his death, his two sons, Lenana and Sendeyo, fought between themselves for the leadership of the group. Neither of them won a decisive battle, so Sendeyo and his followers occupied the country around Loita in present day Tanzania and Lenana's people lived on the Kenya side of the modern border of Kenya and Tanzania. Conflict continued between them while, at the same time, Lenana's group was being attacked by the Kikuyu. On the coming of the British in 1886 Lenana befriended them, finally taking refuge in their administrative centre at Fort Smith in 1894. The British assisted him to fight against his Masai enemies led by Sendeyo and against the Kikuyu. This help given to the Masai of Kenya at the beginning of the British administration made the Masai rather less hostile to their being moved from the Laikipia plateau in 1904 by the then Kenya government to make way for the European settlement.

The Karamojong Cluster of Peoples

The Karamojong began moving from the cradleland south west of Lake Rudolf area during the fifteenth century and gradually spread into Karamoja towards the Suk Hills. They numbered a few thousand. Whilst in this area, their numbers increased greatly and owing to a shortage of water and lack of grazing land, a section of the Karamojong, later called the Iteso, left Karamoja towards the end of the seventeenth century and began to pioneer the present district of Teso in Uganda. Between 1652 and 1733, the Iteso established themselves on the shores of Lake Bisina and in the Kumi and Soroti areas. Although originally pastoralists, the Iteso added agriculture to their pastoral way of life. This was what began the gradual division of the Iteso and the Karamojong into two different peoples. The Karamojong remained primarily pastoral and fewer in number, while the Iteso were both cultivators and cattle keepers and quite numerous. As the Iteso expanded westwards towards Lake Bisina, the Karamojong were beginning a southward expansion towards Mount Elgon and eventually settling in their present areas in Uganda and Kenya by the beginning of the nineteenth century.

8 The Luo-Speaking Peoples in East Africa

The major Luo-speaking groups today are the Acholi, the Langi and the Alur of Northern Uganda, the Jopadhola of Eastern Uganda and the Luo and Padhola of Western Kenya. The cradleland of the Luo-speakers was in the south-eastern corner of the present Sudan Republic. From here the Luo, starting in the fifteenth century, migrated into Northern Uganda where they arrived at the end of that century.

On their arrival in Northern Uganda the Luo-speakers settled at Pubungu-Pakwach on the Nile. After staying here for some time, some of them pushed on westwards towards the Congo where they intermarried with the Sudanic Madi, Lendu and Okebo who had preceded them to this area from the Sudan. This intermarriage gave rise to the present day Alur, a sub-group of the Luo living near Lake Albert.

Another group of the Luo left Pubungu-Pakwach and went north-east into present day Acholiland. They found the western part of this area inhabited by the Madi and the eastern by the Langi, who were related to the present Karamojong and the Iteso.

The Madi, who were under pressure from the Langi, joined the Luo in defence against the Langi whom they defeated. They intermarried with the Luo and this gave birth to the Acholi, another sub-branch of the Luo. In the seventeenth century the Acholi pushed the Langi people southwards towards Lake Kyoga.

Some other Luo under Labongo moved from Pubungu southwards and settled at Pawir or Chope in the bend of the Nile between Lake Kyoga and Lake Albert. South of their settlement was the empire of the Chwezi kings of Bunyoro-Kitara. Labongo and his followers came into contact with this empire and they superseded the Chwezi dynasty by marriage and peaceful absorption. Then the Luo formed the royal dynasty of the Babito of Bunyoro.

Finally, the rest of the Luo still remained in the dispersal area of Pubungu until later, when some of these settlers moved eastwards into present day Budama in Eastern Uganda, whilst others went to Western Kenya. Their descendants are the Jopadhola and the Kenya Luo.

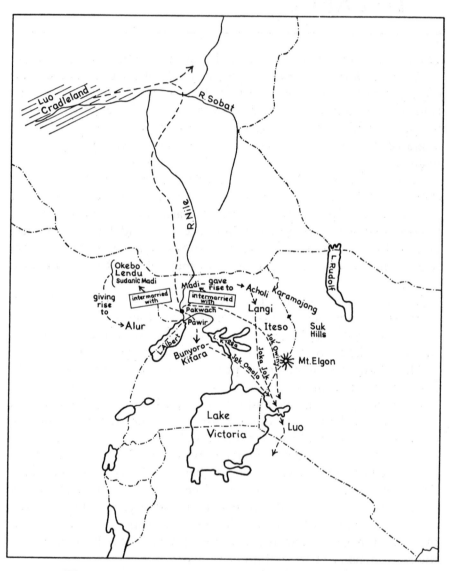

The southward movement of the Luo-speaking peoples
Note: Lake Albert became Lake Mobutu in 1974

The Luo of Kenya

These Luo arrived in Nyanza, South-western Kenya, in four migratory movements:

1. The Joka-Jok travelled from Acholiland between A.D. 1500 and 1550.
2. The Jok' Owiny travelled from Pubungu along the western side of Mt. Elgon, passing Mbale and Tororo.
3. The Jok' Omolo travelled from North Bunyoro between 1540 and 1600 passing through Busoga to Ibanda.
4. The Abasuba were a collection of peoples who had taken on aspects of Luo culture and settled in South Nyanza.

Co-operation developed among these four groups. Through defensive co-operation they developed a number of strong tribes by 1750 and a form of chiefship emerged.

By this period the power of the Masai, the Nandi and of the Abaluyia was rising and the Luo needed a stronger administration for protection against the incursions of such people. This caused the Luo of Nyanza to develop a feeling of unity. They continued to expand and to conquer along their borderland up to 1900.

The Langi

The Langi originally spoke the same language as the Karamojong and the Iteso. They moved out of Karamoja before the Iteso and occupied Usuku, Amuria and the northern Soroti areas, gradually moving westward into the present district of Lango in Uganda. In Lango they assimilated many Luo and, in time, their language became a mixture of Luo and Ateso, with Luo predominating. Whilst in this area, the Langi who were originally cattle rearers changed over to settled agriculture, mainly because they obtained new crops of sweet potatoes and groundnuts and were supplied with iron hoes by the Paluo of Bunyoro. The climate, moreover, was ideal for cultivation.

The Karamojong, the Kumam, the Turkana, the Jie and the Iteso

'Jie' is a collective term embracing not only Jie, but also the

Karamojong, Kumam, Turkana and Iteso. Originally all these people had the same ancestors and their point of origin might have been in the direction of Ethiopia or the Sudan. On arrival in East Africa their ancestors settled in the area of the Suk Hills near the present day Karamoja District of Uganda. Here, as they increased, they found that there was no longer enough water, land or food for them and gradually individual groups started to march away in search of these things. Each group settled in its new place forming a distinct group. The Iteso went to their present land; so did the Kumam, the Jie and the Turkana while the Karamojong remained behind in the original place as the people who were unwilling to move away. All the above groups speak a language closely related to that of the Karamojong.

The migration of those groups from Karamoja took place at the end of the seventeenth century and at the beginning of the eighteenth century and it took a long time before each group finally separated and settled in its present area. By 1730 the Iteso were established on the shores of Lake Bisina in Kumi and the Soroti areas in Usuku. By the beginning of the nineteenth century the population of the Iteso had increased in Usuku and there was a further dispersal in all directions with some Iteso going to Western Kenya where they mixed with the Bukusu. On their migration from Usuku those who remained in Uganda came into contact with the Langi who were in turn in contact with the Paluo of Bunyoro. The latter were bartering iron hoes with the Langi and the Langi also bartered hoes with the Kumam and Iteso. Previously the Iteso had used wooden hoes and their cultivation was limited to small patches of land. With iron hoes the Iteso improved their agriculture and cultivated more extensively. They also acquired two new crops – sweet potatoes and groundnuts. This, together with good soil and climate in the area into which they had moved, made them change from pastoralism to agriculture and adopt a more settled life than their relatives the Karamojong, who remained as pastoralists.

9 The Interlacustrine Kingdoms 1650-1900

The empire of Bunyoro-Kitara which sprang up, probably in the thirteenth century, under the Bachwezi rulers had its centre in the western part of Uganda and included, until the fifteenth century, modern Bunyoro, Buganda, Toro, Karagwe, Ankole, Busoga and some parts of modern Lango. This represented nearly three-quarters of modern Uganda. All these states, however, were not strictly under the Bachwezi as a single political entity. Each state had a ruling class who paid allegiance to the Bachwezi emperors. The Bachwezi emperors sent relatives as their representatives to rule over some states, but the relatives eventually took over the leadership and disregarded the emperors. When the Babito, a Luo dynasty, took over the kingdom of Bunyoro by superseding the Bachwezi in the fifteenth century, this was one reason for the other states starting to withdraw their allegiance and asserting their independence from the Babito kings, thus splitting up much of the area originally belonging to the empire of Bunyoro-Kitara and causing the empire to disintegrate.

Buganda

Up to the end of the seventeenth century, Bunyoro under the Babito was still the most powerful single state in the area of modern Uganda, although Ankole and Buganda had declared their independence on the Babito's taking over power from the Bachwezi. But the Kabakas of Buganda, from the very beginning of the Babito take-over, were intent on annexing land from the Babito's sphere of influence and taking under their hegemony those states which were still paying allegiance to Bunyoro. At this early stage, however, though the Kabakas equipped their fighters with arms to attack Bunyoro these attempts usually ended up with disastrous results. At one time, during the reign of Nakibinge towards the end of the fifteenth century, the Banyoro armies overran Buganda, driving into the centre of the kingdom, and they nearly subdued Buganda. By concerted efforts in the face of a national catastrophe, the Baganda rallied their forces and drove away the Banyoro armies. Even Baganda women took part in the fighting, using whatever weapons they could lay hands on. However, the power of the Babito remained supreme in the area until the second half of the seventeenth century. The position was changed during that period by Kabaka Mawanda who succeeded to the Buganda throne and started to challenge Bunyoro with more success. He seized the counties of Buddu, Bulemeezi, and Singo and made several principalities of Busoga and Kooki into his tributary states, all of which had previously acknowledged the overlordship of Bunyoro.

To retain and rule effectively the new lands which he was conquering, Kabaka Mawanda evolved a new institution – the Bitongole (regiments) – which were administrative posts set up in those parts newly acquired from Bunyoro. Each of these posts was headed by a staunch follower of Kabaka Mawanda, with a group of men at his disposal. In war these groups of men turned into military divisions and they were at the disposal of the Kabaka, led by their respective leaders. The Bitongole helped to prevent the conquered people from rebelling against Buganda and to prevent Bunyoro from reconquering the lost provinces. This institution proved effective and it was continued by the successors of Kabaka Mawanda.

Before the succession of Mawanda to the throne, the Kabakas had adopted a system of dismissing hereditary clan heads, who were originally the leaders of the people both politically and culturally, and from whom the Kabakas had seized power. These men were, at the beginning of the Kabakaship, very influential and they could prevent the Kabakas controlling the population. On dismissing them, the Kabakas appointed clan heads who were subservient to them and who would do whatever the Kabakas wanted. Gradually the Kabakas started to remove the clan heads from political administration. Instead, the Kabakas appointed their followers to political posts and the clan heads were left to administer clan affairs. The new courtiers were liable to summary dismissal if they proved unreliable or inefficient. Kabaka Mawanda continued to dismiss the hereditary clan heads from chieftainships from the middle of the seventeenth century. Many of the hereditary chiefs could not cope with his military programme and so he put in their places his followers who had no hereditary right to their new posts and whom he could dismiss as soon as he was dissatisfied with them. The creation of the Bitongole and the choice of his own chiefs centralized all power in his hand. His followers became malleable and were ready to obey orders in war campaigns against Bunyoro at any time. The policy of removing clan heads from political positions was also followed by the subsequent Kabakas so that the Kabakas' power gradually became supreme; the Kabakas were always sure of support from their people, from whom they could command absolute obedience.

Royal power was further strengthened in the first half of the eighteenth century by Kabaka Semakookiro who eliminated possible claimants to the throne by the execution of his own sons. Once there were no other princes to rally dissatisfied people in opposition to him, he was assured of ruling without a rival. Subsequent Kabakas learnt from him and they executed their sons, and even brothers, to this end. So a rebellion developing around royal princes during the reign of a Kabaka, or at the time of succession, became unlikely. Therefore all people tended to be strongly united behind the ruling Kabaka and to do whatever he told them to, especially in attacking the neighbours of Buganda.

The rise and expansion of Buganda was also linked to its fertile soil and the reliability of its rainfall. In addition the major food crop of the Baganda was matooke, a type of banana which did not appear to deplete the fertility of the soil. Many other parts of the Uganda region which were under Bunyoro were subject to drought and famine, so that the people had to work hard to survive. Yet the Baganda had no trouble obtaining food to feed their families, so that the men spent the greater part of their lives in raiding their neighbours, under the leadership of the Kabakas, thus getting more land and booty. From the 1840's Arabs and Swahilis from Zanzibar started to come to Buganda bringing foreign goods in exchange for ivory and slaves. From that time no wars were fought to get more land from Bunyoro but raids into Bunyoro, Ankole and Busoga continued, presumably to get slaves and ivory for sale to the Arabs and Swahilis. This was the position until the end of the reign of Muteesa I in 1884.

Further land expansion followed after 1893 when the British enlisted the help of the Baganda against Omukama Kabarega of Bunyoro, who had strongly resisted the British take-over of Bunyoro. After Kabarega's defeat in 1896 the counties of Bugangaizi and Buyaga were given to the Baganda as a reward for co-operation. These areas, which later were familiarly called the Lost Counties of Bunyoro by the Banyoro, were included in Buganda by the Buganda Agreement with the British in 1900.

Bunyoro

When the Babito, a Luo dynasty, superseded the Bachwezi in the fifteenth century, the empire of Bunyoro-Kitara gradually disintegrated with the break-away of states that once recognized the overlordship of the Bachwezi emperors, so that only a small area of the empire remained under the Babito as Bunyoro Kingdom. It was, however, still larger than the modern Bunyoro District because then Buganda and Ankole were not strong enough to seize land from it. Bunyoro started to suffer great territorial losses from the middle of the seventeenth century, first to Buganda, then to Ankole and then to Toro. Although by the nineteenth century it had lost considerable areas, it began to show new life when Omukama Kabarega succeeded to the throne in 1870. He was determined to make Bunyoro great once again by winning back to the kingdom the provinces lost to Buganda and to Ankole, and also winning back the whole of Toro, which had seceded in 1830. He also wanted to put an end to the civil apathy and disputes which were going on within the kingdom. He aroused new enthusiasm in his people, who felt that a new era of greatness had dawned. He set up a standing army, Abarusura, attacked Toro and Ankole, and raided the areas that Buganda had taken from the Bunyoro kingdom with some success. His grand programme was stopped by the arrival at Kampala, first of Captain Lugard as officer of the Imperial British East Africa Company at the end of 1889 and then by the establishment of a British protectorate over Uganda in 1894. Captain Lugard found that Omukama Kabarega had already driven Omukama Kasagama away from the throne of Toro. Omukama Kasagama had taken refuge at the court of Kabaka Mwanga at Mengo, near Kampala. Lugard, using the Company's soldiers, restored Kasagama to the throne of Toro. He then marched across Lake Albert and brought back with him the Sudanese soldiers who had been left in the Sudan by Emin Pasha, who was governor of southern Sudan on behalf of Egypt in the 1870's. Lugard stationed some of the soldiers in Toro to prevent Kabarega's attacks on the restored Omukama Kasagama and took the rest to Kampala to strengthen the Company's force. Captain Lugard left Uganda in 1892 but soon the supporters in Britain of colonization started to press for the take-over of Uganda and in 1894 Uganda was declared a British Protectorate.

On the establishment of a protectorate over Uganda, the British withdrew the Sudanese soldiers from Toro to Kampala because it had by then become expensive to maintain them there. As soon as they were withdrawn, Kabarega opened an attack on Kasagama, intent on seeing that Toro gave up its secession. The British decided to start an open war with Kabarega and they enlisted the help of the Baganda warriors. Kabarega put up a determined resistance until he was defeated in 1896, but the British forces did not manage to capture him. He escaped to Lango from where he continued to harass the British administration until he was captured in 1899 and sent to the Seychelles Islands, in the Indian Ocean.

The exile of Omukama Kabarega greatly disheartened the Banyoro. Coupled with the British giving away the counties of Bugangaizi and Buyaga to the Baganda, it made Banyoro feel that they suffered more than any other people in colonial Uganda (although the Kabaka of the Baganda, Mwanga, was also exiled with Kabarega for resisting colonial rule). Perhaps the difference between the case of Bunyoro and that of Buganda was that many influential Baganda, such as Apolo Kagwa, Stanslaus Mugwanya, Zachary Kisingiri and many others, deserted their Kabaka, joined the British and led an army against him. After his defeat, they sat around the same table with the British and negotiated terms that made them the real rulers of Buganda, ostensibly on behalf of Mwanga's one-year-old son, Daudi. But in the case of Bunyoro, once Kabarega was beaten none of the leading Banyoro saw any point in wholehearted co-operation with the British, who had been more sympathetic to the Baganda than to the Banyoro. Moreover, Kabarega appeared to the Banyoro as a man who had come to bring about a new era of greatness, so to them he was the embodiment of their hopes of national regeneration. While on the side of the Baganda, owing to the competitive spirit that had grown among them over the acquisition of political posts under the Kabakas, they had learned that any political power by one man was bound to be impermanent and that it was the duty of far-sighted men to align themselves with the new leader, who was ready to reward them for co-operation. This was the situation during the closing years of the nineteenth century. The Baganda who sided with Mwanga lost heavily, while those who joined the British to crush Mwanga and his forces came to power.

Ankole

Ankole was originally called Karokarungi, or 'the beautiful land', and it originated in the present county of Rwampara in the fifteenth century. When the empire of Bunyoro-Kitara broke up on the coming of the Babito, descendants of the Bachwezi took over Ankole. But it remained small and insignificant until the eighteenth-century when it produced a succession of dynamic kings – Bagabe – who embarked on a programme of expansion.

The Bagabe seized the small counties of Nyabusozi and Kashari from Buhweju, which was an independent state to the north. They also seized areas, as far as the Katonga river in the north, that belonged to Bunyoro. They expanded westwards and absorbed many other autonomous states, mostly through marriage alliances.

Towards the end of the eighteenth century, under Omugabe Ntare IV Kitabanyoro, Ankole armies finally defeated Bunyoro when the Banyoro came raiding the kingdom. From that time Ankole had no further reason to fear the Banyoro forces that had been leading successful attacks into the kingdom for many years. After this conclusive defeat of the Banyoro, Ankole embarked on a still more ambitious plan to expand south-westwards and in this attempt its forces clashed with Rwanda which was expanding eastwards. During Omugabe Kahaya's reign in the early nineteenth century, large Rwanda armies penetrated Shema county of Ankole but they were later driven out by the forces of the Omugabe. The Bagabe of Ankole also attacked Toro and Kooki during the reign of Muteesa I in the second half of the nineteenth century; both of these states were then under the protection of Buganda. Muteesa sent three punitive expeditions against Ankole to avenge this interference and the Baganda armies seized many cattle.

When the British set up Mbarara as the administrative headquarters for Ankole at the end of the nineteenth century, there were still several autonomous states in the area of modern Ankole which were not yet under the Bagabe. These states, however, were quite small in size and their rulers had a few hundred subjects who all spoke a similar language to that spoken by the people under the Bagabe. In 1901, mainly through the efforts of the powerful Prime Minister, Nuwa Mbaguta, the independent chiefs of the neighbouring autonomous states consented to acknowledge the paramountcy of the Omugabe and so their areas came to form modern Ankole, which made an agreement with Britain in 1901.

Toro

The kingdom of Toro was of more recent foundation among the interlacustrine kingdoms. It was carved out of the kingdom of Bunyoro in 1830 by prince Kaboyo, an elder son of a ruling Omukama. This area was quite important to Bunyoro because of its fertile soil and cool climate. It was the grazing area for the cattle of the Bakama. The princes and princesses were born and brought up there. Toro was a good example of how sons and relatives of the Bakama of Bunyoro safely carved kingdoms for themselves out of the area that was under the Bakama and so contributed to the decline of Bunyoro-Kitara when the Babito took over the empire in the fifteenth century. Kaboyo was left in peace by his father, who was of advanced age, and he set up a new dynasty that was related to that of Bunyoro and which had similar royal ceremonies.

When Toro seceded from Bunyoro, it realized that it could not maintain its independence especially if Bunyoro decided to attack it, for it was too weak; so it looked to Buganda as a protector. Buganda's protection became especially important when Omukama Kabarega ascended the throne of Bunyoro in 1870. He was determined to regain Toro and he mounted a determined attack against it. The princes of Toro then fled to the court of Buganda for refuge, and Kabaka Muteesa I reinstated them by force. But no sooner were they restored than Kabarega would drive them away again. The last prince to suffer Kabarega's attacks was Kasagama during the reign of Mwanga II of Buganda. He was reinstated finally by Lugard and the Baganda in 1891 and given Sudanese soldiers to protect him against Kabarega. When Britain declared a protectorate over Uganda in 1894, Toro's independence from Bunyoro was recognized and Kabarega, who was threatening its existence, was exiled in 1899. After signing the Buganda Agreement of 1900, Harry Johnston who was the first British Administrator of Uganda went to Toro and signed an agreement with Omukama Kasagama thereby giving a formal recognition to that kingdom as being independent of any other kingdom in Uganda.

10 The Portuguese in East Africa North of the Ruvuma

The Journey of Bartholomew Diaz

When Muslim Turks gained control of the Mediterranean route from Europe to Asia in the eleventh century, European Christian traders found it harder to obtain the coveted goods of Asia such as silk, gold and spices. They had to pay heavy transit taxes to the Muslim Turks, and traders in Turkish-held territory were often harassed by thieves. Some Europeans therefore contemplated an alternative sea route to India via West Africa, South Africa and the Indian Ocean.

Portugal, a small country with a tradition of adventurous navigation, was the first to discover such a route. In 1487 Bartholomew Diaz, who had been educated at the Portuguese school for mariners established by Prince Henry, was sent on a voyage by King John of Portugal. He had three small ships, manned by Portuguese sailors. They rounded the Cape of South Africa, but ran into severe storms and narrowly avoided shipwreck. Diaz called this the 'Cape of Storms', and the voyagers returned to Portugal with frightening stories of their experiences. Yet the king discerned the possibility of reaching India by this route and named what Diaz had called the Cape of Storms the 'Cape of Good Hope'.

The Adventures of Vasco da Gama

Ten years later the Portuguese king sent three ships under Vasco da Gama to follow Diaz's route and attempt to reach India. The crews were mainly Portuguese convicts whose loss Portugal would hardly regret on a journey of this nature. If they acquitted themselves well they would be released on their return and treated as heroes. From this period up to 1728 the East African coast north of the Ruvuma came under Portuguese influence.

56

In 1498 da Gama reached Mozambique, already an Arab colony ruled by Sultan Khwaza. The reception of the Portuguese was friendly at first. But on realizing that they were Christians, the local ruler became hostile and a few skirmishes between Arabs and Portuguese ensued. Da Gama, with superior weapons, bombarded the town.

Having taken on board two Indian pilots from Mozambique da Gama then proceeded on his way to India, reaching Zanzibar and Pemba. In neither place did he meet much opposition.

It was at Mombasa that da Gama and his men first encountered effective resistance from Arab settlers. Mozambique and Mombasa were allies. The Sultan of Mozambique had sent word to Mombasa to prevent the Portuguese from landing there.

It was a large and prosperous city with a strong Sultan. He prepared for a show of Arab strength against the Portuguese. The Sultan of Mombasa's plan was described as 'tortuous and complicated, such as his oriental mind would naturally devise, and therefore all the more likely to fail'.

He decided to trick the Portuguese into entering Mombasa harbour through an inlet flanked with reefs. There he hoped the ships would go aground and spring a leak. In the confusion the Sultan would attack and defeat the Portuguese. Da Gama sent his two pilots from Mozambique to the Sultan of Mombasa. They joined in the Sultan's conspiracy and returned with the news of the friendly welcome ostensibly awaiting the Portuguese in the harbour. The Portuguese, suspicious however of Arab intrigue, made their way into the harbour through the dangerous channel, where the first ship hit a reef and sprang a leak. The Portuguese realized the Sultan's deception immediately. Tortured by da Gama, the pilots revealed the Sultan's plot. The Portuguese repaired the damaged vessel and sailed north, leaving Mombasa untouched. However, it was to be severely punished in the future.

All along the coast the Portuguese saw more Arab than African communities for the Africans were further away in the interior. Then they reached Malindi. One report states, 'The Malindi Arabs and Swahilis had already heard that da Gama and his men were fearless and ruthless; that they were dressed from head to foot in impenetrable steel; and that they had utterly demolished the great city of Mozambique with cannon fire in pure wantonness, while on their way to seize water, food and women.'

Malindi was a splendid, small town of great wealth. Its riches sprang from the trade it carried on with India exchanging gold, ivory, copper and quicksilver for cloth. But the Malindi Arabs conducted a running feud with those of Mombasa. The feud had lasted several centuries. Having heard that da Gama had been repulsed at Mombasa, the Sultan of Malindi saw in da Gama a possible ally against Mombasa. Da Gama accepted the Sultan's cordial welcome, though wary of Arab treachery after his recent experiences; but he was prepared to be ruthless at the slightest sign of intrigue.

Fortunately for da Gama, and the Portuguese who came after him, Malindi was a true friend and ally. In recognition of that friendship da Gama built a pillar in Malindi which still stands today, though its authenticity has been disputed. Later, when da Gama had returned to Portugal, Mombasa attacked Malindi. But Mombasa was soon to pay a heavy price for its action.

From Malindi da Gama sailed to Calcutta. He returned to Portugal in 1499. He had mapped the route for future voyages, had seen the wealth of the Swahili-Arab towns on the east coast and the tremendous riches of India. He was determined to return with sufficient ships and men to capture them for Portugal.

The Portuguese Looting of the East African Coast

On da Gama's return, King Emmanuel II of Portugal fitted out a fleet of fifteen ships with soldiers to acquire the coastal townships of East Africa and to proceed to India, also to be annexed for Portugal. He intended to build an empire. The expedition was led by Pedro Alvares Cabral, while Vasco da Gama still rested, enjoying the honours of a national hero.

On reaching Mombasa, Cabral took revenge on the Sultan for his treatment of da Gama. He bombarded the city, destroying many buildings. Many Arab and African inhabitants were killed; others fled to the interior. The Portuguese sacked, pillaged and burned Mombasa, then departed for Malindi. The chronicler of the expedition wrote, 'The soldiers looted and burned, carried off shrieking young women, tore jewels and clothes from older ones, and came staggering back to the wharf laden with such spoils and riches as they had never dreamed of before.'

Like da Gama before him, Cabral was warmly welcomed in Malindi and the Sultan was gratified by the punishment meted out to Mombasa.

Cabral reached India and after loading his fleet with valuable merchandise sailed back to Portugal to a tremendous welcome from king and populace.

Two years later da Gama was sent with a powerful fleet to force all Arab and Swahili rulers on the east coast of Africa to accept allegiance to the king of Portugal and pay tribute. The expedition would then go on to India and start colonizing there. This time da Gama had more ships and better crews, and there was no opposition from the Sultan of Mozambique, who realized by now that the Portuguese were not to be trifled with.

Da Gama sailed next to Kilwa to punish Sultan Ibrahim for having plotted against Cabral. Having taken Ibrahim prisoner and put him in irons, he asked for a huge ransom. Ibrahim had to pay a large annual tribute of 1500 gold meticals and acknowledge the supremacy of the King of Portugal. Da Gama saw an Arab ship approaching Malindi with treasure from India and without scruple seized it, killed all those aboard except young boys and took possession of its rich cargo. He then sailed into Malindi harbour to a friendly reception. After building a church there he went on to India, engaged in trading and returned to Portugal. After these pioneering journeys the Portuguese made frequent voyages to India and terrorized the East African coast into submission.

Shortly afterwards more Portuguese arrived on the coast in their thousands to conquer and subjugate the Arabs and the Swahilis, trade with them, convert them and the Africans to Christianity and establish a line of bases along the route to India. Kilwa, Sofala, Mombasa, Lamu, Pate, Pemba and Manda quickly succumbed. Churches were built, run by missionaries, merchants came, and in each town a military fort was set up for the defence of the Portuguese. Many Africans and a few Arabs were converted to Christianity. The Portuguese settlers and merchants enjoyed an easy life, for servants were cheap and plentiful.

Kilwa's Dramatic Surrender

Kilwa was captured by d'Almeida three years after the departure of da Gama. Ibrahim had not paid the promised tribute. The Sultan of Kilwa, having seen nothing of the Portuguese since the departure of da Gama over three years ago, had not unnaturally let the payment of tribute lapse. Perhaps he thought the white men would not return, that they were busy elsewhere, or that they had simply forgotten.

So it was a painful surprise when one day a big fleet was observed approaching and, as they came nearer the Sultan saw to his horror not the lofty pointed sails of Arab dhows, but the purposeful-looking square sails of the Christians.

Sultan Ibrahim was not a very brave or clever man. He seized a few treasures, bundled them on to the heads of his favourite slaves and fled into the bush.

His subjects, unaware of the departure of their sovereign and protector, continued to gaze at the huge fleet bearing down on them. They saw scores of boats, filled with armed men chanting war songs, and rapidly approaching the shore.

Then, like a bush fire, word flashed through the crowds, 'Sultan Ibrahim has gone!' The people melted away; men, women and children departed inland, leaving behind all they possessed, for the white men were close upon them. They vanished into the wilderness behind the towns.

The Portuguese stripped Kilwa of its treasures and d'Almeida appointed a new Sultan in place of Ibrahim. Sofala fell next, in an attack led by d'Almeida's captain. With the capture of both Kilwa and Sofala the Portuguese gained control of the gold from Zambia, which was being shipped first to Sofala and then to Kilwa, where the Arabs either sold it to local Asian traders or took it to Asia.

Meanwhile Arab and African rulers on the coast realized that the Portuguese were their masters. They accepted the need to pay tribute in order to live in peace and save their towns from destruction. The Portuguese would show no mercy at the slightest sign of opposition from the coastal people.

Mombasa was attacked next by d'Almeida. The Sultan there had tried to resist and had gathered a force of 1500 black Africans from the mainland who attacked the Portuguese with bows and arrows. The greater part of these unfortunate men were killed by bullets for a cause they neither knew nor understood. Once again Mombasa was plundered, an event which delighted its enemy, the Sultan of Malindi.

From East Africa d'Almeida sailed to India and became governor there, responsible for looking after Portuguese interests in India and along the East African coast.

Other coastal towns remained unconquered. Alfonso d'Albuquerque sailed from Portugal in 1506 with a fleet to subdue Lamu, Uja, Barawa and Mogadishu. The Arabs of Lamu were notoriously rich since it was the centre for shipping slaves to Arabia and Persia. They submitted without a struggle and agreed to pay tribute to the king of Portugal.

The Arabs of Oja on the borders of Somalia defied the Portuguese. As allies of the Caliph of Egypt they would not join with Christian Portugal. The Portuguese subsequently massacred all the inhabitants, stole the treasures and burned the town to the ground.

At Barawa the Portuguese faced a Somali force of 6000 soldiers armed with bows, arrows and spears. A chronicler wrote, 'The Portuguese were heavily outnumbered, but calling on God and their favourite saints, they attacked the yelling mob.' Forty Portuguese died, sixty were wounded and numerous Africans died. Because they found no treasures in Barawa the invaders decided to vent their rage on the town by burning it completely.

But when they reached Mogadishu the Portuguese realized that they were completely outnumbered by the Somali fighters and departed without a shot being fired. Instead they captured Socotra, held by Arabs from Southern Arabia.

In every defeated town the Portuguese set up a garrison, cleared a harbour for their future landings and built a fort for defence. Thus by 1508, less than ten years after da Gama had made his first historical journey, the whole coast of East Africa from Sofala to Lamu was under the rule of Portugal and paying tribute.

To safeguard their lines of communication the Portuguese defeated Muscat and sacked it. They also took the island of Ormuz, occupied by Persians. Though the Egyptians and Persians came to Muscat's aid, they were all beaten and eventually Portugal gained the mastery of the Indian Ocean. For all these achievements d'Albuquerque replaced d'Almeida as governor of India and the East African Coast.

Colonization of East Africa

Mozambique became the centre of Portuguese activities in East Africa. It took away the gold trade from Sofala and Kilwa and these two old cities dwindled to the status of villages and their walls crumbled.

The Portuguese would not allow Swahili and Arab middlemen to buy gold from the Africans and then sell it to the Portuguese. Many Arabs became impoverished and left the towns; the Arab character of Mozambique, Sofala and Kilwa was obliterated. Some Portuguese became settlers and began farming. Few Portuguese women came, especially at the beginning of the occupation, so there was intermarriage with Africans and Arabs. A large number of Portuguese settled on the island of Pate, whose prosperity increased. Intermarriage on Pate produced a large group of half-castes, still to be seen today in Mozambique.

But the Portuguese were less successful as traders than the Arabs and Africans. Though goods such as gold and ivory from the interior generally reached the coast by barter, both Africans and Arab traders from the coast tried to penetrate the interior to stimulate trade. The Portuguese made no such attempts and also forbade the Arabs and Swahilis to do so, which meant that African traders virtually ceased to bring gold and ivory to the coast.

The government of Portugal became disappointed with the Portuguese traders. Before the coming of the Portuguese about £60 000 worth of gold annually went through Sofala and Kilwa from Central Africa and then was shipped across the Indian Ocean. When the Portuguese took over the figure fell to £4000. After being castigated by Lisbon some Portuguese began to strike into the interior towards the Manika goldfields, establishing a trading post at Sena, one hundred miles up the Zambezi in 1531. A few years later the goldfields were reached and it was agreed that the chief of the Tshikanga would supply gold to Portuguese traders in return for cloth.

Other goods bought by the Portuguese were ivory, garnets, iron ore, oilstone and slaves. Indeed the shipment of African slaves to India for the Portuguese to employ in Goa reached its high mark during the Portuguese occupation of the east coast. Although Portuguese wares such as cloth, beads and bangles reached the interior there was very little contact between the Europeans and the numerous Africans there. Consequently the fighting and hatred which characterized their contacts with the Arab and Swahili colonists in coastal towns was not much in evidence with Africans inland. In 1506, however, Africans from the interior attacked the Portuguese in Sofala and impeded the flow of trade, while in 1580 others attacked a Portuguese garrison at Mozambique and wiped it out.

Jesuits, Augustinians and Dominican Roman Catholic priests also tried to make their way into the interior and win converts. They penetrated as far as the Makalanga country up to the Zambezi valley and established a number of posts. But they never succeeded in winning permanent adherents. On the coast the priests had remarkable success, even converting some Arabs from Islam. However those Arabs who became Christians did so out of opportunism rather than from conviction. For once they became Christians they were treated on an equal footing with the Portuguese settlers and merchants and young Arabs also married Portuguese women. This may explain why, when the Portuguese departed, Christianity and all its churches disappeared from the East African coast north of the Ruvuma and Islam or the African indigenous religions were re-established. What is more, the Portuguese did not encourage Arabs and Africans to become priests and take a leading role in the church. When they were eventually driven out of the territory they took their religion with them, leaving no-one behind to carry it on.

This phenomenon is an interesting one. The Portuguese spent nearly three hundred years on the East African coast north of the Ruvuma. Yet when a second wave of Christian missionary work began in 1844 led by J. L. Krapf there was no trace of the earlier exposure to Christianity. Within a period of only one hundred years after the coming of Krapf, however, Christianity was so firmly established in East Africa that, when the Europeans left, there was no fear of its fading out. It is still gaining strength. This has been due partly to a different approach whereby the role of the people in East Africa as leaders of the Christian church in all denominations has been strongly emphasized.

After the Portuguese defeat of the coastal Arab and Swahili sultans there was an apparent acceptance of Portuguese rule. The governor in Mombasa and his garrisons in all coastal towns and the Portuguese governor general in Goa across the Indian Ocean ensured this. Yet the Arab and Swahili sultans never wholeheartedly accepted foreign rule. It meant subjugation, loss of independence and loss of the Islamic culture and prestige. They inwardly hated the Portuguese. They never ceased to hanker for their former wealth, position and freedom to exploit the natives. Intrigue was rife and they were ready to rise against the Portuguese at the least sign of any leader from the Arab world who might help to drive away the invader.

This struggle against the Portuguese was epitomized by the Sultans of Mombasa. From the beginning they opposed foreign domination. They only submitted after their town was razed to the ground and sacked several times. The Sultan of Malindi, on the other hand, was happy to be an ally of the Portuguese because in this way he could bring about the downfall of his old enemy Mombasa.

To achieve the complete subjugation of Mombasa, d'Albuquerque, Governor General of Goa, built Fort Jesus in Mombasa in 1592. This was a strongly built fort similar to the castles of medieval Europe.

It was meant to protect Portuguese interests on the east coast and the route to India. After its completion the Sultan of Mombasa was deposed and instead the Sultan of Malindi, Hasan bin Ahmed, was installed ruler of both Mombasa and Malindi. He was given half the customs duties of Mombasa. In Malindi, Hasan left his uncle to look after his affairs.

The Arabs of Mombasa never forgave the Portuguese for supplanting their ruling dynasty. Nor were the Arabs in Malindi entirely satisfied with the arrangement, which was to have serious repercussions on the Portuguese.

The Arabs in Mombasa hated Hasan. His uncle in Malindi envied him for his new position of wealth and power. Although Hasan had support in Goa and Lisbon, the local governor in Mombasa, Melo Pereira, wanted him only to be a puppet. Hasan would not accept this role. His position in Mombasa became very difficult, detested as he was by the local Arabs and with his authority undermined by the governor. Pereira soon accused him of high treason against Portugal. Hasan, realizing that his life was in danger, fled into the interior among the Wasegeju people. But Pereira bribed these tribesmen and Hasan was betrayed and beheaded. Lisbon set up a commission to enquire into his death with the result that he was exonerated and his loyalty to Portugal affirmed.

His fifteen-year-old son Yusuf-bin Hasan-bin-Ali was taken to Goa to be educated there before returning to take up his position as Sultan. He spent sixteen years under the tuition of devout Jesuit priests and was converted to Christianity, taking the name of Jeronimo Chingulia, married a Portuguese girl of noble family and returned to rule Mombasa and Malindi. But his position was not made any easier than that of his father. He was suspected by the Arab Muslims and treated with condescension by the Portuguese. Jeronimo hated the Portuguese for this.

Muslim Arabs attempted to persuade him to revert to Islam, alleging that European customs were irreconcilable with those of Islam and Arabs. They began to have some influence on the Sultan, the more so because the Portuguese did not treat him with much respect. Hamilton, who has studied contemporary sources, writes:

'So tension grew in Mombasa. At least one of the Arab priests, when he went to pray at the grave of Jeronimo's father said, "let him not desecrate this holy spot with the unclean ceremonies of the infidels." There were other disabilities also. Allah had created women to be the comforters and cherishers of men. He had ordained by the mouth of his Prophet Mohammed that each man should be allowed four wives, in order to increase the strength of the family, and to divide the household tasks among the women.

But the Sultan had deprived himself of this supreme benefit; and for the rest of his life would have to endure the hardship and in the eyes of many of his subjects the humiliation of owning only one wife, and one family of legitimate children.

This was a point that struck home. It annoyed Jeronimo considerably, when he realized that for a man of his wealth and position to have one single spouse to deck with jewels and silks, when he might be flaunting four of them before his admiring subjects, was a waste of opportunity. He thought longingly of a Portuguese lady named Natalia de Sa, the beautiful wife of a Portuguese noble living in Mombasa, and of the handsome, haughty wife of the new governor, Pedro Leitao De Gamboa, and of her twelve-year-old daughter. He wished he could marry them all, and raise families from them. His hot Arab blood yearned towards women; the thought of his polygamous forebears made his present married state seem ridiculous and unbearable.'

As a result of all these dissatisfactions he organized a rebellion, killing the governor and his wife. All Arab Christians and natives were killed. Jeronimo Chingulia changed his name back to Yusuf. But when the Portuguese in Goa heard of the massacre they sent a squadron which besieged Mombasa. Yusuf succeeded in escaping from Mombasa. When they realized that he had escaped, the Portuguese burned Mombasa and left for India.

Yusuf became a wanderer, first going to Yemen and then to Madagascar. When returning to Yemen in 1635 he was killed by Arab pirates. They did not know who their victim was, but were intent only on seizing treasures from any ship that came in sight.

The Decline of Portuguese Power

Between 1635 and 1668 the Portuguese were losing their power in the East. The strategic islands of Ormuz fell to the Persians. Then the Omani Arabs led by the Imam Nasur launched an attack aimed at driving the Portuguese from their peninsula. The captured Portuguese were tortured and sent as slaves to the Persian Gulf. Imam Nasur died in 1649 and he was succeeded by bin Seif bin Malik, who drove the Portuguese from Muscat.

When Muscat fell in the north, all the towns on the East African coast rose in rebellion. Mombasa sent for help from Imam Sultan of Oman. He came to the east coast towns. Wherever he went the Arabs joined him and massacred the Portuguese and native Christians. The Portuguese, now demoralized, with their fighting spirit gone, were easily defeated.

While all these things were happening in East Africa, Portugal from 1580 had troubles at home. King Sebastian, who had succeeded to the throne a few years earlier, made it his mission to convert the Moors in North Africa and to penalize the Jews in his country by heavy taxes. But in 1580 he was killed in battle while leading his army against the Moors. After his death Portugal, conquered by Philip II of Spain, was engaged in a long struggle to drive out the Spaniards. The Portuguese had little time to defend their East African possessions. Most of the treasures of East Africa had been extracted and now the Portuguese turned their attention instead to Brazil.

Britain, France and Holland, who for a long time had resented Portugal's monopoly of the India trade, made efforts to break it. By 1650 Portuguese ascendancy on the seas was over and Portugal was no longer a power to be reckoned with.

Turkish pirates led by Mirale Bey appeared in the Red Sea and in the Persian Gulf and preyed on Portuguese shipping. They also began to attack Portuguese settlements, until in 1688 Mirale Bey was captured by the Portuguese and sent to Lisbon where he was converted to Christianity.

The Zimbas, a tribe related to the Zulus, left South Africa at this time and moved to the East African coast. They rampaged between the Zambezi and Malindi, destroying houses, devouring food stocks, and even resorting to cannibalism. The Portuguese were not spared but eventually they virtually wiped out the Zimbas at Malindi helped by the Wasegeju, a fighting tribe up-country. The remainder of the Zimbas disappeared into the interior.

The Portuguese from 1622 to 1650 were ejected by the Arabs from Ormuz and Muscat and from all the Arabian coast. The Omani Arabs led by Sultan bin Seif began to attack them in East Africa. In 1652 Pate and Zanzibar fell to the Omani and all the Portuguese there were massacred. In 1660 Faza was captured.

There was little help from Goa or Lisbon for the Portuguese garrisons of the east coast, or if help came it was too late or ineffectual. This weakness was illustrated by the thirty-three-month siege of Mombasa by Omani Arabs in 1696. Mombasa to the north of the

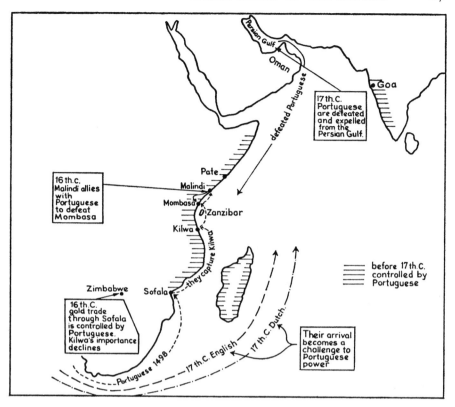

The Portuguese power in the Indian Ocean

Ruvuma river was the chief Portuguese stronghold on the coast, but Portugal could give little aid to her countrymen and in 1698 Mombasa fell to a combined army from Oman and Pate. Zanzibar, an ally of the Portuguese, was soon occupied by an army from Oman. This ended the era of domination by the Portuguese, who withdrew to Goa, in India.

The Portuguese were recalled by the sheikhs of Pate in 1728 to help oust the new overlords from Oman. The Portuguese returned and occupied Mombasa. But, by 1729, they had been driven out once more because their rule was no longer acceptable. The coastal towns wanted independence and, to achieve it, would use Oman or Portugal but would be ruled by neither.

The two hundred years of Portuguese rule were a period of decline and decadence for the city states. Those whose sheikh rulers refused to submit to the Portuguese were attacked, looted, laid waste and taxed heavily. Such was the fate of Kilwa, Mombasa, Oja and Brava.

Their beautiful medieval Afro-Arab architecture was destroyed and anything of value was carried off to Portugal. City states like Malindi, which submitted, were expected to pay high taxes. People became poor, since their trade was destroyed, and the towns were never restored to their former condition.

When the Portuguese discovered that they could readily sail direct from Mozambique to India with the help of the monsoon winds, they no longer needed to follow the coast route up to Mombasa. The northern Arab towns on the coast therefore were visited less and less by the Portuguese.

The Portuguese hated and despised the people of the coast, never attempted to come to terms with them and were hated in turn. There were many attempts to throw off Portuguese rule and Portugal sent numerous punitive expeditions which killed many people, made life unstable and progress impossible.

The Portuguese were interested only in the gold from Sofala and monopolized the gold trade, depriving Arabs and Africans of a share in it. They also put an end to most of the Arab and Persian trade with East Africa and this brought disaster to northern towns such as Gedi. Entrenched hostility to the Portuguese meant that the coastal people assimilated none of their way of life. Even Christianity, which was avidly taken up in the late nineteenth century, did not impress them when it was preached by the Portuguese priests. The only significant legacy left by the Portuguese on the coast – and then by accident rather than design – was to be found in crops from America, such as maize, groundnuts, cassava, sweet potatoes, pineapples, paw-paws and guavas.

11 The Struggle Between the Mazrui Family and the Busaidi Dynasty of Oman on the East African Coast

The Mazrui become Established

Though Oman helped the powerful Arab-Swahili families on the East African coast to drive out the Portuguese, the ruling dynasty was unable to take effective control of the coastal territory. The reason was that the Yarubi dynasty was engaged in repelling the Persians. After a bitter struggle, the Yarubi dynasty's influence was undermined and the Busaidi dynasty came to power.

To control the East African coast, Oman kept a garrison in Mombasa under Muhammed Said el Maamri. But the Arab-Swahili rulers did not want this measure of domination. They had invited the help of Oman to rid them of the power of Portugal, but after the departure of the Portuguese, they expected independence. However, the garrison was accepted for the time being, for fear the Portuguese might return.

Said el Maamri was succeeded by another Oman Arab from Hadramont. He treated the coastal people badly and after complaints Oman replaced him with Muhammed bin Athman el Mazrui in 1740. The appointment of Mazrui provoked a struggle between his family and the Abusaid dynasty of Oman. The opposition of the local Arab-Swahili rulers to Oman rule became a secondary issue. Mazrui immediately renounced his allegiance to Oman and established his family as Mombasa's hereditary rulers.

He attacked and defeated other towns which still paid allegiance to Oman, appointing members of his family as rulers. He began with Pemba, where he put a Mazrui Sultan on the throne. Pemba was particularly important to Mombasa as an ally because it supplied grain. Mombasa lacked water for crops and it was much less fertile than Pemba.

Pate, fearing the might of Mombasa, yet wanting to retain its independence, came to an understanding with the city. An alliance developed between the Sultan of Pate with the Mazrui governor in Mombasa. In 1807 the Mazrui family in Mombasa broke the alliance and placed one of their members on the throne, so that Pate came under direct control from Mombasa.

The Mazrui family attacked Zanzibar in 1753, for it was still under allegiance to Oman. But the attempt failed and Zanzibar remained bound to Oman. The Mazrui next attacked Lamu but were again unsuccessful.

Kilwa, which had become an important slave market, also attempted to throw off the suzerainty of Oman. It failed, however, and Oman appointed a governor supported by an Oman garrison. Mafia, a dependency of Kilwa, also continued to be under Oman.

Thus by 1810 Zanzibar, Kilwa and Mafia were under the sway of Oman. Mombasa, Pate, Pemba and the mainland from Tanga beyond Malindi were all under Mazrui control. The Mazrui were acknowledged by the Swahilis as heads of state in Mombasa. Although there were succession disputes between rival Mazrui claimants, the Mazrui kept their hold on Mombasa and the other areas they controlled. Furthermore, co-operation from the people of the Miji Kenda around Mombasa strengthened their hand.

Open Conflict between the Mazrui and Oman

The Mazrui family seemed to be in a very strong position and set to defy Oman on the East African coast. But in 1806 Seyyid Said became ruler of Oman. He was a man of great energy and bent on re-establishing Oman power on all the coast north of the Ruvuma river. Owing to the increased slave trade, Zanzibar now became prosperous. It paid useful taxes to Oman, money which the Busaidi family used to fight its wars against local rivals and against the Persians. By 1812 Zanzibar was paying £12 000 annually as tribute to Oman. Seyyid Said realized the value of East Africa's coast in maintaining his power, since Oman, as a desert country, was lacking in resources.

An opportunity to attack the Mazrui family soon occurred. In 1809 the Mazrui governor of Pemba, Rizike, wished to throw off his allegiance to Mombasa, but was faced with a threatened revolt at home. Instead of seeking aid from Mombasa, he approached Seyyid Said in Oman. He promised to pay tribute and to permit a garrison on the island.

Likewise there was trouble in Pate in 1819 over the succession to the throne. There were two rival factions, one supporting a Mazrui candidate while the other supported a candidate of the former dynasty. The anti-Mazrui faction asked for help from Oman and Seyyid Said sent a fleet. On the way it conquered Brava and on its arrival in Pate defeated the Mazrui supporters. A supporter of Oman was placed on the throne and a garrison to protect Omani interests was stationed on the island.

On hearing of the fleet from Oman, the governor of Zanzibar attacked the Mazrui sultan of Pemba and took over the island. Meanwhile the Mazrui governor of Mombasa died in May 1823. This weakened the Mazrui family because strife broke out over succession. In the end, Suleiman bin Ali came to the throne, to be succeeded in 1825 by Salim Rashid.

Recognizing the threat from Seyyid Said, Mombasa asked Britain in 1823 to grant it protection through the British governor of India. But Britain was already committed to friendship with Seyyid Said, who claimed to be overlord of the East African coast. In 1798 Britain had signed a treaty with Oman to prevent the French and Dutch from reaching India by way of the Middle East. However, a British naval officer Captain W. F. W. Owen, commander of the survey ship *H.M.S. Leven*, was persuaded by Suleiman to take over Mombasa temporarily as a British protectorate. He did so on his own initiative and with the intention of using the opportunity to abolish the slave trade in Mombasa. In the meantime, official instructions from London were awaited and it was not entirely clear to the British Government what was going on. Owen made terms with the Sultan, whereby Britain would have a share of customs revenues and the Sultan of Mombasa, he rashly promised, should regain his former possessions. A difficult situation existed from 1824 to 1826. The Mazrui family, in asking for British protection, had merely wanted to stave off the Omani threat. Now seeing that the threat was not so great after all, they began to chafe at Owen's presence in Mombasa. Owen's protectorate ended in 1826, when he and his garrison left the island.

Seyyid Said then demanded the surrender of Fort Jesus, but this was refused by the Sultan of Mombasa. It was captured by Seyyid Said after a bombardment in 1828. The Mazrui family agreed to recognize Oman as overlord and was allowed to rule Mombasa and its dependencies, while an Omani garrison was left in Fort Jesus to look after Omani interests. After seven months the garrison was starved out by the Mazrui governor's men and surrendered to Salim. In 1836 Salim died and was succeeded by Sultan Rashid.

Seyyid Said was apparently on good terms with Rashid. But Rashid was soon assassinated, together with many of his leading supporters. The rest of the Mazrui family were deported to Oman where they were all eventually murdered. A few who managed to escape continued to rule in Gazi, a small town north of Mombasa and in Takaungu to the south. The Sultan of Zanzibar directed the affairs of Mombasa until 1840, when Seyyid Said moved to Zanzibar and assumed responsibility for the coastal towns.

From 1728, when the Portuguese left the east coast north of the river Ruvuma, to 1840 when Seyyid Said settled in Zanzibar, there were two events of historical importance. The first was the struggle between the Omani Mazrui family and the Omani ruling family of the Busaidi. For the greater part of that period the Mazrui held their own against the Busaidi dynasty. The second event was the greatly increased settlement on the coast of Arabs from Oman after 1820. By 1840 there were so many Arabs that Arabic culture dominated and influenced Swahili culture.

Once in Zanzibar, Seyyid Said organized trade and this saw the beginning of penetration into the interior of East Africa by the coastal people in search of slaves, ivory, gum copal and rhinoceros horns.

The Involvement of Europeans in East Africa before Partition

Seyyid Said gave the impression that he ruled not only the coast from Cape Delagoa in the north to Malindi in the south, but also the whole interior of East Africa. This impression was passed on to the Europeans and given substance by his Arab and Swahili subjects who explored the interior. They passed as his representatives and browbeat the native chiefs into believing that their ruler was a very powerful Sultan. If the chiefs did not treat them well, he might come and punish them.

In fact the power of Seyyid Said extended only along the coastline. Even some islands such as Pate were independent of him. He tried and failed twice to subdue Pate in the early 1840's. So although Arab and Swahili caravans travelled from both Mombasa and Zanzibar into the interior, he had no power there. Though he had a garrison at Tanga, the ruler of nearby Usambara did not recognize him as overlord. Seyyid Said was wise enough not to insist on his power over the ruler lest it result in repercussions and he treated him as his ally. His main interest was trade, not political power in the interior. His influence, therefore, was only maintained by Arabs and Swahilis in trade posts along the caravan routes up to Lake Tanganyika in the west and Lake Malawi in the south. The African chiefs and their people, believing that these traders had a strong ruler behind

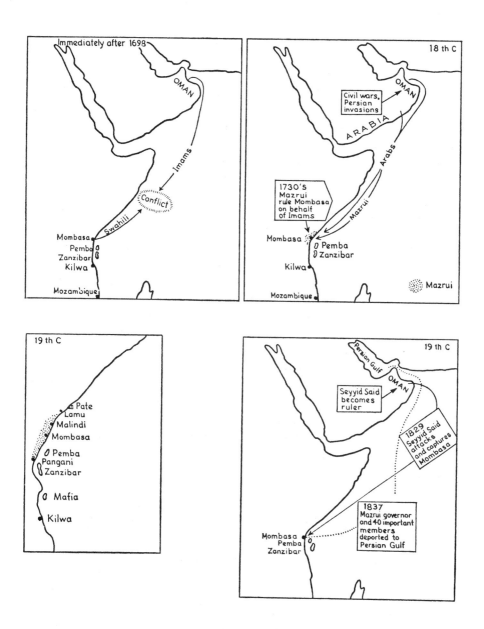

Arab settlements on the east coast of Africa

them, tended to treat them with deference, offered facilities and furthered their advance into the interior. By 1844 Arabs had reached Buganda and visited the court of Kabaka Suna II.

Britain, France, America and Germany, with their interest in trade with Seyyid Said, nonetheless felt that to establish a footing in East Africa they had first to apply to him. In this they were partly justified, because whoever held the east coast controlled the import and export of goods from East Africa.

Thus, while Seyyid Said was struggling to subdue the Mazrui family, he was also engaged in international diplomacy with Europe. Britain and France, however, were interested not only in trade but also in territorial power.

While Britain took the lead in influencing Seyyid Said's East African affairs, there were other countries also interested in having a say in East Africa. From about 1832 the Americans began to trade with Zanzibar. Their interest was purely trade and not territorial acquisition. They introduced the cloth which became known in East Africa as 'merikani,' but they never penetrated into the interior. This was left to the Asians who acted as middlemen. The Sultan actually benefited from increased customs revenue as a result of the Americans' involvement in East African trade.

The Americans were followed by German merchants from Hamburg in 1847. Like the Americans, they exported gum copal, ivory, cloves and hides. The Germans imported hardware, mirrors, beads, soap and cloth. Seyyid Said was pleased at their commercial activities for two reasons. One was that they increased his earnings and the second was that they were not interested in involving themselves in the administration of his territories. Sultan Majid, who succeeded Seyyid Said in 1856, made a commercial treaty with the Germans in 1859. These activities made Zanzibar very important and Kilwa's importance, based on the slave trade, declined.

Zanzibar Passes to British Control

Seyyid Said had contributed to the building of a commercial empire based on Zanzibar which had become a centre of international trade in East Africa. Thanks to his influence, caravans financed by Asians made regular journeys into the interior. But after his death, the decline of Zanzibar began because his successors did not possess his commercial shrewdness. After Seyyid Said's death, Britain was the controlling power in the Sultanate. Since the subsequent Sultans were entirely in the hands of Britain, it was she who had to decide the future development of Zanzibar.

12 The Slave and Ivory Trade

While slaves had been taken from East Africa for many centuries to Arab countries and to some parts of Asia, the slave trade only became important after the middle of the eighteenth century. This arose from the French demand for slaves to work in the sugar plantations on the islands of Mauritius and Reunion in the Indian Ocean and the demand for slaves in Oman and, later, in Zanzibar for labour on the clove plantations. By 1810 about 10 000 slaves a year were being sold at Kilwa and Zanzibar to the French and Arabs. When the French demand declined, owing to pressure at home and in Britain, the Arab slave trade became dominant.

From the 1820's the Arab slave buying increased through the influence of Seyyid Said, who encouraged more Arabs to settle on Zanzibar and Pemba and also secured commercial connections with Europeans, Indians and Americans. These factors necessitated an increase in the slave trade because the Arab settlers in Zanzibar and Pemba needed slaves to work on their clove plantations, while the Americans, Indians and Europeans wanted ivory, which was transported from the interior to the coast mainly by slave porters. Thus even the generally anti-slavery British permitted it because 'no slavery' meant 'no ivory'. By 1839 40 000 slaves were being sold every year in the Zanzibar market.

Slave Routes and Slave Areas

There were three main trade routes from the interior to the coast. These routes had been originally opened up by the Nyamwezi, the Bisa, the Yao and the Kamba. The southern route centred on such ports as Kilwa-Kivinje, Mikindani and Lindi and went through the areas occupied by the Makonde, the Makua and the Yao to the Lake Malawi area. This route was primarily for carrying slaves not ivory. The Yao, who were the main agents in the trade, sold their slaves

76

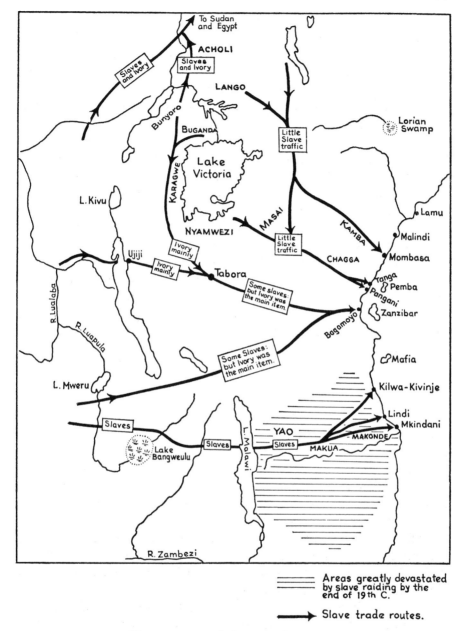

Slave areas and slave trade routes

to the Arabs. As a result of slaving, which caused a lack of men to tend the farms, the Kilwa hinterland and the Lake Malawi region lay wasted and neglected by the end of the nineteenth century.

The second route centred on Bagamoyo, on the mainland opposite Zanzibar and went into the interior towards the Nyamwezi country, where the Arabs and Swahili possessed an important trading centre at Tabora. Tabora was a hub of commerce with routes spreading west to Ujiji and the Congo, north to Karagwe and Buganda and south to Katanga. While there was some traffic in slaves on this network, the main item of trade was ivory.

The third route of penetration into the interior began on the Northern Tanzania and Southern Kenya coasts, from such ports as Pangani, Tanga and Mombasa. Various roads led to the Chagga round Kilimanjaro and beyond through the territory of the Masai to the eastern shores of Lake Victoria. Groups of people such as the Masai would not permit Arab or Swahili merchants on this route and as a result the traders were mostly Kamba.

East Africa was penetrated by another group of traders – Egyptians and Sudanese who were the vanguard of Egyptian penetration and imperialism down the Nile river. They came in search of slaves and ivory and had established themselves in Northern Uganda among the Acholi by the 1850's and had penetrated into Lango and Bunyoro by the 1870's.

Results of the Slave and Ivory Trade

Socially and politically the slave trade shattered many African peoples. Some nations, who previously were numerous, were reduced quite drastically as a result of depopulation. Others used the weapons and wealth from the ivory trade to form themselves into new and larger political groups. On the whole, much human misery resulted. Following the suppression of the slave trade, some nations, like the Yao, found it difficult to settle down to agriculture and give up slave dealing. In addition, the slave trade left a legacy of suspicion among different African ethnic groups, and also between Africans and the descendants of the Arabs and Swahilis.

Economically the slave and ivory trade brought East Africans into world trade and increased the exchange of goods among many ethnic groups. Generally the effects were worse along the southern route, where slaving was the major occupation, than along the central and northern routes, where ivory was more important.

In the latter half of the nineteenth century, it appeared as if trade were leading to political influence. In some areas traders were establishing kingdoms; parts of Acholi were for some time controlled by the trader Abu Saud and in the Congo, Tippu Tip, son of an Arab father and African mother from the Tabora area, set up a state, Manyema, where he controlled trade and administered justice.

13 The Suppression of the Slave Trade

Early protests against the slave trade and slavery were made by the Quakers, both in England and America, as early as the seventeenth century and during the eighteenth century the opposition in both countries increased. We should remember, however, that by the eighteenth century England was the greatest slaving country in the world. In 1772 the Supreme Court of England declared that the British law did not allow slavery in England. English sugar planters from the West Indies, who had brought slaves to England as their servants, were supposed to free them as a result of the Supreme Court ruling.

From this time on, the Anti-Slavery League, led by William Wilberforce and Thomas Clarkson, endeavoured to get a law passed in Britain stopping the slave trade in all British colonies. In 1807 an Act of Parliament was passed in the British Parliament that made it illegal for British subjects to engage in the slave trade anywhere in the world. Britain set up a naval patrol in West Africa to stop her subjects from trafficking in slaves. She persuaded other countries to prevent their subjects from engaging in the slave trade as well. Some countries, such as Denmark and Holland, had already outlawed the trade at the beginning of the nineteenth century and, with British persuasion, Portugal, France and Spain had outlawed the trade by 1820. Despite these laws, ships from most nations continued to carry slaves across the Atlantic until the American Civil War in the 1860's.

The Fight Against the Slave Trade and Slavery in East Africa

East Africa was not affected immediately by the British Slave Act of 1807 because no British subjects were directly involved in slaving in East Africa.

By 1820 Britain had sent a naval patrol to the Indian Ocean but the British officers of the patrol had no right to search French vessels which were suspected of carrying slaves to Mauritius and Reunion in the Indian Ocean and to the West Indies. Since the naval patrol did not have many ships, it was very difficult to stop the activities of the Arab slaving dhows on the long coast of East Africa.

Britain's chief ally was Seyyid Said, Sultan of Zanzibar, who was the main slaver in East Africa. Britain was therefore reluctant to undermine the power and wealth of her ally. Furthermore the slave trade in East Africa did not interfere with British trade as it did in West Africa. Thus if Britain could abolish the trade without expense and harm to her own interests she would. In 1822 Said wanted British help against the Mazrui family of Mombasa so he signed the Moresby Treaty which limited the flow of slaves to his Arabian possessions from his East African lands. However, watching the East African coast was only a minor duty of British ships in the Indian Ocean and the trade went on much as before. The Hammerton Treaty of 1845 followed, which restricted the slave trade to Said's East African possessions but, once again, the trade continued to flourish as before.

In 1870 the British wanted to increase their naval power in the Indian Ocean for political reasons in India. The British government decided that Parliament was unlikely to vote the extra funds needed unless increased naval strength was linked to a humanitarian cause, the anti-slavery campaign. This proved accurate and Parliament agreed to an enlarged naval force in the Indian Ocean for this purpose. The new Sultan, Barghash, who had become Sultan in 1870, was threatened with a bombardment of Zanzibar if he refused to stop the slave trade. He gave in and in 1873 signed the treaty which was the death blow to the slave trade. On the day the treaty was signed the Zanzibar slave market was closed and later a church was built on this site. Suppressing the East African slave trade must have been much simpler than elsewhere in Africa since it was all centred on one market in Zanzibar. However, the British had long believed that no slavery meant no ivory, a product they wanted, and they feared that the Sultans of Zanzibar, if pressed too hard, would turn to France as a 'big brother and protector', a position which would have given France great commercial advantages in East Africa.

Effects of Suppression in East Africa

The first effect of the suppression of the slave trade was to confirm among the Arabs and Swahilis that their Sultan had lost his sovereignty over the East African coast and that he was no more than a British puppet. The Arabs and Swahilis threatened to revolt but feared the British military power to crush their independence. They could no longer be counted upon to give their complete loyalty to the Sultan, however. Furthermore, a disastrous hurricane in 1873 destroyed the clove plantations of Zanzibar while slave labour was now more difficult to get. Of course many Arab-Swahilis had suffered economically from the suppression of the trade in slaves. Thus there were strong economic as well as political grievances against the Sultan's government.

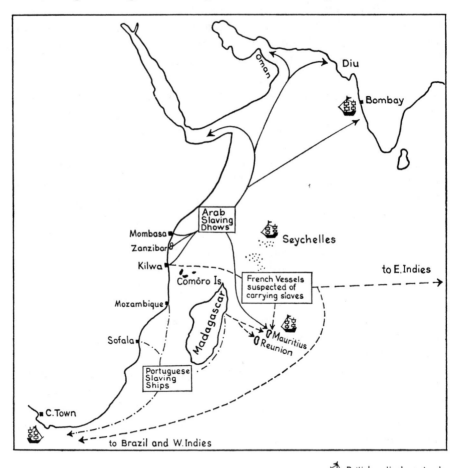

The eastern slave trade

The second effect was to loosen the economic and in part political hold which the Sultan held over East African nations and the Sultan's 'empire' in East Africa began to fall apart. Tippu Tip, a Swahili in the Congo, virtually created an independent state in Manyema and began selling his ivory and slaves to the Belgians in the Congo. Mirambo led a revolt among the Nyamwezi against Arab influence and authority among his people. It would not be long before the scramble for East Africa began, a contest largely between the economically and politically weakened Arabs and the stronger Europeans. The suppression of the slave trade helped to decide that the Europeans would win this contest and, as in West Africa, suppression of the slave trade led to the partition – Britain taking over Kenya, and later on Zanzibar and Uganda and Germany taking over Tanganyika while France agreed to the deal. However, once the British and German administrations had established themselves, they introduced forced labour, an only slightly disguised form of slavery, and this practice was continued in the British colonies despite the proclamation of 1897 which abolished the institution of slavery in British East Africa. This forced labour ended in the early 1920's after a change of British colonial policy because Britain wanted to demonstrate to the world that she was trying to champion the interests of the Africans. Moreover in Kenya British settlers were adopting the system of African forced labour for their farms, using their influence in the Kenya Legislative Council. To discourage this, British administrators gave a lead by abandoning the system of forced labour for public works.

14 The Impact of the Ngoni Invasion on East Africa

The Ngoni originally lived in South Africa, in Northern Zululand. As a result of the wars of Shaka Zulu, the Ngoni under their leader Zwangendaba, had fled from their area in 1820 and were wandering in search of a new home. In 1835 they crossed the Zambezi and marched northwards through Malawi and Zambia and reached the Fipa Plateau to the south of the Rufiji River early in the 1840's. They had learned the military tactics of the Zulus and they used these tactics on their way to the Fipa Plateau, incorporating the defeated people in their ranks as they went. By the time they settled in Tanzania, the additional non-Ngoni peoples were greater in number than the original Ngoni. The incorporated peoples had only partly assimilated Ngoni values, culture and language, and were unable to maintain their unity and create a large centralized state as their relatives had done in South and Central Africa.

The Ngoni Expansion

Zwangendaba died in 1848 and at once the Ngoni people started to feel the absence of his wise and strong rule. They split into five groups, two of which remained in Tanzania and the rest settled in Malawi and Zambia.

The first Tanzania group of the Ngoni to break away went north from Fipa and became known as the Ngoni-Tuta. They went on raiding and met the Holoholo on the eastern shores of Lake Tanganyika. The Holoholo finally adopted the war tactics of the Ngoni and fought on equal terms with the Ngoni-Tuta, whom they defeated.

After rallying from their defeat by the Holoholo, the Ngoni-Tuta turned to harass the Nyamwezi in 1850's. In so doing they upset the Arab trade route between Tabora and Ujiji and raided as far as the southern shores of Lake Victoria. They captured many Nyamwezi whom they incorporated in their ranks. The Ngoni-Tuta disturbed a vast area of central Tanzania, preparing the way for Mirambo to build up a strong Nyamwezi Kingdom because of the many Nyamwezi chiefdoms weakened by the disturbances.

The second Ngoni group was called the Ngoni-Gwangara and it was led eastwards from Fipa to Songea by Zulu-Gama. Here they found another Ngoni kingdom set up by the Ngoni-Maseko, who did not belong originally to the group of Zwangendaba, but had come from southern Mozambique. They had crossed the Zambezi near its confluence with the Shire River, marched to the east of Lake Malawi and reached Songea early in the 1840's. Led by Maputo, the Ngoni-Maseko were stronger than the Ngoni-Gwangara but they were weakened by intrigue among them and the Ngoni-Gwangara drove them away from Songea in the 1860's. They went across the Ruvuma and eventually settled in South-western Malawi. The Ngoni-Gwangara soon split into a northern and southern kingdom.

From Songea the Ngoni-Gwangara raided far and wide between Lake Malawi and the coast till the imposition of German rule in 1886. Southern Tanzania lived in fear of raids by the Ngoni-Gwangara of Songea who were always out to seize captives and amalgamate them in their numbers. At the same time brigands called Maviti started raids in imitation of the Ngoni-Gwangara, but with the intention of capturing people for sale as slaves. Though the Ngoni-Gwangara also sold slaves, their chief objective in capturing people was to incorporate them in their society to strengthen their ranks.

Ngoni Inspired States: Sangu

Sangu borders on the plateau of Fipa on its eastern side. Here there were a number of Sangu chiefdoms quarrelling with one another. As a result of raids of the Ngoni under Zwangendaba, Mwahawangu, one of the many Sangu chiefs, withdrew north-east to Uhehe from whence Mwahawangu returned to his chiefdom. After the death of Zwangendaba in 1848, Mwahawangu taught his followers the military tactics of the Ngoni, conquered the other Sangu chiefdoms and created a united Sangu state. His grandson Merere succeeded him around 1860 and dominated much of the southern highlands from his base at Utengule into the 1870's, after which the Sangu were overshadowed by the Hehe.

The Hehe

The Hehe lived in the southern highlands of Tanzania and they were originally organized in more than thirty independent chiefdoms. From the 1850's, under the leadership of Muyugumba, all were united in one state. He used the military tactics of the Ngoni and Merere lost most of the Sangu state to Muyugumba by 1877. In their expansion the Hehe came into conflict with the Ngoni-Gwangara of Songea. They fought two wars, one in 1878 and the other one in 1881, which were inconclusive and a truce was concluded under the new Hehe ruler, Mkwawa. This brought some peace between the two groups. Together with the Ngoni-Gwangara, the Hehe remained the most powerful state in southern Tanzania until effective German rule was established there.

The Mbunga

The Ndendeuli were living in part of the Songea area in which the Ngoni-Gwangara clashed with the Ngoni-Maseko. The Ndendeuli learned the new military tactics from the Ngoni too. When the Ngoni-Maseko were defeated and fled to Malawi, they left some remnants of their group behind them. These were gathered by the Ndendeuli into their society and a new society developed known as the Mbunga, who were routed by the Ngoni-Ngwangara about 1862, and fled northwards across the Kilombero valley, settling south of Morogoro.

Summary

The Ngoni shattered traditional society in Southern and Western Tanzania. Ethnic groups which failed to imitate their methods had their social organization destroyed and many of them were killed. Their remnants turned into brigands who terrorized the area looking for slaves to feed to the East Coast trade. The other tribal groups which learnt and imitated the Ngoni methods of warfare resisted the Ngoni onslaught and at the same time began taking over parts (or whole states) of those groups whose social equilibrium had been destroyed. This is how the Sangu, Hehe, Mbunga and the Nyamwezi under Mirambo created large states.

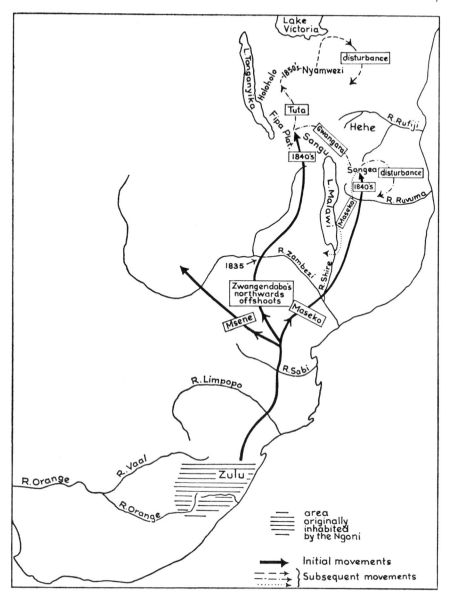

Northward offshoots of Ngoni under Zwangendaba and others

15 The Empire of Mirambo

The Situation of Unyamwezi before Mirambo

The Nyamwezi are found east of Lake Tanganyika and they belong
to the same group as the Bantu of Western Uganda and the Bantu
people of the lake region of Tanzania. They were divided into many
independent chiefdoms which quarrelled among themselves. Within
each chiefdom there were always bitter quarrels as to who would
succeed as the head of the chiefdom when a ruler died.

From the first half of the eighteenth century the Nyamwezi became
commercially minded and they initiated direct trade with the east
coast. From the 1820's, through the influence of Seyyid Said, Arabs
started to penetrate the interior to ensure a steady and adequate supply
of slaves and ivory to Zanzibar. The Nyamwezi continued to send
trading caravans to the coast and some of them acted as porters in
Arab caravans.

Some Arabs settled at Tabora in Unyanyembe, one of the numerous
Nyamwezi chiefdoms. The chief of Unyanyembe, Fundikira,
welcomed them because this gave Unyanyembe an advantage over
its neighbouring Nyamwezi chiefdoms. The Arab traders took a hand
in the direction of the political affairs of Unyanyembe and, after
the death of Chief Fundikira in the 1850's, the Arabs drove out
the new chief, Munywa Sere, for demanding high taxes from trading
in slaves and ivory and installed their puppet, Mkasiwa.

The Rise of Mirambo

While the situation was developing like this in Unyanyembe,
Mirambo became chief of Ugowe, a small Nyamwezi chiefdom. He
then inherited another chiefdom, Uliankuru, through his mother.
Around this nucleus he gradually consolidated his power and influence
and by 1876 his capital at Urambo was quite important as a slave

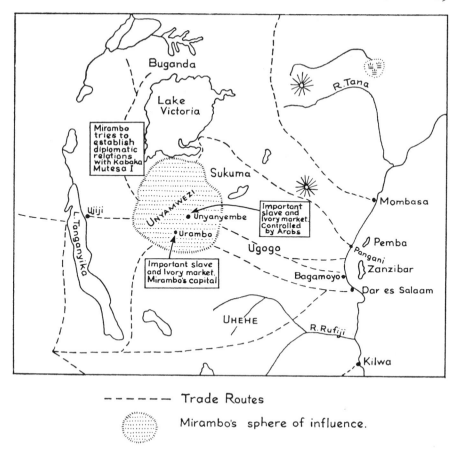

Trade routes and Mirambo's empire

and ivory market, its only rival being the market of Unyanyembe, which was controlled by the Arabs.

Mirambo was a good soldier and he led his army in battle. He acquired guns and he had about 5000 armed professional soldiers plus 7000 other soldiers, which helped his success in attacking other Nyamwezi chiefdoms whose stability had already been rocked by the incursions of the Ngoni-Tuta. The conquered enemies were absorbed and the youths were recruited into the army. He never attacked his neighbours, the Sukuma, to the north, however, because the trade which he wanted to capture was concentrated in Arab hands and those of other Nyamwezi rulers in Nyamwezi country.

By 1880 Mirambo had extended his influence to the west and

north-west of Tabora. In this way he gained control over the territory crossed by the caravan routes from the coast. There were two main routes and one of them proceeded north-westwards through Karagwe to Buganda; the other one ran to Ujiji and beyond. This was a large area and it came to be called the empire of Mirambo.

This large empire brought Mirambo into conflict with the Arabs because their trade routes lay in his territory. He demanded transit fees from the Arabs for protection while passing through his dominion and he also demanded homage from them as a great ruler. The Arabs refused both, so he closed the routes and, from 1871 to 1875, there was a struggle between his forces and the Arabs, during which time trade west of Tabora was stopped. At last, fearing to lose their trade, the Arabs accepted Mirambo's terms and trading was resumed.

Mirambo was at peace with the Europeans. He invited missionaries to settle in his empire, hoping to benefit from their knowledge and skill and hoping for prestige from their presence in his country. Mirambo tried to establish diplomatic relations with Kabaka Muteesa I of Buganda but these did not materialize because Muteesa was preoccupied with warding off trouble from Egypt.

Mirambo's empire, however, had no foundation based on tradition. It was built around his personality. The groups of people whom he conquered continued with their separate traditional institutions and there was little effective administrative machinery at the centre. When he died, in 1884, his empire crumbled.

16 European Travellers in the Interior of East Africa

Early Information

We have two written works which indicate that the East African coast was known to the outside world as early as the first century A.D. One is called *the Periplus of the Erythrean Sea* and the other is the *Geography of Ptolemy*, both written by Greeks. In the ninth century we get even more accurate information of the east coast of Africa from Arab travellers such as al-Masudi. However there was no information about the interior because the people on the coast did not penetrate it. Although they used to get trade goods from the interior, these commodities reached the coast by a system of barter from one tribe to another, so that people from far inland did not actually reach the coast to tell Arabs anything about the interior.

The Nineteenth Century

From the 1820's, as a result of Seyyid Said's involvement in East Africa, Arabs started to fit out caravans for the interior to obtain ivory and slaves. By 1840 caravans were arriving in Uganda and Arabs could then talk about the lakes system in the interior and about the Nile. This information soon aroused the curiosity of European geographers who wanted to know about the source of the Nile and the lakes system in the interior of East Africa. By 1840 the river system of West Africa had been satisfactorily mapped by men from Europe and so geographical interest now centred on the exploration of the system of rivers and lakes in East and Central Africa.

European Interest Aroused

The visits of three German missionaries into the interior and the stories which they heard from Arabs greatly excited British geographers, who were keen to 'explore' the sources of the rivers and the extent of the lakes. In 1844, Dr Ludwig Krapf settled at Rabai near Mombasa to start a C.M.S. mission station there. The Church Missionary Society was a British Society which was then joined by other nationals in Europe to spread Christianity to Asia, America, Australia and Africa. The Germans were interested in this society. Krapf, under its auspices, had worked in Ethiopia for some years. But he failed to make an impression there. So he decided to move to East Africa hoping to do better. He was soon followed by two other C.M.S. German missionaries, J. Rebmann and J. Erhardt.

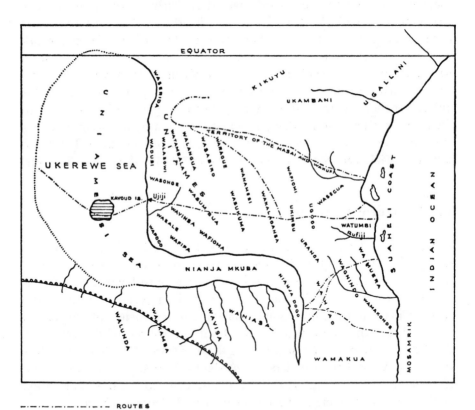

Map drawn by J. Erhardt early 1850 to show the interior of East Africa.

Krapf marched from Rabai to the headwaters of the Tana River and saw Mount Kenya in 1849, while Rebmann in his marches of the previous year had seen the snow-capped top of Mt Kilimanjaro of Tanzania at a distance. Erhardt, on the other hand, using the stories told him by Arab travellers, drew a map of what he thought to be the interior of East Africa showing the lakes system. The map was quite wrong, but this map and the information of a snow-capped mountain on the Equator created much curiosity among geographers.

The Travellers

Impressed by the above information and the map, the Royal Geographical Society of Britain sent Richard Burton and John Speke in 1856 to look for the source of the White Nile in the lakes system of East Africa. They arrived first in Zanzibar.

Burton and Speke left Zanzibar and followed the caravan routes to Ujiji on Lake Tanganyika. Speke went on to Mwanza where he saw and named the great lake, Victoria, after which they returned to Britain. Naturally, the people living around the lake had their own names for it, but the European explorers liked to see themselves as the first men to 'discover the wonders of the world', to feel they were finding new marvels, and the European world turned them into heroes. (No one has suggested, however, that the first African to see either the Alps or the Thames discovered them.) Speke guessed that Lake Victoria was the source of the Nile. In 1860 Speke was sent again, this time with James Grant, by the Geographical Society to East Africa to test his guess and really make sure that the Nile originated from Lake Victoria. On their arrival in Zanzibar they followed the caravan routes to Buganda, where they visited the court of Muteesa I, and later in Bunyoro they met Kamurasi, then Omukama of that kingdom. They visited the outlet of the Nile at Jinja and called the cataracts the Ripon Falls. They then began to trace the Nile north and at Gondokoro they met Samuel Baker, another English explorer who was accompanied by his wife travelling south on the Nile intent on seeing from where the river originated. The Bakers pushed on to Lake Albert which on pure surmise they concluded was the source of the Nile. In the meantime Speke and Grant arrived in Khartoum and sent a cable to the Royal Geographical Society saying that they had solved the mystery of the source of the Nile.

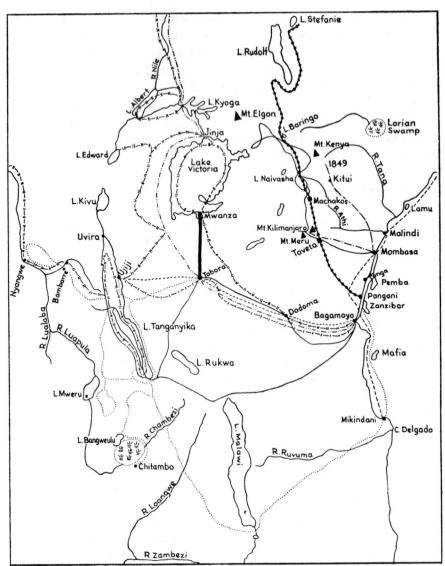

Note: Lake Albert
became Lake Mobutu
and Lake Edward
became Lake Idi Amin
Dada in 1974

─ ·· ─ ·· ─	Rebmann 1848
─ ── ─	Krapf 1849-52
── ── ──	Burton and Speke 1857-59
▬▬▬	Speke
── ·· ── ·· ──	Speke and Grant 1860-63
─×─×─×─	Baker with his wife 1863-64
············	Livingstone 1866-73
─│─│─│─│─	Stanley 1871-72
─║─┼─┼─║─	" 1874-76
────────	Thomson 1883-84
●─●─●─●─●	Teleki 1887

European travellers in the interior of East Africa

Livingstone and Stanley

With the conflicting evidence of the Bakers and Speke and Grant, Europeans were as confused about the Nile as before. So David Livingstone, a kind of wandering missionary, began the search for the source of the Nile in 1866. He started from Mikindani and followed the caravan route to the south of Lake Malawi, then turned north to Lake Tanganyika. Europe lost contact with Livingstone for a year and feared he was dead, so Henry M. Stanley, a newspaper reporter, set out to find him in 1871. The two men met at Ujiji and they examined Lake Tanganyika and found nothing which looked like the Nile. Stanley, having vainly attempted to persuade Livingstone to return home with him, returned to Europe and Livingstone died at Ujiji in 1873. His African servants and friends carried his body back to the coast where it was shipped to England and buried in Westminster Abbey. In 1874 Stanley returned to East Africa and canoed around Lake Victoria to Jinja, again seeing the source of the Nile, travelled around Lake Tanganyika showing it had no connection with the Nile and then followed the Lualaba river to its junction with the Congo and down the Congo to the Atlantic coast in West Africa. He thus confirmed Speke's view that Lake Victoria was the source of the Nile and for the Europeans the mystery was solved.

The Effect of the Travellers

It is less important to know which traveller went where or why he went, than it is to know what all this activity signified and what its end result was. In the first place, the travellers focused the attention of Europe on East Africa, an attention which led to the European military invasion and occupation of East Africa. Now they were scrambling to find the source of the Nile; soon they would be scrambling to own and control East Africa. Neither African nor Arab realized this at the time and almost everywhere these pink and red faced men were offered open-handed hospitality and assistance, despite the fact that they often did not behave exactly as strangers should in a foreign land. Stanley, for example, assisted a revolt against Kabarega in Bunyoro and he nearly exterminated the inhabitants of Ukerewe island in Lake Victoria, using guns which he distributed to his African porters. These islanders were trying to prevent him from continuing on his travels in search of the source of the Nile.

Secondly, almost all wrote travel books, or left behind manuscripts or diaries which were published after their death. Livingstone had travelled along the southern slave route to Lake Malawi and he wrote in lurid fashion about the degradation and sufferings of the slaves. He called for missionaries and travellers to follow in his footsteps to replace the slave trade with Christianity or commerce. The first result was for an intense missionary interest to be aroused and all the great inflow of missionaries and mission societies into East Africa followed.

Thirdly, all the travellers excited the interest of European traders. Almost all, including Livingstone, exaggerated the wealth in Africa which would enrich the European trader and called for white settlers also to seek their fortune in Africa. Many missionaries who followed Livingstone added their voices to the call for white settlers and the ultimate result was the settler colonies of East and Central Africa. Thus the missions followed the travellers and the traders came behind, followed ultimately by the military and the settlers. But credit must be given to such missionaries as Livingstone for, whatever may be the thinking of some people today, they were genuinely interested in bettering the situation of the Africans according to what they thought to be the interests of the Africans.

Finally, the travel books written by the travellers created an image of Africa in Europe and America which persisted for almost a century and is by no means entirely changed today. Many sought, through exaggeration, to be sensational, many sought to highlight the worst features of African and Arab life in order to appeal to the European humanitarian instinct, and many vastly exaggerated the wealth of Africa to draw Europeans towards it. However, many wrote about the customs, politics, religion and history of various peoples which helps us today to reconstruct African life in nineteenth century East Africa. The effects, short and long term, worked both for good and for evil for Africa and in this the travellers were exactly like any other historical phenomenon.

Others

Another European traveller of note was Dr Fischer, a German, who reached Lake Naivasha in 1872 from the coast. There was also Joseph Thomson who travelled across Masailand and reached Mount Kenya, Lake Baringo, Mount Elgon and the north-east corner of

Lake Victoria in 1883-4. He was the first European to demonstrate that it was shorter to get into the interior through Masailand instead of the three old routes (see map p. 94). Finally, Count Teleki, a Hungarian, reached Lake Rudolf in 1888.

The travels of all these explorers in the interior solved the question of the lake and river system of East Africa. By the 1880's the interior was no longer vaguely imagined by the people of Europe but competently mapped and described. Besides identifying the situation of the rivers and lakes, the explorers also observed the flora and fauna of the area, a subject of especial interest to European scientists and settlers.

17 Christian Missionaries

As we saw in the previous chapter, the first East African missionaries were Germans from the Christian Missionary Society. The first was Dr Ludwig Krapf who set up a post at Rabai near Mombasa in 1844. He was joined by J. Rebmann in 1846 and by J. Erhardt in 1849. They found little enthusiasm for Christianity among the people of the Miji Kenda near Mombasa so they turned to travelling in the interior.

In the early 1860's the Universities Mission to Central Africa moved from Malawi, on the Shire River, to Zanzibar because they could not communicate easily with the outside world from Malawi. In addition the Arab traders there were against the establishment of the mission for it opposed the slave trade. A group of the C.M.S. followed the Universities Mission to Zanzibar. All these engaged in the work of helping the freed slaves on Zanzibar. In the 1870's the Universities Mission to Central Africa established mission posts at Tanga and around the Ruvuma River. Within the same period the United Methodists established themselves at Ribe on the coast of Kenya and the London Missionary Society set up a post on Lake Tanganyika. In 1877 another group of the C.M.S. arrived in Uganda at Kampala and started their mission. All these Protestant missionary societies had their bases in Britain.

The Roman Catholic missionaries were from France. The Holy Ghost Fathers arrived at Zanzibar from Reunion in the Indian Ocean in 1862 and, in 1868, they set up another station on the mainland of Tanzania at Bagamoyo. They were followed by the White Fathers, whose work is described later in this chapter.

Spread of Missionary Work on the Coast

After the suppression of the slave trade in 1873 the question of providing for freed slaves became serious. The C.M.S. opened a post near Mombasa known as Freretown to help in the work of rehabilitation. The missionaries taught Christianity, writing, reading and manual skills so that the people could support themselves when they left the mission posts. The freed slaves, after acquiring Christian principles and manual skills, were usually married and set up in what were called Christian villages. This helped to spread Christianity across the nearer parts of the interior. By 1885 the Holy Ghost Fathers had villages of this nature about one hundred miles away from Bagamoyo.

Missionary Work in the Interior

From the coast the C.M.S. set up a post at Mpwapwa in Ugogo and another one at Usambiro, both in Tanzania. The chiefs there liked the missionaries but their presence was not welcomed by the Arabs because they harboured fleeing slaves who belonged to the Arabs.

In 1878 the London Missionary Society set up a post at Ujiji, followed by the White Fathers the following year. The latter also established a post at Unyanyembe in 1881 and later at Tabora and at Kibanga, opposite Ujiji on Lake Tanganyika. Mission activity in the interior depended upon the friendliness, co-operation and assistance of both the Arab-Swahili merchants and the African rulers. The London Missionary Society had to abandon Ujiji in 1883 as a result of Arab hostility and the White Fathers left Unyanyembe in 1889 because Isike, the ruler, was no longer co-operative. However, as a general rule, both the Arabs and African rulers tolerated the missions as being at least harmless and at best institutions of good work. Kings often looked upon the missionary as a diplomatic representative of his homeland – the equivalent of a modern embassy – through which the kings could communicate with European powers.

Missionary endeavour in Uganda came as a result of Stanley's call for missionaries to Buganda in 1875, when he was on his travels to confirm Speke's assertion that Lake Victoria was the source of the Nile. The C.M.S. were the first to arrive at Kampala, in 1877, travelling by the Tabora-Usukuma-Karagwe route. The White Fathers followed them in 1879, travelling by the same route. Both groups of missionaries were given lodgings in the residence of King Muteesa I of Buganda and they started to teach Christianity, reading and writing. An account of their work is given in Chapter 22.

With the notable exception of the Baganda, it did not appear that the missions were likely to have any great success among East African peoples at that time. It was only after the European invasion and the opening of the colonial period that many East Africans began to see that, if they were to adjust to European rule and rise under it, the missions were the institutions which could provide them with the skills to do so.

Missionary Schools and Medical Missions

Both the Catholic and the Protestant missionaries were engaged primarily in teaching Christianity to the people. In some places their success in converting Africans was more rapid than in others, but by 1900 Christianity had spread in all the three East African countries. As a result, the belief of Africans in their various traditional religions began gradually to diminish.

Besides teaching religion, the missionaries engaged in the work of education. They started schools of a rudimentary nature at first, but by the beginning of the Second World War in 1939, these schools, aided by the Governments, had developed into the present-day system with Makerere College at the top. Throughout the colonial era the missionaries controlled the system of education and the Governments were mainly concerned with grants to aid running the mission schools. However since independence the Governments have taken control of the educational system, resulting in two important benefits. One is that all schools have been thrown open to all children on the basis of merit rather than religion. The second result is that a steady Africanization of the educational syllabus has started to develop so that students will be required to learn things that are relevant to their situation and work. A more detailed account of education will be found in Chapter 40.

Another social service which the missionaries have provided since the 1890's is the medical service. They set up hospitals and treated both Christian and non-Christian alike. The work of the medical missions was supplemented by the East African Governments early in the twentieth century. Even now, missionary hospitals are a good example of unforgettably devoted service to the people of East Africa in the name of Christ.

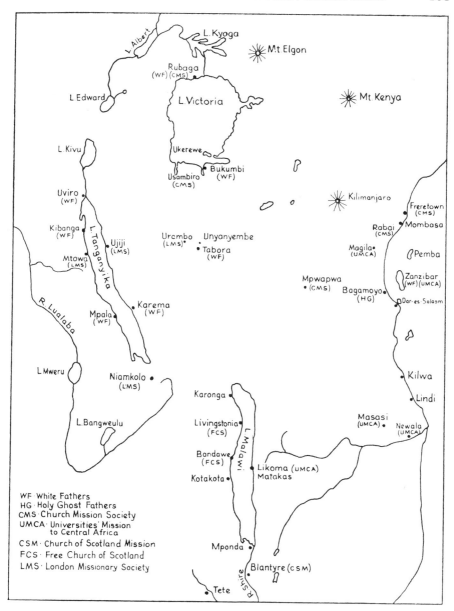

Christian missionary stations at the coast and in the interior of East Africa

Note: Lake Albert became Lake Mobutu and Lake Edward became Lake Idi Amin Dada in 1974

African Clergy

From the very beginning of the missionary era the Catholic and Protestant missionaries realized that they could not spread the faith all alone because of their small numbers. So they taught catechists whom they sent out to help teach the catechism and prayers in remote places. This development was followed by the education of African clergy to man the churches on an equal footing with the European missionaries.

Nearer the independence period the government of the Church was rapidly passing into the hands of these African clergymen and now African control is more or less complete, with African bishops leading the various churches.

18 European Traders

From the 1820's, when Seyyid Said became very much involved in East African affairs, European businessmen started to be interested in trading with Zanzibar. At the time of his death in 1856 there were British, French, American and German traders with stores on the island. However, these European traders never ventured into the interior. They bought the commodities from Africans and Arabs who sold them in the market of Zanzibar and, at the same time, it was the Africans and Arabs who took European imports into the interior. The turn of European traders to proceed into the interior came after European travellers and missionaries had supplied adequate information about the inland areas.

European Individual Traders

The Arabs, Swahilis and certain African groups looked upon themselves as the legitimate middlemen between the African producers in the interior and the European buyers in Zanzibar. Thus any European attempt to enter the interior to trade was bound to run into opposition. In 1881, and again in 1885 and 1886, European business men who attempted to establish themselves in the Nyamwezi area were prevented from doing so. Légère a French trader, was driven away from Unyanyembe and one unidentified German trader was killed in 1886. One Irishman, Charles Stokes, did succeed by allying with the Nyamwezi of Usongo and keeping away from traditional Arab-Swahili markets.

European Trading Companies

Since individual traders could not break into the established patterns of trade, Europeans turned to companies to do so. In 1878 James

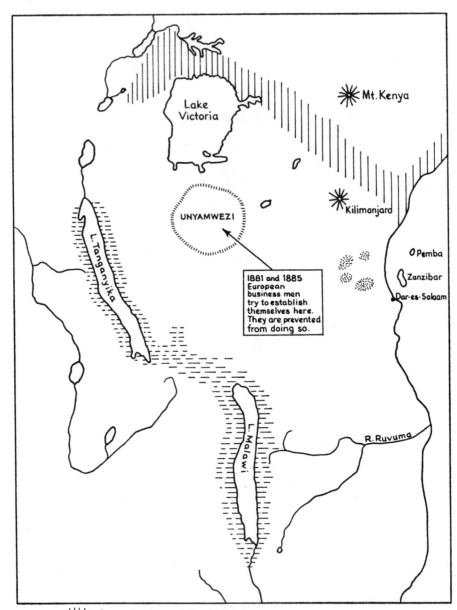

Area of activity of the I.B.E.A.Co.

Area of activity of the Livingstonia Company

Areas annexed by Carl Peters in 1884

European traders in East Africa in the 19th Century

Stevenson, a Scotsman, created the Livingstonia Central African Trading Company which put steamers on Lakes Malawi and Tanganyika. The company supplied European goods to the C.M.S. Missionaries and traded in ivory and other products. This company had some success because it was not directly competing with the Arab merchants who were primarily interested in slaves.

Another Scotsman, William Mackinnon, operated a steamship company whose ships called at East African ports from Aden. He persuaded Sultan Majid (1856-70) to develop the port of Dar es Salaam and opened a direct mail service between Zanzibar and Aden in 1872 which speeded up the mail between Zanzibar and Europe. He attempted to set up a trading company but, although he had secured the lease of all the trade in the Sultan of Zanzibar's East African dominions for fifty years, the British Government refused to support the idea and the scheme collapsed. However, in 1887 he formed another company which secured a royal charter from the British Government. It was called the Imperial British East Africa Company (IBEA Co.). Besides trading it was expected to administer the British 'sphere of influence' obtained under the Anglo-German Agreement of 1886.

As a result of this same agreement, Carl Peters organized the German East Africa Company to trade in and administer the German 'sphere of influence'. Thus, by 1888, the two companies were prepared to break the commercial middleman position of the established trading network dominated by the Arabs and Swahilis. However, neither succeeded in doing so. The British company almost went bankrupt and the German company was virtually expelled by an Arab-African revolt. The failure of their companies brought the European powers into East Africa. Like the missionaries, the European traders had to wait until the military might had done its work before they could become successful. Even after the conquest, European traders had not the resources or the skill to monopolize East African trade. Very largely they continued as before to dominate the trade between the East African coast and Europe while Asian immigrants took over control of the domestic commerce of the interior.

19 The Scramble for Colonies

Imperialism

The word imperialism in recent years has tended to be used in connection with Africa. But we need to remember that not only Africa was colonized by Europeans. America, Asia, New Zealand and Australia were also once colonized. As one historian has written, 'Always these extensions of control over non-European territories had involved trading, missionizing, adventure, settlement, loot, national pride, conquests and wars between rival powers.' So by 1870 it was an established fact that Europeans had long exercised control over other non-European areas.

The use of the word imperialism is regarded by historians as dating from 1850. Between 1870 and 1914 we find what has been termed the 'age of imperialism'. It arose from the search for lucrative markets and secure overseas investment by Europeans with capital resources.

There was a dramatic suddenness in the attempts of European powers to secure colonies. Many European nations with former colonies had lost them by 1870, but they had not suffered economically. By 1815 France had lost most of her colonies in America and Asia. Spain no longer had her large South American empire. Britain had already lost the thirteen colonies in America. In 1822 Portugal lost Brazil. Economists described colonies as burdens on home governments and preached free trade. Gladstone and Disraeli even said that these wretched colonies would all be independent in a few years and were millstones around their necks. Yet within a short time Disraeli reverted to a colonial policy. Bismarck, Chancellor of Germany, was opposed to German colonial aspirations. He said, 'All the advantages claimed for the mother country are for the most part illusory.'

It was strange that after such views there was a reversal of policy and colonialism was soon in full swing. Imperialism was directed at Africa and eastern Asia, the only areas of the world not yet under

European influence. During this time of intense competition in Europe, colonies could bring a country political aggrandisement and economic advantages.

Factors Underlying Imperialism

On the economic side there was a desire to invest accumulated capital, to find markets for industrial goods, to obtain raw materials and to establish overseas settlements for excess population. Raw materials from Africa and Asia such as cotton, silk, rubber, vegetable oils and minerals were very much in demand for European factories. European markets had an abundance of manufactured goods, but a system of protective tariffs at home made industrialists look for new markets overseas. Foreign territories, however, could only be made safe for investment if they were taken over.

Another factor was the strategic one. The ports of Africa and the Far East were valuable naval bases in times of war. Europe was torn by rivalries and mutual distrust and war was ever imminent. Once the partition of Africa came, the powers were confronted with the choice of grabbing advantages for themselves or seeing them snatched by potential enemies. The international situation in Europe, therefore, gave an impetus of its own to the general race for colonies.

Both economic and political interests created imperialism. There were also subsidiary reasons for seeking colonies – the enhancement of national prestige and the provision of additional sources of manpower to defend the mother country. The activities of men like Du Chaillu and De Brazza in Central Africa, H. M. Stanley in the Congo basin or Carl Peters in East Africa acted as a spur. Cecil Rhodes, imbued with the love of money, 'a man of initiative and energetic enterprise', played an important part in the story of imperialism.

Christian missionaries too aided the spread of imperialism. Dr Livingstone of the C.M.S. later turned explorer under British government auspices to open a path for commerce and Christianity in both Central and East Africa. France, even more than Britain, sent organized missions into Africa to convert Africans to Christianity. French missions penetrated into all parts of Africa, setting up schools and medical services usually in the footsteps of explorers and adventurers. Belgian missionaries were active in the Congo as early as 1878 before Leopold took over the Congo.

Then to consolidate their gains, the European countries sent administrators and soldiers. By 1895 only one-tenth of Africa remained unappropriated by European powers.

Colonization

Colonial acquisitions caused no war among the colonizers. Occasionally one power made gains with the encouragement or assent of another. Bismarck encouraged France to expand into Tunisia as a diversion to prevent her fighting with Italy. Though there were usually clashes over boundaries, these never flared into war. In Africa there was always supposedly enough empty land for compensating any aggrieved European power.

To reduce the possibilities of fighting and constant quarrelling among Europeans over the acquisition of African land, Bismarck and the French President jointly called the 1884-5 Berlin Conference.

The events which led to the holding of the conference were precipitated by two men. Leopold II, King of the Belgians, and the French President Jules Ferry wanted to take over a part or the whole of the Congo, while Portugal, supported by Britain, laid claim to the mouth of the Congo which she had seized from the Africans during the fifteenth century.

When Stanley travelled from Zanzibar through Uganda and the Congo down to the Atlantic Ocean, and revealed the Congo's great potential, Leopold began to consider the possibility of taking over the Congo for himself. In 1876 he called a conference in Brussels, the capital of Belgium, of European geographers, traders, merchants, travellers, opponents of the slave trade and any other Europeans who might care to attend. To these he expressed his intense desire to stamp out the slave trade in Africa. He wanted to establish Christianity and promote trade for the benefit of Africans. Such objectives were only a cover for his real motive which was to seize African lands with the support of other Europeans. At the close of the conference, the participants formed the International African Association with Leopold as President and headquarters in Brussels, where he could keep it under close observation.

The Association, directed by Leopold, at once sent several Belgian expeditions to East Africa in 1877 with the aim of establishing posts from the east coast to Lake Victoria. These were to be staging posts for future European travellers in search of better areas for exploitation.

But all such attempts failed because the Belgians leading the expeditions were unfamiliar with East African conditions.

After this the Association turned its attention to West Africa, but simultaneously the other members realized that Leopold was working purely for his own ends. The Association broke up and its so-called humanitarian motive was abandoned. Each country wanted to operate independently and acquire African lands for its nationals.

Leopold engaged Stanley in 1878 to colonize the Congo for him and start trade there. In this Leopold, unlike other heads of state, was not acting on behalf of his countrymen. The Congo was to be his own personal estate, a means of enriching himself and his family.

While Leopold was contemplating this scheme, France, led by Jules Ferry, also planned to exploit the Congo. Before Stanley's travels through the Congo in 1876 Count de Brazza had already explored it, with the backing of the French President, who was now determined to take over parts of the best areas of the Congo exclusively for France. Portugal, earlier than any other European power, had already claimed the area around the mouth of the Congo. When she suspected the plans of Leopold II and Jules Ferry, she became alarmed and enlisted the support of Britain. Then an argument developed in Europe over the ownership of land which rightly belonged, however, to Africans, who were not consulted. France and Britain had already begun to seize land in West Africa and Germany was showing interest in the race. The European powers, not wanting to settle merely the Congo question, wished to lay down rules by which they would allocate African lands by mutual agreement.

Effects of the Berlin Conference

Bismarck, then Chancellor of Germany, the strongest power in Europe, and who claimed not to want African land, called a conference in his capital Berlin. Indeed he gave the impression to the other European powers of being neutral and therefore best able to solve the problem. The historic Berlin Conference took place from November 1884 to January 1885. Three principles were laid down in the acquisition of African land. One was effective occupation. This meant signing treaties with African chiefs of an area on the basis that 'protection' would be given against their enemies. Then the European power in question would set up a fort in which it stationed a few soldiers and that would constitute effective occupation. In signing treaties the African chiefs never imagined they were giving away their power and land to the Europeans. They believed they were entering into normal diplomatic relations with governments of other countries.

The second principle was that an occupying power must allow other Europeans to trade freely in the area if they wished. The third principle was that an occupying power had to abolish the slave trade. After the conference, European powers were in effect given free rein to acquire as much land as they could before another power came to snatch it away again.

The Berlin Conference led to the rapid partition of Africa among all the colonial powers. It also heralded the new era of colonialism. The treaty gave Leopold II rights of possession over most of the Congo Basin and its outlet to the Atlantic Ocean, but other countries had the right of free trade and free use of the river. Both the Niger and the Congo were to be opened to trade with all nations. The treaty was an agreement among the powers to divide Africa amicably and to allow colonial acquisitions without strife and rivalry. Ten years after the Berlin Conference, nearly all Africa had been partitioned. Chartered companies were allowed to develop the different territories, and had monopoly rights for exploitation. Ethiopia and Liberia alone were independent south of the Sahara and the two small Boer republics in South Africa.

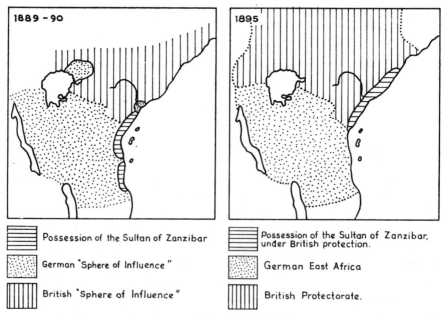

Stages in the Partition of East Africa

20 The Egyptian Scramble for East Africa

Sir Samuel Baker

Egypt was the first to try to annex East African territories to its empire. The movement was led by Ismail who became Khedive of Egypt in 1863. His grandfather Muhammad Ali, who ruled Egypt from 1810 to 1854, had extended the Egyptian empire in the Sudan up to Gondokoro, so that all the northern Sudan was under Egypt. Ismail wanted to extend this empire to the whole of East Africa through the northern Uganda Province, Bunyoro, Buganda and then down to the east coast.

To interest Europeans in his expansionist scheme, Ismail used the pretext of wishing to abolish the African slave trade. European parliamentarians by now believed that this trade should be stopped, and they were likely to be sympathetic to anyone furthering this aim.

In the southern Sudan, Arabs from Egypt and the northern Sudan had enslaved Africans since the days of Muhammad Ali. Government officials in the Sudan had for years been directly involved in the sale of Africans. By the time of Ismail, the Arabs had extended their activities to northern Uganda, among the Lugbara, Kakwa, Acholi, Madi, Alur and other peoples in this area and had reached Bunyoro – Kitara. The Arabs from the north thus joined the east coast Arabs in the capture and sale of slaves for shipment to Asia and to North and South America. Ismail now arrived on the scene, declaring that he wanted to establish sound administration and economic progress in the area by first taking it over and then stamping out the slave trade. In this way he obtained the moral support of the British government which already had connections with Egypt.

Ismail fortunately had Europeans who were already acquainted with African lands as a result of their travels. They had sought the sources of rivers such as the Nile, discovered the presence of lakes and investigated the flora and fauna of African lands. Such information was much in demand by geographers and naturalists in Europe.

In 1869 Ismail appointed Sir Samuel Baker as Governor of Equatorial Provinces, that is northern Sudan and parts of Southern Sudan. He had been instructed to acquire for Egypt southern Sudan, Uganda, Kenya and mainland Tanzania. This was a welcome assignment for Baker, who had earlier hoped to be the first European to see the source of the Nile. He would thereby have achieved an enviable reputation, because this question had exercised the minds of Europeans for several centuries. In 1863, accompanied by his wife, he set off from Khartoum to follow the Nile to Uganda. Baker, however, met Speke and Grant near Gondokoro and was told that they had already solved the riddle of the source of the Nile. They had started from Zanzibar and gone all the way to Buganda and then turning east again, sailed along the river from Bulondoganyi in Busoga to Jinja, where it flows out from Lake Victoria. The news was a great disappointment to Samuel Baker and his wife.

However, to soften the blow, Speke told them that in the neighbourhood of Masindi in Bunyoro there was a lake which he and his companion had no time to explore. Rather than return to Europe with a sense of failure, the Bakers went on to investigate this lake and saw Lake Mwita Nzige, now called Sese Seko Mobutu.

When he was appointed governor, Baker saw a chance to recover his self-esteem. He would in effect have supreme authority over all the territory which Egypt had claimed in the Sudan and also any future gains he might make. Ismail in Cairo was too far away to exercise much supervision.

Baker already knew of the havoc which the Arab slavers were causing in the area. His strategy was to establish a line of military posts in most of the southern Sudan area and in parts of Acholi and Bunyoro with European and Sudanese soldiers to fight against Arab slavers. Posts such as Dufile, Padibe, Patiko, Wadelai, Foweira, Mruli and Kabagambe were set up. The plan achieved some success in reducing the scale of the Arab slave trade. But the Arabs were wily. They frequently outwitted the guards and captured numbers of unfortunate Africans.

In 1870 Baker reached Bunyoro-Kitara, where Kabarega had in 1869 succeeded to the throne after the death of his father Kamurasi. Kabarega and his brother Ruyonga fought to decide the successor to the throne and the ownership of the royal drum, which was the symbol of power. Kabarega enlisted the help of the Arab slavers while Ruyonga called upon Kabaka Muteesa I of Buganda to help him. Unfortunately, Muteesa's warriors arrived too late. By then Kabarega, with the help of the Arabs who had a plentiful supply of guns, used in the hunting of men for slaves, had already defeated Ruyonga and his supporters. Some of these people were enslaved and marched to Egypt.

At once Kabarega began to reorganise his kingdom. He established a new type of standing army of well-trained youths and called them 'Abarusura'. Having done so, he felt that he could dispense with the Arab slavers who had helped him to the throne. He realized that reliance on them would hamper his freedom to develop his kingdom. Further, he knew that the main interest of the Arabs was the capture of his subjects for selling as slaves, and it was on these very subjects that Kabarega wanted to build a strong kingdom. To the Arabs' dismay, he took a strong line and drastically curtailed their freedom of action.

Then he proceeded to infuse a spirit of nationalism into his Banyoro subjects. He reminded them of the past glories of Bunyoro-Kitara when the greater part of present-day Uganda was under its influence. He promised to reconquer what Bunyoro-Kitara had lost to Buganda, Ankole and Toro. The Banyoro responded enthusiastically to such a leader, and his promises of triumphs to come.

At this moment of national reorganization and resurgence, Baker appeared on the scene. He bluntly told Kabarega, a ruler of a great ancient kingdom which was once an empire, that henceforth Bunyoro-Kitara would be part of Ismail's empire. Kabarega's reaction can be imagined. He saw it as an affront from a man without royal blood. Immediately he let loose his soldiers on Baker's men. Baker and those of his men who managed to escape death from the onslaught of arrows and spears crossed the Nile in boats and took refuge at Fatiko, near Gulu in West Acholi. Baker never again plucked up courage to cross into Kabarega's country.

Eight months after this incident, Baker's contract with Ismail came to an end. He had achieved nothing in the way of expanding Ismail's empire. He had not done much either to stop the slave trade. Indeed, after his departure the slave trade increased, because he had enlisted the services of former Arab slave traders, following the old maxim of setting a thief to catch a thief. On Baker's departure, the Arabs resumed the practice of capturing Africans even more zealously, to make up for their losses during his administration.

Colonel Charles Gordon

Sir Samuel Baker was succeeded by Colonel Charles Gordon. A traveller and a soldier, having seen much action in Asia, he was, like Baker, utterly opposed to the slave trade. His vision was even greater. He believed his mission was to take over the whole of East Africa in the name of Ismail to prevent Arabs from the north and the east coast capturing Africans and carrying them into slavery. His troops occupied Kismayu on the east coast. Sultan Barghash requested the British Consul, Sir John Kirk, to send a protest to Cairo at this interference in his dominions. Gordon was then directed by Ismail to remove his troops from Kismayu.

In his gradual occupation of East Africa for Egypt, Gordon wanted to use Buganda as a base. He sent his American chief of staff Chaillé-Long in 1874 to negotiate with Muteesa I. Chaillé-Long asked Muteesa to end his trading arrangements with the Sultan of Zanzibar and to deal with Gordon in Gondokoro. Muteesa did not care much for this idea because Buganda already had close connections with the sultans of Zanzibar. He was aware of the intentions of Ismail, for news of Baker's abortive encounter with Kabarega had reached him. But he was diplomatic and friendly and sent Chaillé-Long away with promises of co-operation which he did not, however, intend to fulfil.

Soon Gordon sent another mission led by his French assistant Linant de Bellefonds. Muteesa reacted coldly and the emissary came away empty-handed. Gordon then sent an Egyptian general, Nuehr Aga. Muteesa decided to show his feelings openly this time. He put Aga and about seventy-five of his men into custody. After a week of fear and uncertainty, they were allowed to go free. He had shown Gordon that he was bent on clinging to his independence and that he had forces at his command to defend it. Gordon at that point gave up all hope of using Buganda as a stepping stone to acquire for Egypt the rest of East Africa.

Gordon decided to concentrate on Acholi and the southern Sudan. But even there he made no headway. The Africans hated him and his Arab soldiers, because Baker's garrisons had turned into semi-official slaving posts. In Acholi people displayed great hostility to any Arab who appeared in their midst. They drove away the troops in all the garrisons but Fatiko. Even there the soldiers could not move freely outside their fort without being in danger of their lives. Gordon's rule did not extend further than the fort of Fatiko and when his term of office came to an end in 1876, he had been no more successful than his predecessor.

Emin Pasha

Two years later Edward Schnitzer, a German doctor, but known to history as Emin Pasha, was made governor of the Equatorial Province. This was now officially the area from Gondokoro down to Bunyoro. In 1879, Gordon was made overall controller of the Equatorial provinces of which there were now two – the northern Sudan and the southern Sudan, plus Acholi as far as Bunyoro.

Gordon realized that it was impossible to extend further than Fatiko in west Acholi. So he advised Emin Pasha to withdraw his garrisons from Mruli and Kabagambe in Bunyoro. But his advice was not taken and in 1880 Gordon left the Khedive's service in disgust.

After the departure of Gordon, Ismail's ambitions to extend his role in East Africa came to an end. In 1881 a revolt led by Muhammad Ahmed in northern Sudan stopped all development. The Sudanese resented the high taxes levied by Ismail's men. The money was not used for the benefit of the Sudan. Much of it was sent to Cairo where Ismail spent it on lavish projects; that which remained in the Sudan was diverted by officials into their own pockets. To add to the injustice, the people in the southern Sudan were the victims of the slave trade in which Ismail's officials openly engaged. The rebellion that finally erupted, known as the Mahdist revolt, spread like wildfire fanned by Islamic fervour. It was seen as a holy war against the Christian officers of Ismail, but its character was both political and religious. The Egyptian administration was driven out of northern Sudan. Emin Pasha, who was south in Gondokoro, was cut off in 1883 from all communication with Khartoum and Cairo. But with exemplary courage, he organized his soldiers, who were intensely loyal, into a force that held its own against the Mahdist attacks. He left the area in 1887 after pressure from Stanley. (See Chapter 39.)

The direct result of Ismail's involvement in Uganda was to alarm both Omukama Kabarega and Kabaka Muteesa I. Kabarega realized that a trained and strong army was a necessary pre-requisite to independence. Muteesa tried to ally with the Sultan of Zanzibar and he struck up a diplomatic friendship with Sultan Majid which continued with his successor Barghash.

At this critical juncture, Muteesa was paid a visit at his court at Mengo in 1875 by Stanley. The explorer was on an expedition to study rivers and lakes and to confirm Speke's claim that the Nile did in fact flow out of Lake Victoria (a claim that had met with some scepticism in Europe). Stanley discussed with Muteesa the possibility of sending teachers to his country. Muteesa at once accepted the idea, hoping it might lead to an alliance with Britain and be a means of obtaining guns. In this way he would be in a stronger position to defend his kingdom against Egyptian expansionism.

21 European Colonization of East Africa

Germany and Britain divided East Africa between them while France gave her blessing. They followed the rules which they and other European countries had made at the Berlin Conference.

German colonialism in East Africa was led by Carl Peters. In 1884 he founded the Society for German Colonization in Berlin to launch a determined drive to acquire colonies in Africa. Several German societies had been founded with the object of securing land in Africa, but they tended to be slow and calculating in their approach. Carl Peters was too impatient to associate himself with them. His plan was to start in East Africa, using Zanzibar as base to gain colonies for Germany on the mainland. British interests, however, represented by the consul, Sir John Kirk, Sir William Mackinnon and General Lloyd Mathews in Zanzibar, would hardly allow German colonial schemes in East Africa to prosper. To protect their position, the British claimed that all land in East Africa belonged to the Sultan of Zanzibar.

Rival Claims

Peters was not to be put off by such claims. He refused to accept that the Sultan's power was of any importance outside Zanzibar and said he certainly could not be considered overlord of all the East African mainland. In November 1884 Peters arrived in Zanzibar with Count Joachim Pfeil and Dr Carl Jühlke, all young men determined to carve out areas for Germany. They were disguised as mechanics, to avoid detection by the British representatives in Zanzibar. Having crossed secretly to the mainland, they signed a treaty of friendship and eternal protection with an African chief and hoisted the German flag in the area. Moving on farther they made treaties with the chiefs of Usagara, Uzigu, Uguru and Ukami. All these gave Carl Peters protectorate powers over their lands in perpetuity. The implications of these treaties were not clear to the chiefs, who signed them in good faith as normal diplomatic alliances with another power whose sovereignty and integrity they respected.

With these treaties in their pockets, Carl Peters and his two colleagues hurried back to Germany. Peters asked Bismarck to accept the treaties, in view of the Berlin Resolutions which had just been formulated. Bismarck accordingly gave them a charter and Peters formed the German East Africa Company to take effective possession of the lands and administer them.

On hearing Peters' claim, the British Chamber of Commerce in Manchester, which already had become interested in East Africa, protested to the British government and asked it to forward the protest to Bismarck. One of the British merchants concerned was Sir Harry Johnston who had also signed treaties with chiefs in the region of Taveta and Mount Kilimanjaro. Supported by his British colleagues in Zanzibar, in particular the consul, Sir John Kirk, Sultan Barghash ratified the British treaties. The Sultan was given to understand that the Manchester Chamber of Commerce would develop trade in the area between the east coast and Lake Victoria. The result was the formation of the British East Africa Association to resist the claims of Peters.

Britain at this time had troubles in Egypt which led to a dispute with France. In 1882 Britain had taken charge of the Suez Canal to control the sea-route to India and China. France, her partner in building the Suez Canal, did not support this partial take-over of the canal. Britain, to counteract French opposition, was seeking German support in Egypt and was prepared to lend her weight to Germany's claims in East Africa. When Sir John Kirk asked Britain to send a protest to the German government on behalf of the Manchester Chamber of Commerce over the Sultan's lands, he received orders that the British East Africa Association should not trespass on the areas claimed by Germany. Instead Kirk should help the Germans to consolidate their claims, so long as they recognized what the Anglo-French Agreement of 1862 had given to the Sultan of Zanzibar. The supposed British guarantee of protection for the Sultan's dominions proved a disappointment to Sultan Barghash and to Kirk who had assured the Sultan of British integrity.

The Fashoda Incident

This was one example of the way in which the scramble for African lands was always subordinated to European domestic politics. Another may be seen in Carl Peters's struggles in Uganda which Germany chose to ignore. The same thing happened over Fashoda* in 1896 when Britain and France almost went to war. Britain wanted to control the Nile valley on which Egypt depended, and was also contemplating a continuous stretch of territory from South Africa to Egypt.

The French had other plans that were at variance with this project. They wanted one continuous belt from Dakar to the Gulf of Aden, from the basin of the Congo and French West Africa across the upper parts of the Nile and joining Ethiopia and French Somaliland in the east. The 'missing link' was the gap between the southern part where effective Egyptian power stopped in the Sudan and the northern boundary of Uganda where Britain ruled. Fashoda was the strategic point in this gap where there was already a disused fortress, established by Sir Samuel Baker, which could prove crucial to the control of the Nile.

The race to Fashoda was won by the Frenchman Major Jean-Baptiste Marchand after one year's march from Gabon in West Africa. He rebuilt the fortress and hoisted the French flag on 6th July, 1896. He signed the usual treaty with the local chief who placed himself permanently in the protection of France against other European powers. After twenty days, General Sir Herbert Kitchener, Britain's representative, arrived from Egypt with five gunboats and some 2000 men, a force much stronger than Marchand's handful of Senegalese soldiers.

Both men had their countries behind them. Before starting the march, Marchand had been told by the French Foreign Minister, 'You are going to fire a pistol shot on the Nile; we accept all its consequences.' Public opinion in Britain and France favoured war. But Marchand and Kitchener kept their heads and did not fight. They asked their governments to decide on the next move. In the end it was agreed that Marchand should leave Fashoda, lest hostilities result, in which case their common rival Germany would reap the benefit. In March 1899, therefore, Marchand withdrew. Though France was excluded from the Nile valley, she made gains to the west of the river and Britain agreed not to seek any territorial influence to the west.

*Fashoda, in the Sudan, is now re-named Kodok.

German Acquisitions by Threat of Force

Jühlke now came to the fore in the race to sign treaties in the Kilimanjaro region, Peters having stayed behind in Berlin. In May 1885 Sultan Barghash of Zanzibar sent troops to Usagara and dispatched General Mathews to Kilimanjaro in an attempt to forestall Jühlke. Mathews was successful in this and hoisted the Sultan's flag in Teita. He signed about twenty-five treaties with chiefs in the district, among them Mandara, the most powerful chief of the Chagga. Jühlke then arrived a few days later. Mathews also signed a treaty with Mandara. There was nothing untoward in this diplomatic formula in the eyes of African chiefs, who had no thought of actually ceding their sovereignty. Unfortunately, to the whites it was evidence of Africans' unsophisticated minds and lack of understanding and they took advantage of them.

Jühlke also took under protection Witu at the mouth of the Tana river which was ruled by Simba, who was violently opposed to the Sultan of Zanzibar and his claims to be Simba's overlord. The treaty Simba signed with Jühlke was, as he understood it, for the supply of arms to fight Sultan Barghash but not for Germany to have control of his land. Jühlke's interpretation was quite different, however, and he had every intention of acquiring rights over the land.

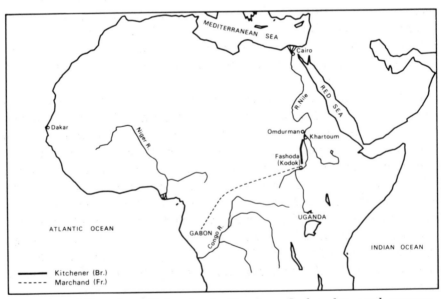

British and French ambitions in the Southern Sudan, late 19th century

Sultan Barghash, on hearing the news that some of the land over which he claimed overlordship was being taken by Germany, sent a strong protest to Bismarck and to Britain and America. These two countries had no great interest in the matter. Besides, the Sultan's claims were difficult to substantiate. Bismarck's answer was to send a squadron to Zanzibar harbour in August 1885 and threaten to blow up his palace unless he agreed to all the German claims. Without the support of Britain, Barghash could do nothing but acquiesce.

Partition of East Africa

Since there were doubts about the extent of the Sultan's power, Britain, France and Germany set up a commission to investigate the situation. France was included as a matter of courtesy, as a party to the Anglo-French Agreement of 1862. The Sultan's claim was now recognized as extending over the islands of Zanzibar, Pemba and Mafia, and on the mainland ten miles inland from Ganghi Bay in the south to Kipini in the north. Kismayu, Brava and Merika towns and a ten-mile radius around them were also included. Mogadishu, too, was given to the Sultan with a five-mile area round it. Britain took over Kenya, while Germany took over mainland Tanzania. All this was laid down in the Anglo-German Agreement of 1886. Towards the end of the year, Germany agreed with Portugal that Cape Delagado should be the northern boundary of Portuguese Mozambique. To avoid high administrative costs in their 'spheres of influence', Britain and Germany relied entirely on trading companies, namely the Imperial British East Africa Company and the German East Africa Company.

Meanwhile there was a struggle for Uganda by Germany and Britain. The I.B.E.A. Company sent Frederick Jackson in 1889 to investigate the Buganda area and to take over Equatoria Province, where Emin Pasha had been cut off from Khartoum by the Mahdist revolt. As described in Chapter 39, Stanley had been sent to meet Emin Pasha at Gondokoro to persuade him to leave the province, to further Britain's plans for taking the whole of the Nile valley into her sphere of influence.

In July, Peters also secretly left the coast and went to Uganda and arrived before Jackson at Mengo, the seat of Kabaka Mwanga, king of Buganda. He found Mwanga and the Christians threatened by the Muslim community, which had the backing of Arab traders who came in search of slaves and other commodities.

At this juncture Father Lourdel of the French White Fathers sent letters on Mwanga's behalf to Jackson, asking for help against the Muslims. Jackson had in fact already been in correspondence with Buganda requesting a treaty and concessions, but there had been little enthusiasm from the Baganda. Now in their hour of danger they were willing to agree to terms in return for British assistance. The letters, however, fell into the hands of the unscrupulous Peters, who saw his opportunity.

Peters was received warmly by Mwanga who, encouraged by the Roman Catholic White Fathers, signed a treaty of protection with Germany. Peters then hurried back to the coast with Buganda added to the list of German acquisitions, delighted at having stolen a march over Jackson. Jackson then arrived at Mwanga's court and tried hard to conclude a treaty. But Mwanga refused and Jackson left Buganda a disappointed man.

Unfortunately for Peters, Buganda and later Uganda were assigned to Britain by European diplomats without knowledge of what Peters had negotiated in Buganda. It was crucial to Britain to have the whole of the Nile valley in her sphere of influence because if any other power controlled Uganda, Britain's hold on Egypt could be jeopardized. The flow of the Nile, vital to Egypt, could be tampered with or diverted.

At this time Germany's strategic position in Europe and the development of her navy took precedence over other matters. She therefore granted Britain Witu and Uganda. This arrangement secured the British hold on the Nile, in return for Heligoland, an island in the North Sea which had formerly belonged to Britain. It was further arranged that Britain should take over as a protectorate all the possessions of the Sultan of Zanzibar as laid down in the 1862 Anglo-French Agreement. All this was formally recognized in the Anglo-German Agreement of 1890 in Brussels.

So East Africa's fate was decided, by Europeans sitting at conference tables in Europe. It was done without reference to the Africans and their interests and often the Europeans had no clear picture even of the extent of the African territories which they were dividing among themselves.

22 European Teachers Come to Uganda

Ismail of Egypt failed to take over Acholi, Bunyoro, Buganda and other areas further to the east. But King Kabarega of Bunyoro and King Muteesa of Buganda were uneasy about the threat to their independence.

While Charles Gordon was persuading Muteesa I to accept the rule of Egypt, Stanley arrived at the court of Muteesa I at Mengo in 1875. His journey of 1000 miles was no mean feat in those days before modern transport; the railway from Mombasa to Kampala was not yet built. Stanley, as we have seen, had come from Britain on a geographical exploration of East Africa and the Congo.

King Muteesa welcomed Stanley at his court. Stanley saw that in the large Buganda population there was scope for the teaching of Christianity. He discussed the Christian religion with King Muteesa and told him that if he wished teachers could be sent out to Buganda to teach not only the word of Christ but also the elementary skills of reading, writing and arithmetic. Muteesa was in favour of the plan, as he still had at the back of his mind the idea that any contact with Britain could lead to military assistance. Stanley therefore wrote to *The Daily Telegraph* in London appealing for teachers.

The Arrival of the Missionaries

This was a time of great interest among Europeans in missionary teaching and, as we have seen, many teachers were already at work in Africa in the north, south and west.

The British party, including the Reverend Alexander Mackay, arrived in Uganda in 1877. They were followed in 1879 by two Frenchmen, Father Simon Lourdel and Brother Amans of the Society of the White Fathers. King Muteesa received them all warmly and allowed them to stay in his palace. He showed a keen interest in Christianity. At the same time he was watchful and wary in case their religious teaching should prove to be a cover for a political intrigue to take over the country.

The missionaries, however, worked hard at their task, learning the Luganda language and Kiswahili. Their position at court was an advantage to them. There they came into contact with men of influence, the chiefs and their entourage and through them had access to all the king's subjects.

Mackay, with the aid of a printing press, printed text-books and books of prayers which were distributed to his pupils. The study of reading, writing and Christian doctrine was taken up by many, including some of the chiefs and their servants, amongst them young boys. It was felt that King Muteesa would look favourably on those who had extended their education in this way. Others, however, would have none of it and felt the new religion cut across their own beliefs.

Unfortunately there was ill feeling between Mackay and Father Lourdel who vied with one another for pride of place in the king's esteem. He failed to understand their disagreements. He had assumed that as both were Europeans and of the same faith they would work in harmony. His main concern was that they had not provided him, through their governments, with military weapons as he had hoped. When he took them to task they explained that they had come solely to teach his people and not to help him fight his enemies.

Muteesa therefore took no further interest in their work of education and conversion. In any case, by 1880 there was no longer any threat from Egypt. The attempt to take Acholi, Bunyoro and Buganda had been abandoned. Emin Pasha was fully occupied in Equatorial Province, as the Sudanese people were engaged in trying to drive out the Egyptian army.

Another factor which influenced the king's attitude to the Christian teachers was the presence at his court of Arabs established there before the arrival of the Europeans. They were on good terms with Muteesa and he had adopted some Islamic practices, such as prayers and fasting. More important, they supplied him with guns and joined in his military campaigns. The Arabs resented the Europeans and falsely alleged to the king that the Christians were in league with Ismail.

These allegations, together with murmurings from certain of his chiefs who distrusted Christianity, claiming it deprived the king of the respect and honour due to him, produced in Muteesa a marked coolness towards the Europeans. They were now working under difficulties and in 1882 Father Lourdel and Brother Amans left for an island south of Lake Victoria. They wished to continue their teaching away from the unfriendly atmosphere of the court. Mackay, however, remained.

Christians in Danger

Muteesa was still unreconciled to the Christians when he died in 1884. The new king, his son Mwanga, at first was friendly towards the teachers. He invited Father Lourdel and Brother Amans to return to Mengo and gave encouragement to Mackay to continue his work.

Soon, however, like his father, he conceived a dislike of Christianity. He saw in it a challenge to his authority, when pupils of the missionaries sometimes refused to obey his orders because their religion prevented them. Although a sincere and courageous conviction on their part, their attitude angered the king deeply.

The Arabs once again sowed the seeds of distrust and claimed that the missionaries' teaching was dangerous to Mwanga. In 1885 the king ordered his executioner Mukajanga to kill three young Christian boys who were under Mackay. They were the first Christian martyrs of Uganda. In the following October Bishop Hannington, newly appointed as bishop of Eastern Africa, was murdered on his way to Kampala after Mwanga had sent orders to Chief Lubwa of Busoga. There was a belief among Baganda that a foreigner who came by that route would bring danger to their country.

After this Mwanga continued his campaign of vengeance with further atrocities. In June 1886 he decreed that thirty-seven Christians who had refused to renounce their faith should be burned to death at Namugongo, fifteen kilometres from Kampala. Some were his own chiefs; others were boys of only twelve. Yet in spite of this the remaining pupils of the missionaries continued their instruction secretly by night, and would then pass on their knowledge to others.

Eventually Mwanga decided to rid himself of both Christians and Muslims. With the support of some of his chiefs he planned to expel all foreigners and put them on an island in Lake Victoria. The Christians and Muslims united and prepared to fight the king and his followers, but he fled to the Sese Islands. They appointed his brother Kiwewa king in his place, but he ruled for only a short time before being killed. Disputes had in the meantime broken out once more amongst Christians and Muslims. Kalema, another brother of Mwanga, then became king, with the support of the Muslims.

Then in 1890 he was driven out and took refuge in Bunyoro and the Christians restored Mwanga to the throne.

23 Uganda Becomes a Protectorate

In 1886 Britain, France and Germany divided East Africa between Germany and Britain, Kenya and Uganda being allotted to Britain. The British government proposed to administer its new East African territories through the Imperial British East Africa Company headed by Sir William Mackinnon.

The Role of Lugard

In 1890 the company sent Captain F. D. Lugard to Kampala as its representative. He arrived there in December and set up his quarters on the hill known as Lugard Hill in the Old Kampala area. He found King Mwanga newly restored to his throne and made an agreement with him by which Lugard promised to protect King Mwanga and his people. One of the conditions for protection was that all dealings with Europeans should be through the British company and that Buganda should be open to trade with other countries, while European missions should be permitted to teach religion to the people. This agreement was intended to last for two years.

Captain Lugard feared that the few soldiers he had at his disposal could not quell any rebellion that might arise in the country. So he decided to go through Ankole, Toro, Bunyoro, Acholi and across Lake Sese Seko Mobutu and bring back the trained Sudanese forces which Emin Pasha had left behind in the Sudan after Stanley's departure.

When Lugard arrived back in Kampala in 1890, he found two rival kings, Kabarega and Kasagama contesting the throne of Toro. Lugard decided to back Kasagama who was residing in Kampala, having been ousted by Kabarega. Lugard returned to Toro, and restored Kasagama to the throne leaving with him sufficient Sudanese forces to sustain his power.

Lugard's journey to the Sudan also brought friendships with other chiefs in Acholi and Ankole and the presence of the Sudanese soldiers in Uganda is recalled by the establishment of small family settlements of Nubians at Bombo, Entebbe and Arua.

Tensions Build Up

On his return to Kampala from the Sudan, Captain Lugard found considerable disagreement between the Catholics and the Protestants on the question of government appointments. There was also a strong difference of opinion about the seat of the Imperial Company's administration. Several directors of the Company thought that the headquarters should be in Mombasa, seeing little profit in the considerable expense of maintaining an armed force in Uganda without the prospect of a profitable trade in that country.

Such a decision to leave Uganda at this stage did not suit Lugard's policy. He had signed an agreement with King Mwanga which was intended to last for two years. Only one year had elapsed, so that Captain Lugard had to stay in Kampala for another year. He feared a Christian rising which would imperil the lives of the European teachers especially those belonging to the English C.M.S. Thirdly there was the fear of renewed rivalry between Kasagama and Kabarega. All the efforts that Lugard had made to create friendships with the king of Ankole and other chiefs, as well as the stationing of Sudanese forces in Uganda, would have been in vain.

During this period Bishop A. R. Tucker of the C.M.S., who had succeeded Bishop Hannington in Kampala, heard that it was the company's intention to leave Uganda. He was afraid that if the company departed, the lives of the missionaries would be in danger, and their work wasted. So he appealed for financial support for the company from Christian benefactors in Britain. This resulted in sufficient funds being given to the company to enable it to stay in Uganda for another year.

What Captain Lugard had feared, happened at last. In January, 1892, the Catholics and Protestants still disagreed over the disposal of offices in the government. King Mwanga was on the side of the Catholics, Captain Lugard supported the Protestants. The two sides began fighting. The Protestants won the first battle because of superior weapons. Mwanga and his followers retreated to Bulingugwe island in Lake Victoria, only to be summoned back by Captain Lugard.

When they returned he made a new arrangement for sharing offices between Catholics and the Protestants which was accepted as a fair compromise by both sides. So peace was restored.

British Administration Begins

After settling these matters, Lugard returned to Britain in August 1892. He left Captain Williams in charge of Uganda on behalf of the company. In London Captain Lugard told the British government to end the system of rule by the company because the company had insufficient funds to carry out the administration. The C.M.S. in Britain supported him.

At last the British government sent Sir Gerald Portal, who held an important position in Zanzibar, to Uganda to prepare the way for starting a British administration. He arrived in Kampala in March 1893, and signed an agreement with King Mwanga and his chiefs on behalf of the British government. Sir Gerald Portal promised that Britain would protect King Mwanga and his people. In return King Mwanga would allow the British government to collect taxes. This was the end of the rule of the Imperial Company and the beginning of the direct responsibility of the British government in Uganda. After this Sir Gerald Portal returned to Britain in May and in June the following year the British Parliament declared formally that Uganda was its protectorate.

24 Uganda 1894-1920

When Britain declared Uganda her protectorate in 1894, kings and chiefs in various parts in the country lost their independence of action. They had to act according to the instructions of the British representatives in their areas. At once, a campaign was started by the British officers to bring all the different parts of Uganda under the administration, either peacefully through treaties if their native rulers accepted the British rule or by force of arms if they resisted.

Kabarega of Bunyoro

We have already seen Kabarega's clash with Captain Lugard of the Imperial British East Africa Company early in 1891. When the British officials set up their administration in Uganda Kabarega did not come to terms with them. He still wanted to win back Toro for the old kingdom of Bunyoro and also to keep that kingdom's independence. So he started to attack Kasagama of Toro who had been restored to the throne by Lugard.

The Commissioner for Uganda, Colonel Colville, mounted an attack on Kabarega in January 1894. He was helped by Baganda collaboration and by the Sudanese soldiers left behind by Lugard. Kabarega was defeated in two engagements but he refused to make a treaty with the Commissioner. He fled with some of his followers across the Nile to Acholi where he stayed for some time with Chief Awich of Payera. From Acholi he went to Lango and harassed the British administration from there for five years. After Kabarega's defeat, a chain of forts was built through Bunyoro, separating the west from the east of the country to prevent further trouble. In 1897 Kabarega was deposed and his young son, Yosiya Kitahimbwa, was installed as Omukama.

Mwanga of Buganda

Though Kabaka Mwanga had at first co-operated he soon felt the limitation of his power by the British administration. At the beginning of 1896, he was punished by the British Commissioner for having allegedly smuggled ivory and sold it without the Commissioner's permission. After that incident he could no longer tolerate the interference of foreigners.

Disillusioned and resentful, he escaped early in July from his palace at Mengo and went south-west to Buddu county 128 km away where, on his arrival, he gathered a force of his Baganda subjects and staged a resistance against the British administration. He was defeated by the British forces aided by Baganda collaborators from Kampala and subsequently banished to Mwanza in Tanzania. The British installed his year-old son, Daudi Chwa, as the Kabaka and set up three regents for the young Kabaka.

Mwanga soon escaped from Mwanza and secretly joined Kabarega in Lango where they staged a more concerted opposition to the British administration. They were finally tracked down by the British forces and sent into exile on the Seychelles Islands, in the Indian Ocean, in April 1899.

Awich of Acholi

In 1898 Major Macdonald from Kampala was in Acholi, signing treaties with chiefs officially accepting the British administration, but Awich, chief of Payera, refused to sign a treaty. At the same time Awich was using former followers of Kabarega and the Sudanese, who had revolted and run away from the British administration, to raid other Acholi chiefs. It was from the British administrative headquarters at Nimule that a campaign was set on foot in 1898 to capture Awich. He was finally captured in 1901, by Major Delme-Radcliffe who carried him to Nimule as a prisoner. The British however reinstated him as chief of Payera in March 1902, in spite of which he remained discontented with British rule. In 1912 there arose in Payera the Lamogi Rebellion, which was a protest against the registration of firearms. This rebellion was blamed on Awich, who was banished to Kampala and his area of Payera was divided between his two sons.

British Control

Nearly everywhere in Uganda colonial rule was established by force either directly by the British or by their collaborating agents, the Baganda, even in Buganda itself. Yet everywhere this foreign rule was resisted, with disastrous consequences for the resisters, the most notable of whom were Kabarega, Mwanga and Awich.

In the Ankole area the king of Igara committed suicide because of British pressure and his neighbour the king of Kajara fled to

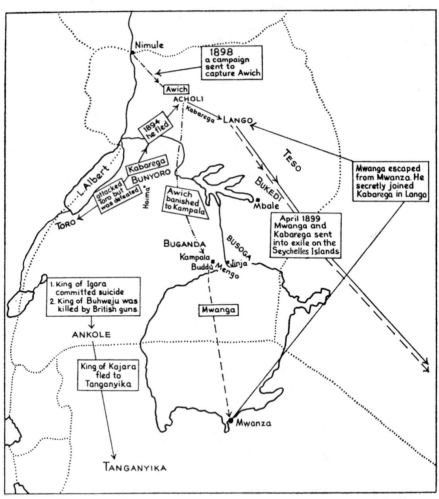

Resistance and collaboration in Bunyoro, Buganda and Acholi
Note: Lake Albert became Lake Mobutu in 1974

Tanganyika, while the king of Buhweju was killed by British guns, while trying to resist.

In Busoga chiefs were threatened with deposition if they did not co-operate; in Teso and Lango British rule met with opposition which was defeated only by the guns of Semei Kakunguru, the Muganda agent of the British, about whom more must be said.

He was a Muganda general who knew well how to fight and how to rule after fighting. He helped the British to fight against Kabarega in 1894 and to capture him and Mwanga in 1899. In 1893 he was appointed by the British officers to rule in Bugerere from where he went on subduing the people of the east to the rule of the Uganda Protectorate, sometimes using force to make the people obey his orders. From 1894 to 1904 Kakunguru was busy in both the northern and the eastern parts of Uganda. He brought Bukedi under the Protectorate, and also Teso, Lango and some parts of Acholi, setting up his headquarters at Budaka in Bukedi. While he was there he governed and directed all that area which he had subdued as its ruler or king. He was a good administrator, however, setting up laws and enabling people to travel from one place to another without fear of being attacked by others. He also built roads. He preserved the system of chiefs, although instead of using the local title for each kind of chiefship, he used the Ganda titles, such as saza-chiefs, gombolola-chiefs, miruka-chiefs and mutongole-chiefs. About 1908 the British had his headquarters built for him at Mbale. In 1912 he was made Secretary General of Busoga, after which he started to disagree with the young British officers and he became a private citizen. He died in 1928, having performed valuable work in the early years of the Uganda Protectorate.

The Sudanese Mutiny in 1898

In the end it was the turn of some of those who had collaborated with the British to resist – the Sudanese soldiers. These soldiers had been Emin Pasha's soldiers whom he had left behind in the Province of Equatoria (Southern Sudan) in 1888, and whom Lugard used to crush the Catholics in Buganda as we have seen in the previous chapter. When the British Government took over the administration of Uganda, it used these soldiers to capture Kabarega and Mwanga. When ordered to march north to prevent a possible invasion of Britain's rights in Uganda by the French in 1898, they mutinied.

They were underpaid, their pay was in arrears and they were tired of the hard life of constant fighting so they shut themselves up in a fort near Jinja. Britain had to order Indian soldiers from the coast to attack them and, with the collaboration of the Baganda, the Sudanese soldiers were defeated. With the defeat of both the Uganda resisters and the rebellious Sudanese soldiers, British rule in Uganda was established with no further serious challenges.

Political Development

When the British started their administration in 1894 they had very few officers available, so they used Baganda chiefs as their agents in many parts of Uganda, especially in the western and eastern areas. These chiefs introduced the system of administration then prevailing in Buganda, which was familiar to them. This system was based on saza, gombolola, miruka and village chiefs. The British officers always took over as soon as these agents had set up the administration.

From 1898 there had been a process of bringing all parts of Uganda under the administration either by treaty or by force. This process was finished by 1919. The most famous treaty, or agreement, which was made during this time was the 1900 Agreement with the Baganda chiefs which rewarded them with land titles for their collaboration with the British.

As new parts were brought under the protectorate, some Baganda agents were used to help run the administration, who ran into resistance everywhere. This hostility to the British Baganda agents was shown up dramatically in the Nyangire Rebellion by the Banyoro in 1907. The Banyoro bombarded the saza and gombolola headquarters where the agents were stationed. The agents ran for protection to Hoima, the British administrative headquarters. The Baganda agents were not removed but the Banyoro were satisfied by the British officials' promise that no more Baganda agents would henceforth be appointed. The British also promised to replace the Baganda agents with Banyoro of ability whenever such people came forward. The Banyoro were also given permission to report on any inefficient Muganda agent and if the charges against him were found to be genuine he would be replaced. The last Muganda agent to be removed from Bunyoro was James Miti in 1930, who was expelled as a result of accusations brought against him by the Banyoro, as had been the trend in other places where Baganda agents had been placed. By

1930 most of the Baganda agents had been withdrawn from non-Buganda areas.

Economic and Educational Progress

From 1904 to 1920 the government was engaged in encouraging the planting of cotton on which Uganda's economy came to rely. Governor Sir Hesketh Bell (1905-10) was identified with this growth of the cotton industry in Uganda. He also encouraged the building of roads throughout the country to help transport the cotton and other goods. The cotton growing helped the people to get cash and pay their poll tax. This poll tax was introduced in 1905 and it had to be paid by every man who was eighteen years of age or above. The result was that in 1916 the British Treasury stopped paying its annual subvention to the Uganda Treasury to help run the administration as it had become self-supporting.

As for education, the Roman Catholic societies of the White Fathers, the Mill Hill Fathers and the Verona Fathers and the Protestant C.M.S. were responsible for it with very small grants in aid from the central government. The proceeds from the sale of cotton helped parents to send their children to school. By 1920 attendance at a mission school had become something much coveted by parents for their children because the old African way of education had been overtaken by school education. Parents who wished their sons and daughters to rise under the new order had to see that their children attended these mission schools.

25 Kenya 1895-1920

Introduction

Under the Anglo-German Agreement of 1886 Kenya was administered by the Imperial British East Africa Company and not, therefore, directly financed by the British Government. Then in 1895 the company withdrew, because its funds were insufficient to cover both its trading and the administration of Kenya and Uganda. On 1st July, 1895 the British government formally declared a protectorate over Kenya. The East Africa Protectorate* extended from the coast to the Rift Valley. The adjacent territory, from the Rift Valley to Lake Victoria was the eastern province of Uganda and it was transferred to Kenya in 1902, with the object of placing the railway – which had reached Kisumu in 1901 – under one management and of providing land in this fertile region for settlers from Europe.

Troubles on the Coast

The British Foreign Office had originally envisaged a single administration covering the East Africa Protectorate and Uganda in the style of the German protectorate which jointly administered Tanganyika and Rwanda-Burundi. Such a policy, however, proved impossible. Uganda had its own problems, not least the aftermath of religious wars and the opposition of King Kabarega to the protectorate. It was decided that Kenya should be governed from Zanzibar by the British Consul, Sir Arthur Hardinge.

This decision provoked a rising among the Mazrui. They had disputed the sovereignty of the Sultan of Zanzibar and had hoped that on the departure of the Imperial British East Africa Company they might regain their independence. Instead they saw the British government taking over. Under Mbarak bin Rashid they rebelled, only to be defeated by troops from India and driven from Mombasa.

*The name 'Kenya' was not adopted until 1915.

They burned a number of towns on the coast before crossing into Tanganyika, where the German governor, von Wissmann, granted them asylum. After the defeat of the Mazrui the British used the Liwalis and their subordinates as local agents on the coast.

Trouble broke out next among the Herti Somalis near Kismayu and the Ogaden Somalis. The latter were an aggressive people who frequently attacked their neighbours in their search for water and pasture-land and on one occasion they raided the British post of Yonte. A punitive British expedition arrived in April 1898, but the final quelling of the Somalis was not achieved until 1901.

The Protectorate Reaches into the Interior

The British government based its administrative network on the chain of old trading posts stretching along the route from Mombasa to Uganda. The route followed the Teita Hills, Machakos, Kiambu, from Lake Baringo across the Uasin Gishu plateau to Mumia's in the Kavirondo Gulf and then on to Buganda. Posts had been set up at Ndi, 160 km from Mombasa, Dagoretti, Mumia's and Eldama Ravine north of Lake Nakuru and already each had a nucleus of European settlers.

The approach had to be cautious, as hostility from local peoples could have overthrown the whole plan and Britain lacked the necessary troops to use force. The Masai in particular might have offered resistance, but it happened at this time that they were engaged in civil war, with Sendeyo and Lenana fighting for the succession and were, moreover, harassed by cattle disease and famine resulting from locusts. Smallpox also took its toll in the last ten years of the century and the Masai were in no position to oppose the British.

The Masai, who were used to various traders passing through the country, imagined at first that the British would not stay long. However Lenana, leader of the Kaputie and Matapatu Masai, made friends with the British when Fort Smith was established south of Kiambu near Nairobi. He was glad to accept aid and shelter for his followers at the Ngong settlement in 1893 where Francis Hall taught methods of agriculture, so that they could make up the losses they had suffered as cattle farmers.

Sendeyo, leader of the Loita Masai, then realized that with the British on the side of his brother Lenana he could not hope to claim the title of Laibon. He therefore made terms with Lenana and his people also settled near Ngong.

Trouble broke out in 1895 when the Masai attacked the Kikuyu at Kendong. A British trader, Andrew Dick, and some fellow Europeans in a nearby camp then attacked the Masai and killed more than a hundred of them before Dick himself was killed. Lenana feared British reprisals, so he negotiated a settlement and led the British to believe that the Kikuyu and Swahili porters had been to blame.

Punitive expeditions against the Kikuyu, Kamba and Nandi followed. As a result, British rule extended to the Teita hills and by 1900 the Kamba were governed from Fort Ainsworth. The Masai and Kikuyu were similarly controlled from Fort Smith, later renamed Fort Hall.

In the Kavirondo Gulf Mumia, king of the Wanga, co-operated with the British and from this base they brought other groups in Western Kenya under British rule. It was a favourite tactic to employ the services of a friendly chief to subdue adjoining territories.

Yet not all the neighbouring tribes submitted without a struggle. The Nandi in particular were in a better position than some to resist, since they had escaped the prevalent diseases and their cattle had not been infected as elsewhere with rinderpest and pleuro-pneumonia. The murder by the Nandi in 1895 of a British trader named West and later attacks on officials provoked open conflict with the British. An assault on the Nandi, together with the Keyo and Tuken, under the leadership of F. J. Jackson, failed completely. Then, by establishing strategic posts, the British gradually managed to bring under control the Keyo, Marakwet and Tuken on the edge of the Rift Valley. In the Kerio Valley the British subdued the Pokot and Turkana. By 1910 posts had been set up at Mayale, Archer's Post, Marsabit and Mount Kulal. Another, at Seneuli, prevented Somali encroachment on land there, since they had by then reached the Tana river in their wanderings. Among the Boran a post was set up at Wajir. The British presence was not welcomed by any of these peoples and it was established solely by force of arms.

The Nandi finally gave in after five attempts to repel the British. In the meantime the Sotik were crushed in 1905 with help from the Buret, and the Gusii were also brought to submission. At this time there was inter-tribal warfare, with attacks on tribes which were already under British rule by others still determined to resist. The defeat of the Nandi came in 1905. Their 'orkoiyot' or leader and 600 of his warriors were killed and the people were driven out of the Tinderet hills.

In 1908 the Bukusu were defeated with the loss of more than

200 men. The heavy death toll brought warnings from London to the officers in command, but by then the damage was done and the territory had been taken over.

The area between the Rift Valley and Lake Victoria was systematically annexed and fifteen companies of the Kenya African Rifles stood by in 1902 to put down opposition wherever it might arise. The Luos in the Kavirondo Gulf had attacked the invaders in 1897 but were crushed and the Luos to the north of the Gulf put up little fight. The Nyanguoni resisted but were overcome by superior military strength. Once again, stations were set up by the troops, at Kahanga among the Luhya, at Kericho among the Kipsigis and at Karungu among the southern Luos.

The story of the establishment of British rule in Africa was everywhere one of greater military power. Such resistance as was made could not match the strength of organized troops and there were often collaborators who would work with the invaders. The fact that resistance by Africans to the Germans in East Africa received greater prominence has resulted in an impression, albeit a false one, that the British rule was by comparison introduced in a humane and enlightened manner.

With Britain in control, life changed for the Africans. Weaker groups were now safe from the attacks of stronger groups. The army built new roads and improved communications. Agriculture came to the fore and new crops were introduced. By this means Africans who were not stockbreeders had a source of income and could contribute taxes to the revenue. It was now apparent that a new power had come into the land, a power that could decide disputes among tribes and make laws.

Administration

At first the British attempted to govern their East African colonies through local chiefs, by the Village Headmen Ordinance of 1902. The system proved virtually unworkable. Powerful chiefs often refused to co-operate and lesser chiefs with little authority found themselves in high positions as mere puppets of the British. Such leaders were often ineffectual and sometimes corrupt and commanded little support from the tribes.

The system was replaced by another based on the traditional Kenyan councils of elders and given legal force in 1911 by the Native Tribunal

Rules. The people knew and trusted the councils which had power
to try minor cases. However, the councils' additional duties of
collecting the poll tax and recruiting labour for the government and
for private settlers were resented. It was felt that this was foreign
domination and that it was unjust that Africans having been obliged
to give up their best land to settlers should then have to work for
the newcomers who all too often paid them not in wages but in
kind.

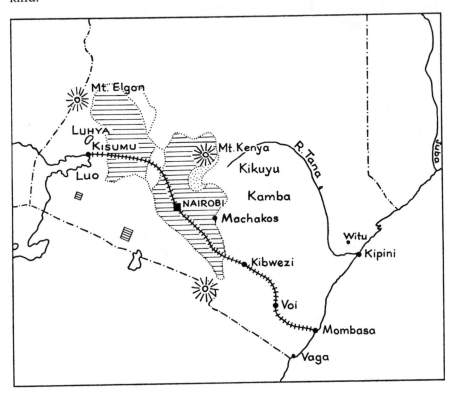

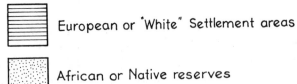

European or "White" Settlement areas

African or Native reserves

African and European areas in Kenya

The Arrival of the Settlers

Although Europeans began to settle in Kenya in 1896 the biggest influx was from 1903 onwards. The Commissioner, Sir Charles Eliot, hoped that by encouraging settlers he could make the railway pay and also relieve the British Treasury of some of the colony's administrative costs. The railway had reached Kisumu in 1901 and from there steamers, dhows and canoes plied to Entebbe, Jinja and Port Bell in Kampala. Settlers arrived from Britain, New Zealand, Australia, Canada and South Africa with the aim of setting up a European type of society. The country's African character was disregarded.

Settlement soon turned out to be heavily biased in favour of the incomers and the rights of the Africans were often ignored. The settlers were vocal in claiming their 'rights' and formed the Colonists Association (1902) and the Planters' and Farmers' Association (1903). On their insistence a Legislative Council was formed with Britain's agreement in 1906. Sir Charles Eliot's enthusiasm for the success of the white settlement project led him to overlook the Africans' claims. The position was not helped by such men as Lord Delamere and Captain Grogan who were aggressive and unscrupulous in furthering the prosperity of the whites despite the efforts of government officials to preserve land for the Africans. When Lord Delamere was appointed land officer by Eliot he reserved 100 000 acres of land near Nakuru for himself and other settlers received 5000 acres each in the Kenya highlands. These people became the principal landowners and subsequent settlers had to be content with smaller amounts.

Gradually the settlers created for themselves a rich enclave of whites in Kenya. Poor Europeans were discouraged from settling, from fear that they would accept menial work which it was felt the Africans should do. This served to keep a distance between the Africans and the whites. Asians were segregated in many towns, but led by A. M. Jeevanjee of the Indian Association they put up a determined fight for a share of Kenya. Largely to consolidate the hold of the white settlers the capital was changed from Mombasa to Nairobi in 1907. The former railway depot supplanted the ancient city, and the Arab-Swahili influence in the Kenyan culture was diminished.

First Effects of the Settlers on Kenya

By 1905 Kenya was under the direction of the Colonial Office in London and the new administrator, Sir James Hayes, had the title of Governor, whereas his predecessors – Sir Charles Eliot, who resigned in 1904 and Sir Donald Stewart – had been merely Commissioners.

The Masai people were among the first to feel the effects of white settlement. Between 1903 and 1913 they were moved several times to make way for British settlers and their leader Lenana acquiesced in this. Under the Masai Agreement of 1904 they were put into two reserves, one south of Ngong and the other at Laikipia Plateau, and they were forbidden to cross from one to the other least they spread cattle disease to the lands of Europeans which lay between the two territories. Then the northern reserve was required as farmland for settlers so the two Masai groups were amalgamated in the remaining reserve. Legalishu, the leader of the Laikipia group, was not in favour of this change and thought that the land allotted, though larger than the original southern reserve, was insufficient for all the Masai.

The creation of reserves for African peoples became the standard practice. But whereas the Masai had been consulted, because of their leaders' good relations with the British, other tribes were not. Another factor in the treatment of Africans was the attitude of settlers from South Africa who were accustomed to using Africans for cheap labour, with a system of recruiting them to work on settlers' land, often for payment not in cash but in kind. In 1907 a Commissioner for Native Affairs was appointed to regulate the employment of Africans. In return for living on settlers' land they had to give 180 days' free labour each year and registration was compulsory. Under the Masters and Servants Ordinance it was an offence for an employee to break a contract once he had been recruited by the local council.

In these measures the Africans had no voice. On the Legislative Council and the Land Board were settlers' representatives who looked after their own interests. In 1909 by the so-called Elgin Pledge they debarred Indians from the Kenya highlands and Africans were compelled to leave their own lands in order to work on the farms of white settlers.

During this time the missionaries continued their work, gaining converts and attracting pupils to their schools. The Africans who came under the influence of the missionaries were generally pro-British. It was argued by others, however, that the missionaries, like the settlers, took land for their churches, schools and farms and that the imposition of the Christian religion was simply another form of subordination by the Europeans.

Changes brought about by World War I

While the British government was involved in the war of 1914-1918 the settlers took advantage of the situation to strengthen their hand. They extended the period of their land leases from 99 years to 999 years. They took even stricter measures to prevent Asians from settling in the highlands and segregated them in still more of the towns. The mobility of African workers was severely curtailed by the issue of an identity card called *Kipande* without which no African could travel. A system of elected representatives to the Legislative Council was introduced, but neither Africans nor Asians were eligible for election, thus leaving all the power with the settlers. The country changed its name from 'The East Africa Protectorate' to 'Kenya', after Mount Kenya. All these steps were approved by the Colonial Office, which also acceded to the settlers' demand that the next governor should be a military governor. He arrived in the person of General Edward Northey in 1919.

By the time that General Northey took office there was no longer the conflict of opinion that had existed earlier between moderate officials in the administration, who upheld the rights of Africans and Asians, and settlers demanding white supremacy. The official policy was now that European interests were paramount in Kenya. New land was needed for additional settlers coming under the Soldier Settlement Scheme at the end of the war. It became customary to dispossess Africans of the areas required without even reference to London. More labour had to be recruited for government projects and for settlers and was obtained by the notoriously harsh circulars issued by General Northey. Another move in the settlers' favour was the abolition of income tax in 1922 and the imposition of high tariffs on imported wheat and flour, so that Asian importers should not spoil the local market.

African Rights

After the war there was a reaction in London against the settlers' pursuit of self-interest to the detriment of the Africans and Asians. General Northey was recalled in 1922 and replaced by Sir Robert Coryndon, former governor of Uganda. Discriminatory measures against Asian citizens were rescinded. The settlers countered with a plan to seize the railway and telegraph system and kidnap the new governor.

The growing animosity between white settlers and Asians, who demanded direct and equal representation and an end to segregation, resulted in a conference in London in 1923 called by the Colonial Secretary, the Duke of Devonshire. Representatives of both sides attended. The outcome was the Devonshire White Paper, a compromise. It rejected control of Kenya by either European or Asian settlers and also the principle of equal Asian and European representation, but it did declare that the highlands were to be reserved for Europeans. Most important, however, was the declaration of 'African paramountcy' in Kenya.

The White Paper did not, however, materially change the position of the Asians and Africans. The advantages were still with the settlers. Lord Coryndon, in an attempt to help African agriculture, sponsored the growing of coffee and cotton, thereby depriving the settlers of some of their labour force. When the new governor Sir Edward Grigg took over on the death of Coryndon in 1925 he sided with the settlers and encouraged further European immigration. Increased numbers of whites would be likely to strengthen the case for self-government. Grigg when in the Colonial Office had already put forward a proposal in 1923 for an East African Federation. However, when the idea was studied in 1927 by the Hilton Young Commission it found that Africans did not want federation. It reiterated the policy of African paramountcy laid down in the 1923 Devonshire White Paper and recommended an East African High Commission to deal with matters of common interest and promote co-operation between Africans and settlers.

The settlers, not content with these findings, still pressed for a federation. In 1931 the British Government set up a select commission to examine the question again. African opinion, particularly in Kenya and Uganda, had hardened against the idea. Two prominent men from Kenya, Chief Koinange of the Kikuyu Association and Ezekiel Apinde of the Kavirondo Taxpayers' Welfare Association went to

London to give the commission their views. Both were moderates and not violently opposed to the colonial administration. Through interpreters they made it clear, however, that they were not in favour of any move which would lead to European supremacy in East Africa. It is worth noting that the more extreme anti-colonial views of Jomo Kenyatta and P. J. Mockerie, both of the Kikuyu Central Association and both fluent English speakers, were not allowed expression.

Still the settlers, led by Grogan and Delamere, persisted in a spirit of defiance towards the Colonial Office. In 1931 Sir Joseph Byrne was appointed governor and he was determined to carry out the policy laid down by London. He ignored the demands of the diehard settlers, who tried to manipulate the Legislative Council for their own ends, and was instrumental in passing measures which removed some of their previous privileges from the Europeans. The most notable was the levying of income tax, hitherto paid only by the Africans.

Gradually the influence of the fiercely pro-European group waned. Lord Delamere, a sick man for some time, died in 1931. The campaign was carried on for some years by Lord Francis Scott and Major F. W. Cavendish-Bentinck, but they resigned from the Executive Council in 1936, frustrated at their lack of success. On the death of Sir Joseph Byrne in 1937, Sir Robert Brooke Popham became governor, with a more conciliatory attitude towards the settlers, and their hopes of obtaining a ministerial form of government began to rise once more.

26 Kenya 1920-40

Troubles and Unrest

Africans did not take kindly to the colonial administrative arrangements in their areas. From 1912 tribes were divided into separate locations. But in certain places, notably Nyanza, which had a high density of population, members from one tribe crossed over into the locations of other tribes in search of land, leading to tribal conflicts during the 1920's and 1930's.

Another source of friction in this area resulted from the British appointing Wanga chiefs to rule over places outside Wanga territory. The kingdom of Wanga was unique in Kenya, for it had a centralized system of government like the kingdoms of Uganda. The British considered that chiefs with experience of such a system would make better rulers. Accordingly Wanga chiefs were put in charge of Luo, Nandi and other Kipsigis locations. Mumia, the Wanga king, was created Paramount Chief of North Kavirondo in 1909. This arrangement provoked great hostility, the more so because Mumia had earlier collaborated with Swahili and Arab slave traders. He had obtained guns from them and terrorized other tribes, extending his territory and capturing people to sell as slaves. From the start he worked with the British, earning bitter hatred on account of his Wanga chiefs who levied government taxes and recruited labour for government projects and settlers.

During the 1920's and early 1930's non-Wanga peoples actively opposed Wanga chiefs and urged their removal.

In view of the opposition, the colonial government removed the headquarters from Mumia's to Kakamega. Some Luo locations were taken from north Kavirondo and administered by Luos from Central Kavirondo.

Mumia died in 1926 and was succeeded by one of his sons. But the new leader was not respected. Tribes began to appoint their own chiefs in opposition to Wanga chiefs. The colonial government in

146

1934 began to withdraw Wanga chiefs from non-Wanga districts, much to the relief of the tribesmen concerned. Disputes now arose among Luos and Luhya because of clan feuds and because rival churches were being established. The acrimony even extended to football matches, where bloody fighting would break out.

Rivalries between Luo and Luhya resulted in a split in the Kavirondo Taxpayers' Welfare Association in 1925 and the Luo virtually took it over. In 1934 the Luhya formed the North Kavirondo Central Association to fight for the creation of a Luhya paramount chief, namely Mulama, Mumia's brother. The government rejected the idea and dismissed Mulama from his post as chief of Mumia's. With him the Wanga dynasty ended.

New Religious Movements

Another remarkable development in Nyanza during the 1920's and 1930's was the formation of breakaway Protestant churches. The first was the Dini ya Roho (the religion of the spirit), formed in 1916 among the Luo in the Kaimosi region. The followers of this religion spoke strange languages, attributed to the inspiration of the Holy Spirit. At times they were possessed by the Holy Spirit and would make prophecies. They spent much of their time marching through the villages with drums beating, seeking to show their disregard for earthly things. When so many people were struggling for material benefits, the unworldliness of this sect presented a strange contrast.

Mumboism also developed early in the 1920's among the Luos. It rejected western ideas. Mumbo was a god to whom sacrifices were made. The faithful wore skins, were unwashed, had long hair and were of striking and distinctive appearance in a society which was fast acquiring European habits. All this was an expression of opposition to colonialism and the discarding of African customs. The cult spread to Gusii and South Kavirondo. But it died out when its leaders were deported to the coast in the 1930's. They were thought by the government to be subversive.

Another religion was found among the Suk – the Dini ya Musambwa (religion of the spirits of the dead). It, too, was pledged to oppose western ideas and stop de-Africanization. The cult became prominent after 1945.

Questions of Native Rights

African awareness was further aroused by the Native Lands Trust Bill of 1929. The Colonial Office wanted to grant to those Africans who had been removed from their reserves in favour of settlers other land equal in size and value. The Legislative Council, which was dominated by settlers, refused to pass the bill. The governor, Sir Edward Grigg, pressed by the Colonial Office had to force the bill through by using his casting vote.

The Kikuyu Central Association was at the centre of the opposition to the settlers on this issue and its general secretary was Jomo Kenyatta. The association ran a Kikuyu paper to educate the people and to make them aware of the white man's oppression. The association at first collected money to further its activities. But the governor refused to allow this in view of the association's vocal opposition to the government and the missionaries.

In 1930 the government, still adhering to its policy of African paramountcy, declared that suitably qualified Africans should be permitted to sit in the Legislative Council. But to qualify they had to be trained through the local native councils, formed in 1925. The councils were unlike those promulgated by the 1902 Village Headmen Ordinance. The latter were either controlled by the heads of small clans and families or by the age-old system of assemblies of elders. The local Native Councils of 1925 were representative, presided over by the district commissioners. Their members were elected and the councils covered more tribes than those of 1902 and consequently were larger. Their duty was not to pass laws but to suggest improvements in the law to the government. They dealt with land improvement, education, roads and the registration of births, marriages and deaths. They also levied taxes for education and other communal services.

The local native councils deprived Africans of a quicker road to political maturity. The young and educated in particular saw these local native councils as retrogressive. They were not the places in which to fight for the causes that mattered. This young generation wanted to rub shoulders with the white men in the Legislative Council where decisions that affected the Africans were taken. Though the Colonial Office was sympathetic to the Africans' wish to join the Legislative Council, it was left to the discretion of the governor to choose the time. It was also for him to decide the proportion of African representatives in the Council.

The Land Problem

By 1926 the land question had become extremely serious for the Africans. Reserves had been marked out in 1905 and by 1926 there were twenty-three of them, fast becoming over-populated. One difficulty was that the government was able to re-allocate the land as it wished.

Although these twenty-three reserves were gazetted in 1926 to allay African fears and to make it hard for the administration to alienate reserve land, the Africans were dismayed when, in 1932, gold was found on the Kavirondo Reserve at Kakamega and the government removed the land from the reserve area to sell it to European prospectors. The Africans living there were compensated with money, but they could not obtain land elsewhere, which was all they cared about.

The grievances of Africans about land became so acute that the Secretary of State for the Colonies set up a land commission in 1932, headed by Sir William Morris Carter. The recommendations of the commission did not satisfy the Africans because they set aside for the white settlers a further 43 253 square km of good land. Despite the fact that some land was added to the reserves, the situation was left almost as before. The best land in Kenya was now in the hands of the white settlers. This was particularly disastrous for the Kikuyu people who lived on the periphery of white settlement and had lost the best of their land to the settlers. As they were close to Nairobi, the Kikuyu would have had a ready market for their crops in the town, where prices were good. Unfortunately there was no means by which they could move to free land. They had to be content with being allowed to grow crops on the settlers' land and keep their animals there. In return they had to contract to do 180 days paid work per year. The arrangement benefited the settlers, who were assured of a source of labour. Africans who stayed in the reserves did not have this obligation. But the squatters – principally the Kikuyu, Nandi and other groups of Kipsigis – and the people in the reserves were all desperately short of land. Their desire for it was sharpened by the fact that there were large tracts of land unused but fenced off by the settlers.

In Nyanza and in other areas there was relatively little alienation of land. In these areas many people were recruited to work on settlers' farms. Their greatest complaints were about labour laws that greatly restricted their movements and also the very low wages.

Developing Political Awareness

In 1921, as a result of General Northey's pro-European policy in Kenya, the Africans formed their first political organizations to protect their interests. One, formed in Nyanza province, was called the Young Kavirondo Association and was dominated by the Luo and Abaluyia. The other, the East African Association, was formed in Nairobi and dominated by the Kikuyu. The Young Kavirondo Association was deflected from its more radical policies by the influence of Archdeacon Owen of Nyanza who was in favour of working through official channels. In 1923, it changed its name to the Kavirondo Taxpayers and Welfare Association. The East African Association was proscribed and its president, Harry Thuku, was deported to Kismayu on the coast after trying to extend the association beyond the Kikuyu. The group was re-formed as the Kikuyu Central Association in 1924 at Fort Hall and began to petition for more liberal treatment of Africans.

These associations were inter-tribal. They did not attack the colonial system, but wanted redress for specific grievances – the failure to provide land for tribes and the interference, as they saw it, by the Church of Scotland with Kikuyu customs and values. These were the main issues in the 1920's.

The Beginning of the Nationalist Movement

The African nationalist movement was founded in the 1930's. Whereas in the 1920's African political activities concentrated on specific issues, the new movement attacked the actual colonial system. The Kikuyu Central Association was the driving force.

After 1930, however, the Kikuyu Central Association was torn by factions. There was a split led by Chief Koinange, who eventually came back to the fold in 1937. When Harry Thuku returned from exile in 1931 he stayed in the Kikuyu Central Association for a time, but finding it too radical he formed the Kikuyu Provincial Association in 1935.

Despite this state of affairs, the Kikuyu Central Association continued to be the most influential political body. It used the independent schools – built after the Kikuyu break with the Church of Scotland in 1929 – to spread political ideas. In 1937 the son of Chief Koinange returned from a long study tour in Europe and

America and set up the Kenya Teachers' Training College to produce teachers, mainly for the independent schools. From here political ideas reached many educated and semi-educated Africans.

The Kikuyu Central Association gave rise to sister associations elsewhere in Kenya, among them the North Kavirondo Central Association, founded in 1934 by the Abaluyia, the Ukamba Members Association and the Taita Hills Association in 1938. The Kikuyu Central Association also infiltrated the trade unions, which were very active, chiefly in Nairobi and Mombasa. In fact its activities much alarmed the government at the time of the labour trade union strike in Mombasa in July 1939. World War II was then imminent and the Kenya government feared an invasion by the Italians from Somaliland. Because the defence of the country and the Empire was now paramount, it banned the Kikuyu Central Association and its sister associations.

Apart from such organizations there were also numerous ethnic associations formed in the towns during the 1930's to help provide social services. Town councils were then composed entirely of settlers who had no interest in making amenities available to African inhabitants and workers. The new groups acted as channels of African opinion and played a part in mobilizing nationalist forces after 1945.

The Economic Situation

During this period the economy was affected by two depressions. The Europeans managed to survive by growing maize, which was easy to cultivate and much in demand in the world market. They were helped by the measures taken by the Kenya government, which expanded the railway network to serve the whole of the territory and kept its freight rates down to the barest minimum. It also raised import levies to protect home producers and allow them to sell their wheat, meat and dairy produce in East Africa in the face of foreign competition. In addition the government provided various social amenities. Unfortunately there was no thought of similar benefits for the African areas.

The Africans actually suffered in consequence of the steps taken to help the white settlers. They were not allowed to be independent producers of cotton and coffee; their output now dropped drastically compared with their record exports of the 1920's. The settlers considered Africans purely as a source of cheap and plentiful labour, so that if the Africans engaged in production on their own account the settlers would be deprived of their work force.

In 1932, when the depression was at its worst and the situation seemed hopeless, the government called in Lord Moyne to advise on economic policy. Acting on his advice it once more allowed Africans to grow their own crops of coffee, cotton and maize for export. Gradual recovery from the economic crisis took place after 1933 and from that point onwards the Europeans switched from maize-growing to a system of large plantations of sisal, coffee, tea and pyrethrum.

27 Tanganyika Under the Germans

After the partition of 1886 both Britain and Germany decided to rule their respective territories through trading companies, to reduce the cost of administration. Through the influence of Carl Peters the German East Africa Company was formed to take care of the German area. By 1887 the company had set up ten centres in the immediate hinterland where there were plantations of coffee and cotton. These centres also served as trading stations. But they soon proved a failure owing principally to the opposition of Arabs, who saw all Europeans as a danger to their trade in slaves and ivory and to their political control. Europeans would no longer allow the trade in slaves which was still the main source of Arab livelihood.

The company tried to trade in local products such as ivory, gum copal and a few others. But it met with the formidable competition of the already established Indian firm of Sewa Hadji and of Charles Stokes, an Irish merchant who had formerly been a missionary. To get revenue Carl Peters persuaded the Sultan of Zanzibar, Said Khalifa, successor to Sultan Said Barghash who had died in 1884, to allow the company to collect customs duties on the coast. It was also to regulate commerce, improve communications and dig for minerals. The company subsequently began to raise the German flag in all coastal towns. This was greatly resented by the Arabs who realized that their political influence and their commercial traffic in slaves and ivory were threatened. Already the British and Germans were waging a campaign against the slave trade and it had become very difficult to sell slaves in Zanzibar and in many coastal towns.

To resist the Europeans, who were poised to ruin their political power and commercial supremacy, the Arabs on the coast raised a revolt in 1888, led by an Arab half-caste called Abushiri in Pangani. Abushiri had always refused to recognize the Sultan of Zanzibar. He was readily joined by an African leader of Swahili origin, Bwana Heri, chief of the Zigua who had also refused to recognize the sultan.

He therefore resented being handed over to German rule by the sultan.

The Arabs supported by some Africans drove out all the Germans from the coastal towns except Dar es Salaam and Bagamoyo.

Since the revolt was aimed at both Germans and British the two European powers joined forces to crush it. The British aided the Germans by their naval patrol which was in the Indian Ocean trying to stop the Arabs from shipping slaves across the Indian Ocean. The German government sent in Captain Hermann Wissmann with a small number of troops. In 1889 he began to organize the German forces, consisting of Sudanese soldiers, some Zulus from Portuguese Mozambique and a large number of Tanganyika askaris. He then set out to crush the revolt systematically. The rebels were not well co-ordinated. Faced with such formidable opposition, Abushiri fled from Pangani and went into the interior after his forces were defeated on the coast. Wissmann set up a post at Mpwapwa and the insurgents lost heart. Abushiri was betrayed by the local people and captured by the German forces who hanged him publicly as an example to other rebels. Bwana Heri fared a little better. Seeing that all was lost, he surrendered to the Germans and was pardoned. By early 1891 all the rebellious spirits were crushed.

The German Government Steps in

By 1891 the German government realized that a trading company was not equal to the task of administering a colony. It had not enough money to run the administration and its forces were inadequate to crush any opposition. Moreover its main interest was bound to lie in trading and making profits. So the German government took over the administration of Tanganyika and left the company to concentrate on commercial activities. The government appointed Julius von Soden as the first governor. Wissmann, who had done much to crush the Arab revolt, was not appointed to a senior post on the grounds that he had not shown sufficient ability to organize the colony's finances, which by 1891 were in a chaotic state. But he was given the task of organizing a system of steamers on Lakes Tanganyika, Malawi and Victoria, which he did with some success.

The governor, the head of the administration, had power to issue local decrees. One such decree that greatly affected the Africans at this early period was the African Hut Tax, passed in 1897 to help increase the country's revenue. But the tax brought in very little money because the system of a cash economy was still in its infancy. Many people were allowed to pay the tax in millet, groundnuts and in sheep and goats.

Agriculture was introduced and Africans were encouraged to grow cotton. Areas were allotted various crops considered best suited to them. To develop modern crops botanical gardens were set up at Dar es Salaam. Two experimental agricultural stations were established at Kwai and Amani. The government created plantations which were in due course sold to businessmen. It also began to undertake public works, building offices, roads, bridges and railways and the town of Dar es Salaam was modernized.

Administrative Problems

The problem of the governor was now to enforce his decrees. He had only 165 German soldiers. He recruited about 1800 African soldiers, the majority of whom were Nubians from the southern Sudan. To overcome the difficulty chiefs in the interior were persuaded to co-operate. Those who considered this an abdication of their power refused, but were deposed and replaced by chiefs more ready to fall in with the German plans. On caravan routes military posts were set up to safeguard communications. Similar posts were also established at centres of trade, missions and government centres, headquarters of chiefs and the sultan's agents. German government officers were posted at a number of district headquarters where they were virtually their own masters.

Local chiefs continued to act as leaders of their people but they were answerable to the local German officers. A system of non-traditional chiefs was inaugurated, whereby Arab and Swahili chiefs from the coast (called 'akidas') were put in charge of groups of villages. Each village still had its traditional chief called a 'jumbe'. But the akidas were much disliked by the people because they had no local ties. They tended to enforce German orders very rigorously. The akidas were also inclined to over-ride the orders of the jumbes. The German administration owed much to the assistance given by the akidas and the jumbes, considering the size of the area and the small number of Germans who had to administer it. But the jumbes could not always be relied on to carry out German orders. By 1903 German East Africa – Tanganyika, Rwanda and Burundi – was divided into twelve civil and sixteen military districts, each headed by a German officer.

African Resistance to German Rule

When Germany took over Tanganyika many chiefs and their people did not relish the prospect of losing their independence. Along the German route of penetration into the interior there were many attempts at resistance, but they were systematically crushed by the Germans, who had the advantage of possessing superior weapons. The pattern of conflict was no different, however, in British and French territories. There too the more outspoken chiefs and their people made armed attacks on British and French headquarters. The number of revolts in Tanganyika against the Germans does not imply that foreign rule was necessarily harshest and least welcome there. All imperialists threatened the loss of political independence and freedom for Africans to follow their traditional culture and economic way of life. The German East Africa Company was replaced in 1891 by the German government administration because from 1887 the company had shown its inability to run the territory. The Abushiri revolt emphasized this failure in no uncertain terms. But even the German administration did not find the position easy, particularly as it was immediately faced with revolts led by the African chiefs.

In June 1891 the administration was dealt a blow by the Wahehe of Iringa. The Wahehe led by chief Mkwawa ambushed a German force commanded by Emil von Zelewski at Lule-Rugoro and 300 African askaris lost their lives. Only four German soldiers and thirteen African askaris escaped. It took some time for the German administration to recover from this shock and the Wahehe did not suffer retribution until 1894. The Wahehe were encouraged by this feat and for some years blocked any German advance into their country. Their chief Mkwawa lived in a fortified palace at Kalenga near Iringa. Like a castle of mediaeval Europe, it served as a refuge for many of his people when attacked. But in October 1894 the Germans, having crushed several powerful chiefs, launched an attack on the fortress at Kalenga. Mkwawa soon realized that the odds were against him. He left the fortress and decided to fight in the countryside. His followers around Iringa capitulated to the Germans. Out in the countryside, Mkwawa had no difficulty in obtaining a large following and began a guerrilla warfare which lasted until 1898.

In this year Mkwawa was betrayed by some of his people and finding further resistance hopeless, took his life rather than be captured by the Germans. The guerrilla warfare, however, led to the systematic extermination of the group. Presumably it was this fear of extinction that led some of the Wahehe to betray chief Mkwawa to the Germans.

Between 1891 and 1894 the Germans were engaged in action with several other groups of people. At first the Wanyamwezi living on the central trade route co-operated with the Germans. Owing to their long-distance trade connections, the Wanyamwezi were accustomed to meet foreigners and have dealings with them. Soon they realized that the Germans had come to take their land, control their trade and also rule them. Led by their chief Siki in 1892, they began to fight against the Germans and closed the trade route for a number of months. They were dislodged only by a superior force under Lieutenant von Prince. But rather than submit, Siki committed suicide.

The Wagogo also rose against the Germans, but their effectiveness was blunted by their disunity. They therefore engaged in sporadic attacks until their resistance was worn down.

In Bukoba three chiefs took up arms but were soon silenced. Tagaralle, chief of the Ujiji on Lake Tanganyika, mounted a determined campaign to prevent a German advance in his country, but was soon quelled. The longest struggle the Germans had was with the Yaos from 1890. Led by their chief Machemba, the Yaos put up a strong fight. The Germans nevertheless refused to give up in the face of opposition. They regarded the area as important on account of its economic potential. In the end Machemba fled to Portuguese Angola and his people then submitted to the Germans. A military post was set up on the Ruvuma river to prevent Machemba's return.

Such resistance did not deter the Germans. They continued their advance into the north-western region towards Rwanda. The Belgians in Zaire were facing a revolt among the people of Manyema. In 1898 they were driven by the Africans out of the region east of Lake Kivu. The Germans took advantage of the difficulties of the Belgians and occupied their territory of Rwanda, an arrangement later ratified by agreement between the Belgian and the German governments. The Germans offered tokens of friendship to King Muesi of Burundi in order to bring his territory under their control, but Muesi refused to co-operate. When persuasion and peaceful diplomacy failed, the German administration sent Captain Bette in 1903 to take over

Burundi by force. With the conquest of Burundi the occupation of German East Africa was complete. It left those who had resisted convinced that they could not dislodge the Germans and that it was wiser to co-operate. When, twenty years later, the next uprising against the Germans came, areas which had earlier faced the Germans in open combat did not fight a second time.

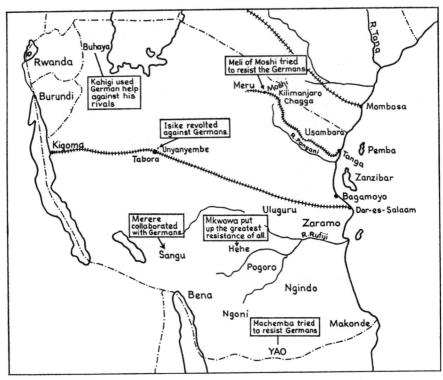

The Germans in Tanganyika: Resistance and collaboration by African Chiefs

28 The Maji Maji Rebellion

As the German administration spread into the interior, it came in contact with chiefs and their subjects who had never before experienced foreign rule. Like their counterparts on the coast, and others already mentioned, they resisted in defence of their independence. In July 1905 a rising took place. This was known as the Maji Maji rebellion, on account of the 'medicine' which warriors drank or sprinkled on their bodies as a protection against the German guns. It was believed to turn bullets to water.

The area affected by the rebellion was extensive, including much of the southern highlands and territory to the east and west, and numerous tribes were involved.

The Situation before the Rising

By 1905, when the Maji Maji rising began, the German administration and missionaries had been in Tanganyika for about twenty years. They had already found collaborators among the chiefs and keen followers among the people. This was achieved by defeating hostile chiefs and replacing them with those more acceptable. Some were traditional and others were akidas. Such chiefs were readier to comply with German wishes. German rule had also brought about stability in tribes which formerly suffered from constant raids and wars with stronger and more belligerent tribes.

Chiefs and people were now enjoying a spell of tranquillity. Some social services were available, notably medical care from the administration and the missionaries. People from the tribes were employed as cooks, workers on plantations, instructors in the mission churches, teachers in schools and askaris. Chiefs around forts and mission posts were in the habit of exchanging visits and gifts with neighbouring German officials and missionaries. The latter in particular brought gifts of cloth which was greatly prized and not easily obtained at that period. The general atmosphere tended towards a friendlier relationship between Germans and Africans. The Maji Maji rising, therefore, came as a surprise to the Germans and the people as a whole, particularly the Christians.

The Causes of the Rising

There were obvious reasons why the people in the area of the Maji Maji rebellion rose up against the Germans. The first was hatred of harsh discipline and forced labour. By 1905 tax was no longer paid in millet and goats but in currency. Money was difficult to come by and men had to walk long distances to work on German plantations in Morogoro, Iringa and Mpwapwa in order to earn the three rupees necessary to pay the tax. By order of the Germans, chiefs were obliged to conscript men to work on roads, railways and plantations. While working the men had to be away from home for some months.

Furthermore, a cotton scheme had been started by the German administration in the coastal districts south of Dar es Salaam. By 1905 cotton-growing had spread to Morogoro and Kilosa. Every chief had to establish a plot of about two acres or 0·8 hectares on which his men had to work communally. Because of the poor yield in Kilosa, very small wages were paid after the sale of the cotton and the men were resentful. Their sense of grievance was all the greater because the money paid to each man was less than the three rupees he had to pay in tax. Discipline was strict on the roads, plantations and cotton gardens. Failure to obey German officers meant whipping. Even chiefs were whipped in public for failing to follow instructions from German officers or their African representatives. But it should be emphasized that neither the tax payments nor the harsh working conditions on German schemes really affected the majority of the people in the area of the Maji Maji rebellion. Only those in the neighbourhood of Iringa, Mpwapwa, Kilosa and Morogoro, which were remote from the central administration, were concerned.

The second main cause of discontent was the destruction of tribal customs and traditions. For example, in pre-German days a chief was a leader. He commanded respect and had to be treated differently from the men he ruled. Now he could be whipped in public and ordered about just like his subjects. Traditional ways were ridiculed by missionaries and discouraged, especially among the young who were becoming Christians and attending missionary and government schools. Many chiefs, elders and medicine men and women saw great danger in this, since it meant the disintegration of the whole basis of African life. Naturally they were angry and alarmed. They knew that once the Germans began to settle and establish their headquarters in their midst, the threat to African freedom and culture would be even greater. Stories of German harshness were rife and spread fear amongst those not yet under German influence.

Organizers of the Rebellion

Medicine men and women in traditional Africa were a very powerful group, with a double role as priests and dispensers of medicine. They were held in great respect by the chiefs and their subjects and consulted by all on religious and medical matters.

In a situation where chiefs and their subjects seemed to be gradually accepting the Germans as a power that had come to stay, and prudence dictated that it was wiser to come to terms with them, the medicine men and women saw the total destruction of all they stood for. At least the chiefs would be left to rule, though with less power and deference from the German overlords. But the medicine men and women would lose everything.

Medicine men of Kolelo, who were mediums of the famous spirit of the Uluguru Mountains, evolved a plan which, they hoped, would dislodge the Germans, not only from their area, but the whole of Tanganyika. The mysterious 'medicine' already mentioned was made from maize, sorghum seed and water and was said to give immunity from bullet wounds. Millet stalks were to be worn, to show that the warriors were not like ordinary men. Although they probably knew that the concoction did not have the powers claimed for it, the medicine men felt that if the majority of people rose up in arms against the Germans, they would outnumber the foreigners. Even if large numbers of Africans were wiped out, they would still be superior in strength. They might even succeed in exhausting the Germans' supply of bullets so that they would have nothing left to shoot with.

The medicine men easily convinced their immediate followers of the power of the medicine and its capacity to help them drive out the Germans from Tanganyika. The next step was to convince the chiefs who had to lead the people. Certain of the medicine men were given the task of approaching them, while their followers tried to cover the whole territory very rapidly, making certain that the Germans had no inkling of the plan beforehand. Chiefs who agreed to fight approached their fellow chiefs to persuade them to join the movement also.

Reactions To The Plan

The idea appealed to some chiefs more than others, for a variety of reasons. Chiefs who had been very powerful and in the habit of attacking others for booty and land had been weakened by the coming of the German administration. They could now no longer prey on other tribes. Some of their lands had been confiscated as a result of clashes with the Germans in the early days and the territories given to chiefs more acceptable to the administration. This state of affairs existed mainly around the German forts. There the chiefs, harbouring a grudge, welcomed the idea of striking a blow against the Germans and being restored to their former grandeur.

Chiefs who had been given German support received with misgiving the proposals to drive out the Germans. They had become friendly with the foreign rulers, though the Germans would have punished them severely for any disobedience. They also knew beyond doubt that Africans could not hope to beat the Germans. Many such chiefs, therefore, though they put up a show of agreement with the rebels, were in fact half-hearted in their support. When fighting broke out they fought on the German side or refused to fight at all.

Other chiefs would not commit themselves. Though they liked the idea of driving out the Germans they feared that the 'medicine' might not after all have the power ascribed to it. They thought it wiser to watch the progress of the fighting first. If it looked as though the Africans were winning they would join in, to avoid being left out when the time came for sharing out the spoils. If they saw that the Africans were getting the worst of it they would either remain neutral or throw in their lot with the Germans against their fellow Africans, rather than suffer the German wrath afterwards.

In addition there were various tribes at loggerheads with one another. When fighting broke out, they did not make a common front but simply began to fight amongst themselves. Some tribes such as the Wabena and Ndendeule had taken refuge in the area between Ubena and Ungoni in the Lukumbura complex. Others had gone to the area between the Mahenge plateau and Ubena, where there was a mixture of people belonging to different tribes and no leaders to unite them in an effective force. They included the Wabena, Ndendeule, Pogoro, Wangindo and Wamwera. Far from joining the Maji Maji rebels, they were liable to turn against them. The Maji Maji fighters were told by their leaders to kill any Africans who refused to join them. So when they arrived here, instead of going to fight the Germans they fought their fellow Africans, burning villages and looting, which further weakened the uprising. Attacks on Africans also occurred in Mbuyuni and Gogo near Mpwapwa. Some chiefs were less interested in dislodging the Germans than in seizing from them such useful articles as cloth and domestic ware. Others were intent on capturing people from weaker tribes or enemy tribes as slaves.

Moreover, German officers and missionaries were on friendly terms with some of the chiefs and the people, who were persuaded to fight with the Germans. Many Christians and Africans receiving medical care and other benefits from the missionaries would not agree to join the fighting. They even gathered around the mission posts and formed a guard against the Maji Maji fighters.

The Fighting

The rising of the people, initiated by certain chiefs and medicine men, began in July 1905, though not simultaneously throughout the region. When one chief felt ready he mobilized his people and marched to a mission station, a German fort or Asian shops or began attacking the akidas. Then chiefs elsewhere would also go into action, in sporadic forays.

The Zaramo workers were the first to revolt. They refused their wages and decided to fight. The Matumbi joined them and together they drove away the akidas and settlers from their hills. The rising spread through the cotton area around the middle and lower Rufiji River and then to Ulunguru, the Makonde Plateau, Lukuledi and the Kilombero valleys, when the Pogoro and the Mbunga tribes joined in. However, by November 1905 the Germans had regained the southern highlands. The Ngoni and the Bena in the west, who had just joined the rising, were attacked and crushed. In the east the Ngindo, with other groups, fought longer, but after the death of their leader Abdalla Mapanda in January 1907 they gave in.

In some places they managed to surprise the Nubian soldiers and African askaris led by Captain Hauffman Forck of Mpwapwa, who suffered some casualties. But by and large, popular belief in the power of the 'medicine' soon disappeared and it was realized that the medicine men had been bluffing. Time and again the rebels were mown down by German machine-gun fire or scattered in disorder to take cover in the forests. In the end it was each man for himself and the struggle against the Germans was abandoned. Cultural ties had proved worthless as a means of uniting Africans against the Germans and the lack of a strong central organization proved their undoing. After the rebellion finally died out it took about two months for the German administration to hunt down all the rebels and bring them to trial.

Results of the Maji Maji Rebellion

The rebellion and the famine that followed it are estimated to have cost the lives of 75 000 Africans. The tragedy was that, of those who died, not all were killed by the Germans and their allies; a large number fell at the hands of Maji Maji fighters. After the rebellion the Germans executed many ring-leaders and sympathizers. The economic effects were dire, since the fighting had disrupted African life and villagers had fled so that crops were untended or destroyed and there were grave shortages of food.

Apart from a minor recurrence in 1908 there was no further resistance to the Germans in Tanganyika. Those Africans who had sided with the Germans, however, emerged richer and more influential, having acquired servants and livestock captured from rebel tribes. The Germans in their turn learned their lesson and improved their methods of colonial administration which had previously irked the Africans.

29 After Maji Maji

After the Maji Maji rising in 1906, which had occurred at almost the same time as the Herero rising in German West Africa, Germans at home voiced concern about the way in which their African colonies were being administered. The whole colonial system depended on the colony buying manufactured goods from the mother country and selling to her its raw materials and commodities. But risings caused instability and destroyed confidence in businessmen wishing to invest in the colonies. The Germans also wished to set a good example of colonial management to Britain and France. There was already a feeling in Europe that ideally both the Europeans and the Africans should benefit from the system. This philosophy was later expounded by Captain Frederick D. Lugard in his book *The Dual Mandate in British Tropical Africa*.

Tanganyika under Rechenberg

In Tanganyika all governors up to 1906 had been professional soldiers. The German government decided to reverse this state of affairs. It appointed in that year Governor von Rechenberg who had been a judge in Tanganyika and later served as German consul in Zanzibar. He was convinced that African interests should be paramount and that settlers should not be allowed to exploit Africans.

With this in view he encouraged the establishment of government and missionary schools. The C.M.S., the Holy Ghost Fathers, the U.M.C.A., the White Fathers and the three Berlin mission societies of Germany played a prominent part. Secondary education was introduced and technical schools followed later for all types of government work, for example in government departments, on plantations, in schools and on the railways. The medical service was also expanded by the government and the missionaries. One great contribution to the health of East Africa resulted from the research of Dr. R. Koch who discovered atoxyl, a remedy for sleeping sickness, which had been the scourge of East Africa and which was not finally eradicated until the 1940's.

The economic position of the Africans was also improved. Seeds from the experimental agricultural stations were distributed free to Africans, whereas the settlers had to buy them, though at a low price. Rechenberg believed that Tanganyika should not be primarily a plantation colony where Africans would automatically work on settlers' estates. They should also be helped and encouraged to grow their own crops. They could then sell them on the German market and buy German goods in exchange.

But the governor's philosophy was not shared by the German settlers. They wanted cheap and plentiful labour on the plantations and this would not be readily available if Africans were to become independent farmers and smallholders. The settlers suggested a poll tax for Africans to induce them to seek work on plantations. Failing that, they argued, the government should compel Africans to work there. Rechenberg rejected these demands and it became necessary for plantation owners to attract workers by higher wages. The settlers likewise opposed education for Africans. They did not appreciate the fact that even on plantations it would be to their advantage to employ skilled workers.

The Administration of Schnee

Rechenberg was succeeded as governor by Dr. Heinrich Schnee in July 1912. While not wishing to depart from the principles of Rechenberg, Schnee tried to reconcile the settlers to government policies. Rechenberg's treatment of the German settlers had been high-handed and uncomprising. Schnee, however, shared the settlers' view that areas such as the fertile land between Tanga and Kilimanjaro should be given over to plantations. Labour, therefore, should be made available at relatively low wages to encourage these enterprises. But only government officials were authorized to recruit such labour, as a safeguard against exploitation by private employers, and the rate of wages was fixed. The arrangement was acceptable to Africans and employers alike and the supply of labour was assured.

Between 1909 and 1914 the number of workers in government and missionary establishments and on plantations rose from 70 000 to 172 000.

On the administrative side, Schnee decided in 1913 to make half the membership of the Tanganyika Advisory Council (a type of parliament) consist of German settlers. Thus the running of the colony was shared in some measure with the settlers.

The years from 1906 to 1914 were a time of considerable prosperity in Tanganyika. Plantations of rubber and sisal, imported from Florida, flourished. Cotton-growing proved successful, especially in the valley of the Rufiji river. Coffee in the Usambara region, where it was originally grown, showed a decline, however. But in the Bukoba area small robusta coffee gardens yielded well. A remarkable crop of copra was produced in the coastal areas by Africans. The Mwanza region produced a good supply of nuts, also grown by Africans.

Communications were also considerably improved between 1906 and 1914 and the number of miles of railway lines grew. Mombo, Buiko and Moshi were all connected by railway by 1912 and the settler community of Kilimanjaro was well served. The central railway was opened, a section at a time: Dar es Salaam to Morogoro in 1909, Morogoro to Tabora in 1912 and Tabora to Kigoma near Ujiji on Lake Tanganyika in 1914. The length of this line was 1 252 km.

All this development was encouraged by the state which also attracted funds into Tanganyika. Prices of cotton, sisal and other commodities were guaranteed so that settlers and Africans could be sure of the rate even when world prices fell. The ending of tribal wars and attacks on government establishments and the disappearance of the slave trade brought about stability and economic growth in the country. Settlers increased rapidly, so that by 1914 there were 4 107 German settlers in Tanganyika. A steamship service was started between Germany and Dar es Salaam which greatly facilitated the trade between Germany and Tanganyika.

Tanganyika during the First World War

But the prosperity ended abruptly in August 1914 with the outbreak of the First World War. Since Britain, one of the nations fighting Germany, controlled the seas, Tanganyika was cut off from Germany. All the British in East Africa were automatically at war with Germans in neighbouring territories. Both groups prepared to fight, supported by their mother countries.

The German government sent in General Paul von Lettow-Vorbeck to command its forces in German East Africa. He was a very courageous man with a mastery of war tactics in the bush superior to that of the Allied Forces commanders. He had a small force of 260 German and 2000 African soldiers. This was augumented by German settlers and their African servants in Tanganyika. With the gallant and unwavering support of the African soldiers, Lettow-Vorbeck managed to out-manoeuvre the Allied Forces until August 1918, when an armistice was signed in Europe.

He was convinced that the decisive battle of the war had to be fought in Europe, not in the colonies. But he wanted to divert as many Allied Forces as possible to the subsidiary action in East Africa. And this he certainly achieved. From his stronghold in Kilimanjaro he engaged the Allied Forces, which included British, African, Belgian and Indian troops, led by General Smuts of South Africa, throughout many months in a series of guerrilla skirmishes. By skilful tactics and strategic withdrawals he continued to outwit them with his few German and African soldiers. His position was made worse because Tanganyika was cut off from supplies of arms from Germany. Lettow-Vorbeck was pressed hard by the Allies in the early part of 1918, and finally crossed into Northern Rhodesia. There he received word of the signing of an armistice on 11th November 1918, though it was not clear whether the terms were unconditional surrender or the evacuation of the German force.

Lettow-Vorbeck then disbanded his soldiers and ordered them to hand over their weapons. But he was never defeated. He achieved his aim of occupying the forces of the Allies in Africa while the crucial campaigns were fought. The Allies had believed that the people of Tanganyika would rise against the Germans. Instead they rallied to the German cause and contributed to the success of Lettow-Vorbeck's strategies by the provision of men and supplies. Earlier risings against the German rule in Tanganyika had given a false impression of the harshness of the Germans, and in fact there was evidence of similar discontent in the territories administered by Britain and France. What was overlooked, however, was the extent of the benefits brought to Tanganyika by the German administration.

Since Tanganyika was the only one of the East African territories where fighting took place, it suffered a setback in economic development as a result. The German settlers enlisted and the plantations became run down and neglected. African agriculture was similarly affected and the piecemeal government attempts to remedy the situation were of little avail.

30 Uganda 1920-39

Political Development

In 1919 some European planters and businessmen voiced a desire for a Uganda Legislative Council through which they would make their wishes known to the government. The higher officials in the Protectorate administration supported the idea as they wanted to secure the co-operation of the European planters and businessmen. When the governor, Sir Robert Coryndon, asked the Colonial Office about such a council he was given permission to set one up.

In 1921 the first session of the Legislative Council opened. The Council consisted of the Governor, the Chief Secretary, the Attorney General and the Chief Medical Officer for the administration, with the non-indigenous community represented by three appointed members, comprising two European businessmen and one Asian. However, the Asian community refused to associate itself with the Legislative Council because they felt that they should have had two representatives like the Europeans. They finally agreed to attend the Council in 1926 when Governor Gowers promised them a second representative in the future.

The Africans were not invited to sit on the Legislative Council. It was taken for granted that the official members would look after their interests. Nor were the Africans keen on being members of the Council. They looked on their local councils as the real source of influence. However, even if they had been interested in the Legislative Council, it would not have been acceptable to the colonial rulers that Africans attend it. Africans began to be represented only in 1945 and it was also about this time that Africans began to sit on Legislative Councils in the rest of East Africa as well.

At the African level the political situation can be looked at from two sides: from Buganda and from the rest of Uganda.

In Buganda this period saw a clash between the old Baganda chiefs and the British administration. The chiefs, still accustomed to the

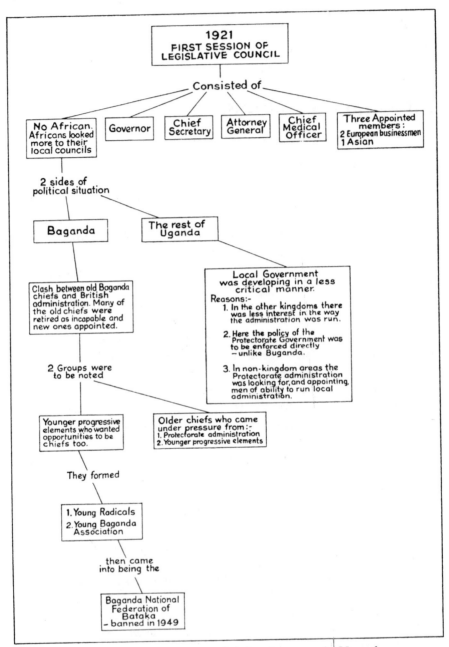

Political and administrative developments in Uganda

degree of autonomy accorded them during the first two decades of the twentieth century, wanted to retain their independence. They had been left mostly to their own devices during the earlier period because the Protectorate officials had felt that the Baganda chiefs were efficient and just in the execution of their administrative duties. But during this period a new group of British officers came to run the Buganda provincial administration. They were determined that they should have more control over Buganda than the agreement of 1900 allowed. They began to look for excuses to interfere and they found them in the inefficiency and oppression of the Baganda chiefs over the peasants. The chiefs' inefficiency was particularly shown by the administration of the Buganda Treasury. It was also found out that they were oppressing the peasants by making them pay various rates for staying on land which the chiefs had been given by the 1900 Buganda Agreement. The provincial administration brought pressure to bear on the chiefs to change their ways. Many of them were retired as incapable and new ones, especially those who had been educated in mission schools, were appointed. These men owed their appointments very much to the provincial officers of the Protectorate so they were ready to co-operate.

While the older chiefs were under pressure from the Protectorate administration, the younger progressive elements in Buganda were profoundly dissatisfied with the chiefs and their sons, who usually succeeded them as chiefs. Progressive elements consisted mostly of young men who had graduated from the mission schools but who were sons of people outside the chieftain hierarchy established in 1900 under the Buganda Agreement. The young men wanted opportunities to become chiefs too, but such opportunities were very few because the Buganda Agreement had entrenched the old chiefs and their offspring in power. They formed the Young Radicals and the Young Baganda Association to oppose the chiefs. Their influence was small but in these associations lay the seeds of future political activities.

Besides this pressure on the chieftain hierarchy, there was the grievance about the distribution and registration of land as arranged by the 1900 Buganda Agreement. In 1900 as a means of rewarding those chiefs and their followers who helped to defeat Mwanga and Kabarega the British divided part of the land in Buganda among them leaving 23 309 sq km for the use of the British Government for the good of the people. As a result of this grievance the Buganda National Federation of Bataka was formed, which wanted two things.

First, some traditional lands that belonged formerly to the clans had been given away to chiefs under the 1900 Buganda Agreement, so the Federation sought permission from both the Buganda Government and the Protectorate administration to rectify the situation. Secondly, some traditional clan lands had been registered in the names of the present heads of clans. This meant that such lands did not belong to the members of the clans as a group but to an individual, who could sell it to other people or bequeath it to his children. The Bataka Federation nearly forced a revision of the 1900 Buganda Agreement in 1924 because the Kabaka, Daudi Chwa, was sympathetic to its claims and he advised the Governor of Uganda to alter the arrangement. But the chiefs persuaded the Governor not to accept the claims of the Bataka Federation. The Governor then declared that, though there was some injustice done as regards the land titles, it was impossible to change a decision of twenty-five years' duration. The Bataka Federation continued to agitate until it was banned after the 1949 riots in Buganda in which it figured prominently under the leadership of Miti Kabazzi, Semakula Mulumba and Father Spartas Sebbanja Mukasa.

Outside Buganda, local government was developing in a less critical manner. This was partly due to the fact that in the other kingdoms of Bunyoro, Ankole and Toro there was less interest in the way the administration was run, while, in the rest of the districts, the administration was offering jobs to men of ability without caring about their family connections. Another important reason for the difference was that, outside Buganda, local government meant to enforce the policy of the Protectorate Government directly while in Buganda the officials had to observe the semi-independent state which the 1900 Agreement had created in the Buganda kingdom. The problems which arose outside Buganda were therefore mainly matters of either administrative organization, or they were due to the scarcity of trained African personnel to take up the numerous posts which the new colonial administration created.

During this period the powers of the African courts outside Buganda were widened by the Native Law Ordinance, so that these courts could alter African laws which were becoming obsolete, and the chiefs were awarded fixed salaries.

Another important episode was when Bunyoro renewed its campaign for the return of the Lost Counties in Mubende, which had been given to Buganda by the British because the Baganda had helped them in the wars against Kabarega. At the same time, in Bunyoro and in Busoga, people were clamouring for land titles as in Buganda. Both the request to return the Lost Counties to Bunyoro and to start a land system similar to that of Buganda were disallowed by the Protectorate administration.

Economic Development

In 1920 a commission was set up to sketch a new policy of development after the war. The commission supported European plantations instead of African peasant agriculture which had been the policy of the Government and which had taken root after 1900. The commission also recommended compulsion of Africans to work on planters' plantations. However the report of the commission was not acceptable either to the Governor, Sir Robert Coryndon or to Mr. Simpson, the Agricultural Officer, and the Colonial Office. Colonial policy at this time was against any compulsion of Africans to work for settlers.

Discouraged by the official attitude, the planters were further discouraged by the slump after the war and, finally, by the great depression which started in 1929. In addition to these difficulties there was the problem of transport, which made plantation business unprofitable in Uganda. The result was that the planters of coffee, rubber and cocoa started to sell out their holdings and by 1933 most of them had ceased to operate.

African cotton farmers were also hit by the economic slump. However, the Protectorate Government agreed to buy the entire crop during these years at a minimum fixed price. This assisted the cotton farmers and even increased the area under cotton cultivation, which had started to drop drastically in the early 1920's.

Other crops grown by Africans at this time were coffee and tobacco with the latter limited to the western region. Tea and sugar-cane were grown by Asians on plantations of which the Lugazi sugar estates were the earliest, begun by an Asian businessman, Nanji Kalidas Mehta, in 1923.

During this period there was a desire by Africans to enter into the cotton buying and ginning industry, but the opposition of the European and Indian buyers and ginners through their Association, backed by the Protectorate Government, kept Africans out of this sector of commerce. Africans were expected only to grow cotton.

From the days of Sir Hesketh Bell, who was Governor from 1905 to 1910, the Protectorate Government carried on an active programme of road construction. This was continued in the period under discussion, and it helped the economy grow. There was also a further extension of the railway which reached Kampala in 1931, thirty-five years after it had begun from Mombasa to open up Uganda, which extension, northwards from Tororo, linked Soroti and Mbale to the main line. The construction of roads and branch lines helped to bring traffic from the production centres into the main lines of communication by train and lorry.

Education

This period witnessed greater government participation in the running of education. This, as we have already seen, had been almost entirely left to the Christian missionaries. There were two forces that brought about this increased participation. There was, in 1924-5, the Phelps-Stokes Commission which came from America and examined the situation of education in East Africa. The commission recommended that the governments in East Africa should give more assistance to missionary bodies in educational work. At the same time the Colonial Office issued a new policy on education in the British colonies. This policy also urged the colonial governments to take a more active part in providing education in Africa.

Greater government participation in education resulted in increased grants to the mission schools. Better school buildings were constructed and, through the Government inspectorate, standards were set up which had to be followed by all schools. Teacher training colleges were built to produce teachers of a recognized standard. Secondary education began to be offered on a very limited scale and in 1935 the first Ugandans sat for the Cambridge School Certificate Examination.

With the support of Sir Philip Mitchell, who was Governor of Uganda from 1935 to 1940, Makerere which had been set up in 1921 by the Protectorate Government as a technical school, was recommended in 1937 by the De La Warr Commission from Britain to become a school of higher learning for all East Africa. This required a step-up in the output of secondary school students throughout East Africa to feed Makerere College, so Uganda increased her output of secondary school students, some of whom would go to Makerere.

Other social work, such as the medical service, was carried forward

by both the Government and the missionaries. During this period
the medical service was engaged in the fight against sleeping sickness,
a disease which was bred by the tsetse fly and which was a terrible
menace to the people.

31 Tanganyika 1920-39

After Germany's defeat in the First World War, the League of Nations became responsible for all the former German African colonies in East and West Africa. This body was similar to the present United Nations Organization, which replaced it after the Second World War. On behalf of the League of Nations, Britain undertook to administer that part of German East Africa which came to be called Tanganyika and Belgium undertook to administer Rwanda and Burundi.

Political Development

Sir Horace Byatt was the first Governor from Britain to head the administration of Tanganyika. He continued roughly to follow the German system of relying on African chiefs and akidas for local administration.

He was faced with the problem of setting the economy on its feet. It had been destroyed by the 1914-18 war, part of which had been fought in Tanganyika but not in Kenya and Uganda. With this problem to be solved, much Government work was not attended to and Byatt has been criticized as having had no clear Governmental policy.

Byatt left Tanganyika in 1925 and was succeeded by Sir Donald Cameron. Governor Cameron charted a clear course for Tanganyika's political development. He did two things in this respect: first, he set up indirect rule and, second, he incorporated the settlers into the work of the Central Government by setting up a legislative council in 1926.

He divided Tanganyika into eleven districts. The British officers looked for the people who possessed traditional authority in these districts. On the whole, this system operated successfully, but among the Gogo there was no paramount chief, among the Chagga there were several and among the Masai the 'laibon' was not a political leader but a religious one. It was in these ethnic groups that efforts to find traditional rulers ran into difficulty. On the coast there were no chiefs so the Government chose new officials, who were as hated by the people as the German akidas. These local chiefs collected taxes, administered justice and carried out some executive tasks. Local authorities had treasuries which paid for minor services and the wages of minor workers. To make sure that the system of indirect rule was working as arranged, Cameron created a Secretary for Native Affairs who was directly responsible for its operation.

In December Cameron set up the Tanganyika Legislative Council. It had not been requested by the settlers, unlike the similar assemblies in Kenya and Uganda, and they were taken by surprise as they did not think the Colonial Government would create a council except under pressure. Five of the latter represented European businessmen and planters, the other two representatives were Asian. All members were nominated by the Governor, not elected.

The Tanganyika Legislative Council worked smoothly; there were few conflicts mainly because the white settlers were of different nationalities and they did not think of themselves as one people, whereas in Kenya the British element predominated. No Africans were nominated to the Legislative Council; they were limited to local government. The limiting of Africans to local government made them complain that indirect rule was a deliberate device to stop them advancing politically.

Concentration on tribal and clan heads as administrators delayed the development of nationhood among the different ethnic groups of Tanganyika. The numerous associations which developed during this time were ethnic-centred and concentrated on local politics. Everywhere in rural areas associations sprang up to oppose the privileged position of the chiefs, to secure power within ethnic groups and progress for each ethnic group individually. The earliest of these associations was the Bukoba Bahaya Union, formed in 1924.

The Tanganyika African Association was organized in 1919 by young men who had been educated to secondary school level under German rule, but who were denied opportunities under the new administration. This association was inter-tribal and it became the focus for African political opinion. It was this association which gained a wider role and national status in 1954 when it changed its name to the Tanganyika African National Union (TANU).

Economic Development

There was a slow recovery economically in Tanganyika after the First World War for two reasons. One was that many German settlers went back to Germany to fight during the war and abandoned their estates and they were not allowed to return after the war. There were many new British settlers who wanted to buy the abandoned German estates but Governor Byatt was reluctant to sell the estates as he wanted to examine the whole land tenure system first, so that land was not allocated indiscriminately. The estates began to be sold in 1923 and, justly, a large amount of land was set aside for African use. As a result of this delay in selling the estates, the economy did not revive quickly after the war.

Secondly, Government labour policy made it hard to get workers for the estates. Africans could not be forced to work for settlers. Moreover, conditions of service safeguarded the African labourers, with wages set at a reasonable level and many settlers felt that they could not afford to pay such wages.

Many Africans preferred to work on their own fields instead of labouring on European farms. Since work was seasonal, those Africans who offered themselves for plantation work might spend a short time there and then go back home for the greater part of the year.

European settlers grew sisal, coffee and sugar around Moshi and tea in the Usambara mountains, but difficulties in getting adequate labour forced many settlers to go to Kenya so that the population of planters in Tanganyika grew very slowly. The result was that the settler problem in Tanganyika was never as acute as in Kenya.

Transport

During this period new roads and railways were built and old ones extended. The central railway from Dar es Salaam, Morogoro, Kilosa, Tabora and to Kigoma on Lake Tanganyika was repaired soon after the war. Then a line between Tabora and Mwanza was started in 1928 which opened up an important area around the southern end of Lake Victoria and improved communications with Kenya and Uganda by lake steamers. In the following year a line from Moshi to Arusha was also completed. Trade connections with the Belgian Congo (now known as Zaire) were developed too and the central railway carried imports and exports for the Belgians. A fuller account will be found in Chapter 42.

Education

During the 1920's the Colonial Government paid more attention to educational needs. In 1920 a director of education was appointed to organize and supervise the school system. Rapid progress began from 1925 as a result of two forces – the Phelps-Stokes Commission and the new British colonial policy on education. Both encouraged the Colonial Government to assist the missionaries and other voluntary agencies in their endeavour to give education facilities to Africans and this was taken up with vigour by Cameron when he became Governor in 1925.

Something worthy of mention in Tanganyika's educational development at this time was the attempt to blend African with European culture and make the schools important and relevant in community life. Great emphasis was laid on tribal culture being taught to boys and girls. Elders who were supposed to know the cultural background of the various ethnic groups were invited to their neighbouring schools to lecture and to participate in the educational activities of the schools.

Unfortunately, this kind of education was dropped because of mounting opposition from Africans who saw no way of equalling their European rulers, whom they wanted to replace, if they were to be educated under such a system.

It should be noted that the Germans had created the finest educational system in East Africa. Africans in Tanganyika had access to secondary school education of a high standard long before this was available in either Kenya or Uganda. This education was provided in Government-run schools. In the other territories the British had merely left education in the hands of the missionary societies. When the British took over Tanganyika, they were obliged to continue to operate and expand these Government-owned schools.

32 Zanzibar 1890-1964

The Working of the British Protectorate

In 1890 Zanzibar officially became a British Protectorate under the direction of a British Resident. Indeed Zanzibar, from the days of Sultan Seyyid Said, had increasingly been made to rely on the advice and direction of the British consuls in Zanzibar because the British wanted to prevent other European powers becoming the 'protectors' of the Sultans and of their interests. When Zanzibar was declared a protectorate, the running of the Government still remained under the management of the Arabs who paid allegiance to their Sultan as head of that Government. The British officials were supposed to be 'advisers' but, in 1891, on the grounds of gross inefficiency and injustice in the running of the Sultan's Government, the British Resident took over all control and seized the Government's finances, appointing European officials to control Government departments. In 1896 the Resident placed on the throne of the Sultan a candidate of his own schooling and so the independence of Seyyid Said's dynasty was totally broken.

The personal rule of the Sultans was replaced by that of an educated Arab aristocracy, which remained privileged in education and in the civil service. When the Slave Emancipation Decree was passed in 1897, the British Government compensated the aristocratic Arab slave owners and safeguarded their economic position. British rule was based firmly on the Arab settlers, just as the Sultan's had been in the nineteenth century, and it did not envisage the Africans as having a share in the administration of the country.

The Africans had very few opportunities to rise. During the 1920's Africans formed the African Association in Zanzibar, of which Sheikh Abeid Karume was a member in 1934. This Association linked together ambitious African workers with the small group of mission teachers on the island and it was the first expression of African political feelings.

The Rise of Nationalist Feelings

After the Second World War Africans and Arabs became more politically conscious. The Arabs became alarmed at the progress of the Africans and they planned to replace the British by a mass movement to gain political control of the situation before the Africans became fully conscious politically. They also planned to create an Islamic state in Zanzibar.

As a result of this idea, Seif Hamoud, a journalist, organized the Arab Association which subsequently demanded a ministerial system of government. The British ignored its demands. Meanwhile many more Arab Associations were formed with Ali Muhsin, another journalist, uniting them all in the Zanzibar Nationalist Party (ZNP) in 1956. When the Government arranged direct elections to the Legislative Council for six seats, in 1957, the Africans and the Shirazi* people were not organized to fight the elections. The African Association formed in the 1920's had never been an effective political body. In 1938 the Shirazi Association based on Pemba had broken away from the African Association. In the face of imminent elections, the two associations reunited to form the Afro-Shirazi Union, which later became the Afro-Shirazi Party (ASP). They won three seats in the 1957 election and two other seats were won by independents from Pemba who joined the Afro-Shirazi Union in the Legislative Council. The sixth seat was won by the Muslim League; the Zanzibar Nationalist Party won no seat.

Between 1957 and 1961 three important things happened, of which one was the intense hostility which grew up between the Arabs and the Africans. The Afro-Shirazis boycotted Arab trade and in turn Arab landlords evicted Afro-Shirazi squatters from their land. The second thing that happened was the reorganization of the Zanzibar Nationalist Party along TANU lines as in Tanganyika, with a youth wing, social services and all the techniques of mass nationalism. By 1961 both the Afro-Shirazi Party and the Zanzibar Nationalist Party were well matched. The third thing that happened during this period was a split in the Afro-Shirazi Party with the Pemba Shirazi leaders breaking away to form the Zanzibar and Pemba People's Party.

Two elections were held in 1961, one in January and another one in June and a final election, leading to independence, in 1963. In these three elections the Zanzibar Nationalist Party of the Arabs and

*The Shirazi people were Africans who through marriages had connections with the early Arabs who came from Shirazi on the Persian Gulf.

the Zanzibar and Pemba People's Party formed an alliance and won the last two elections, although the Afro-Shirazi party secured the majority of votes and declared that the elections had been rigged.

Nevertheless, in December 1963, the two parties, ZNP and ZPPP, led Zanzibar into independence. The Afro-Shirazi nationalists, who were seeking economic equality, realized that Arab rule could not ensure this as the Zanzibar Nationalist Party represented the privileged landed aristocracy while the Afro-Shirazi party represented the unprivileged and landless people. It is against this background that the Zanzibar revolution of February 1964 took place, overthrowing the Arab-based Government.

The Sultan and members of his family fled the country to Britain. The Afro-Shirazi Party formed a Revolutionary Council led by President Karume. He at once sent to President Nyerere of Tanganyika for help in keeping law and order on the island. Nyerere sent him a hundred policemen and the situation was contained. Meanwhile, outside countries began to recognize the Republic of Zanzibar.

On 22nd April 1964 the Union of Tanganyika and Zanzibar was formed under the name of Tanzania. President Nyerere became President of Tanzania and Sheikh Abeid Karume became the First Vice-President of the Republic. The Union Parliament was in Dar es Salaam but Zanzibar retains its own Parliament and Government to run local administration.

33 Islam in East Africa

From the earliest days of Islam there were converts from other races and it is recorded that an Ethiopian negro and former slave named Bilal was appointed by the Prophet Muhammad as the ruler of Medina in recognition of his devotion. Within a century of the Prophet's death Arabs had spread the message of Islam to Iraq, Syria and Egypt. They established themselves in Africa under Uqbah ibn Nafi in present-day Tunisia, Algeria and Morocco and in the ninth century the Aghlabid dynasty flourished there.

Among the first converts were some of the inhabitants of the East African coast, where Muslim immigrants came from the Persian Gulf. In 813 the founder of the Shafite school, Idris es Shafi started to teach and actively seek new members for the faith. A group of Arabs of the Zaidiyah Shiite sect also sought refuge on the coast and settled in the neighbourhood of Shungwaya on the coast of Kenya. For hundreds of years thereafter Islam was confined to the coastal region. There was a fear of the unknown interior of Africa and a reluctance to penetrate the hinterland.

Arabic and Islamic culture exercised a strong influence on the coastal towns, particularly in the Middle-Eastern style of architecture. Each Arab trading post usually had its own mosque and baths. Gradually the Arab settlers were absorbed into the indigenous Bantu population and a new culture developed with a mixture of African and Middle-Eastern characteristics. The basic language was a Bantu-based Swahili with strong Arabic influences.

Muhammad ibn Abdullah ibn Battuta (1304-1377) of Tangier, a great Muslim traveller, spoke of Mombasa as a most important place which attracted crowds of pilgrims to its 'great mosque' when he visited the city about 1332. The stone-built houses, the food, the costume and the hospitality were akin to those of the Arabs. Arab rulers had introduced large-scale agriculture, plantations of palm, sheep and poultry-rearing for their own use. In addition there were the traditional African products – ivory, Sofala gold, coconuts and coconut oil – which were bartered for manufactured goods – the cloth, metalwork and beads of India, Persia and Arabia. For this was the great era of Arab commercial supremacy in the Indian Ocean. He also remarked on the missionary zeal of the Arab-Africans: 'The inhabitants of Kilwa are addicted to 'Jehad' or Holy War for they occupy a country contiguous to that of the infidel Zinj.'.

In 1498 Vasco da Gama was astonished at the riches of Mozambique. The robes of velvet and silk and gold thread, the turbans of silk and gold worn by the Sultan and his retinue revealed a wealth unknown to the western European nations. By the end of the fifteenth century colonies were established on the East African coast and a new religious element, Christianity, was introduced. However, it did not impinge greatly on the Islam faith and when the Portuguese were driven out by Arabs from Omani in the seventeenth century few traces of Christianity remained.

Sultan Seyyid Said, the most famous of the Omani rulers, invaded the East African coast in the early part of the nineteenth century and settled in Zanzibar in 1840. His rise to power brought a great influx of Arabs to the coast. During this period of Arab expansion trade increased, and the chief commodity was slaves. Many were shipped to Muscat, for the Arab way of life and teachings did not condemn the institution of slavery. Arab, Swahili and African caravans started to penetrate the interior in search of slaves and ivory. The Muslim traders took their faith with them. Some remained permanently in the interior, making their homes at the supply depots and resting places on the trade routes. Some feared to return to face their creditors in Zanzibar; others made a profitable living by supplying the caravans that passed through. They formed a nucleus of Muslim communities in the interior, and they converted some of the Africans who came in contact with them.

Unlike the Christians, the Muslims did not go out in a body with the express intention of making mass conversions to their faith. Conversion occurred at the request of an individual. They did not have enough money to set up schools and produce literature. However, the faith spread into the interior of Kenya, Tanzania and Uganda and went on spreading during the European missionary and colonial period. Buganda, in particular, was radically changed by the coming of Islam.

The penetration of the interior by Europeans assisted the spread of Islam because the Europeans took with them Swahili Muslims as soldiers, skilled workers of all kinds, interpreters, domestic servants and traders. These people made many converts through personal encounters with individual Africans.

The first formal Muslim mission to the interior of East Africa started in 1935 at Tabora in Tanzania and it was opened up by the Ahmadiyya Mission which became active all over East Africa. Its head was Sheikh Mubarah Ahmed. In 1954 he completed the remarkable task of preparing a Swahili translation of the holy Koran with a commentary. Today a large amount of Muslim literature is published and reflects the recent educational attainment of Muslims in East Africa, which has stimulated a demand for Muslim literature.

For a long time Muslims used the village Koran schools to teach religion and some secular subjects. These schools were conducted by teachers who were mostly versed only in the Koran. Pupils here learned mainly by rote, so that the standard of achievement tended to be very low. However, the British Government became involved in education in Zanzibar after 1907 and had a considerable influence on the running of the school system, although the Muslims were rather suspicious of the Government's intention in offering this education. The result was that it grew quite slowly, up to 1939, gaining momentum thereafter. In the rest of East Africa the Muslims were reluctant to send their sons and daughters to Christian mission schools or to Government schools which were frequently Christian-orientated. They feared that the Christian teachers in those schools would convert their children to Christianity. Moreover, the Christian mission schools were not too willing to accept Muslim boys and girls. The belief during the colonial period was that each denomination should provide education strictly for its followers. This way of thinking has been changed only recently by the independent Governments, which aim at giving equal opportunities to all citizens regardless of their beliefs about God.

The Ahmadiyya Mission did not set up hospitals like the Christian missions but the Muslim followers of H.H. the Aga Khan started to set up schools, hospitals, dispensaries and libraries for their members after the First World War. Like the early Muslims from the coast, the members of the Aga Khan community do not support missionaries who want to convert others to Islam. They believe that conversion should be a personal choice by the individual.

Today a great majority of Africans are Muslims. A good number of African heads of state are Muslim. With an egalitarian attitude to their non-Muslim subjects, they are engaged in the introduction of mass education and the eradication of poverty. During the British rule of India, Indian labour and skill was routed to the British African colonies where substantial Indian communities, both Muslim and non-Muslim, resided. Three distinct groups emerged in Africa: Europeans, Asians and native Africans. With the coming of independence Afro-Asians either decided their loyalties lay with the new states or emigrated. As a result, thousands of Muslims emigrated to Britain and other countries from Kenya, Tanzania and Uganda.

The Ismailis, coming from both East African and Afro-Asian stock, have, over the years, established their own denominational schools, places of worship and religious education, business and industry. The community provides funds for promising members for higher studies abroad. Similarly, the body of Muslims, who mainly follow the Shafite school of Islamic law, are flourishing and their literature on Islam is in Swahili, English and Arabic. As in the rest of the Muslim world, the practice of Islam in East Africa varies, some people being more orthodox than others. A course on Islamic Studies is offered in the major East African Universities. But the main means of transmission of the rudiments of Islam to the younger generation, and the spreading of the faith in society as a whole, is still the mosque.

Despite the absence of much missionary activity, East Africa has a considerable number of Muslims, now well over four million people.

34 Uganda 1939-75

The Political Situation

After the Second World War most political dissatisfactions were centred in Buganda although they were not expressed by the Baganda alone. They were typical of the feelings of many people in Uganda.

The Movements of 1945 and 1949

In Buganda, many people were politically discontented, feeling that the Lukiiko (the Buganda Parliament) did not represent their interests, although many proposals affecting the populace were passed by the Lukiiko. This discontent was increased by the reforms of Sir Charles Dundas between 1940 and 1944 which gave Buganda a greater degree of self-rule than the other parts of Uganda. These reforms made the old type of chiefs more powerful. Many people felt they should have greater representation in the Lukiiko, by men of their own choosing.

Besides these political grievances there were economic ones. After the war, I. K. Musazi formed the Uganda African Farmers' Association which conducted a campaign against the exploitation of the African farmers by the Asian and European businessmen. Yet the Buganda Lukiiko seemed not to care. The members of the Association were joined by the Bataka Party formed in the 1920's. They demanded the right to market their own produce and they asked the Kabaka to make the Lukiiko more representative of the ordinary men so that it could air the people's grievances. Failure to redress these demands led to riots in 1945 and 1949 in Buganda. The Uganda African Farmers' Union, led by Musazi, and the Bataka Party, led by Kabazzi Miti and Semakula Mulumba, were both banned after the riots of 1949.

Constitutional Development

In 1945 three Africans were nominated to sit in the Legislative Council – one from Bunyoro, one from Buganda and one from Busoga. In 1950 the number of Africans was increased to eight. Three years later the Legislative Council became a miniature National Assembly with Government and Opposition, an arrangement made by Sir Andrew Cohen, who became Governor in 1952.

During Cohen's term of office, from 1952 to 1956, constitutional development went forward quickly. His idea was to see Africans in local governments, running their own affairs through a majority of elected members. Secondly, he wanted to make the Legislative Council the focus of power and authority, so that all people in Uganda should think of themselves as Ugandans instead of as members of particular ethnic groups led by their councils.

While he was developing this theme, the Secretary of State for the Colonies Mr. Oliver Lyttelton made a disturbing speech in June 1953 whereby he resurrected the idea of the East African Federation of the 1920's and 1930's. Muteesa II, then Kabaka of Buganda, supported by the Lukiiko, opposed the federation of East Africa and demanded independence for his own province of Buganda. This demand for independence ran counter to Sir Andrew Cohen's idea of creating a united Uganda, so he deposed Muteesa II and deported him to Britain in November 1953 for breaking the 1900 Buganda Agreement, which required him to co-operate loyally with the representative of the British Government in Uganda.

Sir Edward Muteesa returned to Uganda immediately after the Buganda Agreement of 1955 had been accepted. This agreement redefined the political position of Buganda within Uganda. Buganda had to develop as an integral part of Uganda and so it could not be independent.

While these negotiations about the kingdom of Buganda were going on, constitutional development of the central government was going ahead. In 1955 the Africans in the Legislative Council were increased to 30 in number, a ministerial system was introduced, with three African ministers out of eleven, and 1958 was set as the year for direct elections of members to the Legislative Council.

Political Parties and the Fight for Independence

In 1952 I. K. Musazi, the President of the banned Uganda African Farmers' Union, together with Abu Mayanja and J. W. Kiwanuka, formed the Uganda National Congress (UNC). One of the aims of the Congress was to unite all peoples of Uganda and so bring independence to the country.

In 1954 another party called the Democratic Party led by M. Mugwanya was founded and it was soon followed by the Progressive Party of E. M. K. Mulira. With dynamic leadership by Musazi and J. W. Kiwanuka the UNC was in a better position, until 1958 when Ben Kiwanuka took over the leadership of the Democratic Party.

These three parties fought the 1958 elections. The outcome of the elections did not indicate the real political situation in the country because the Lukiiko of Buganda opposed the elections and did not participate. The Lukiiko feared the elections because it would have no control over directly elected people in Buganda once they joined the Legislative Council.

In 1959 the Protectorate Government set up the Wild Commission to pave the way for self-government and then independence. The Commission recommended direct elections in all Uganda in 1961. While the Commission was going ahead with its work, the UNC split and the splinter group led by A. M. Obote united with another recently formed political group called UPU to form the Uganda's People's Congress.

By 1960 the political situation became clearer with two strong national political parties – the Democratic Party and the Uganda People's Congress – poised to oppose one another. Both parties contested the elections of 1961, together with the old UNC. The Lukiiko of Buganda boycotted the elections. However, this did not stop progress. The DP won the elections and Ben Kiwanuka, the President of the DP, became Prime Minister, with Milton Obote as leader of an active opposition.

Later in 1961 a constitutional conference was held in London attended by all leaders of the political parties and the representatives of the local governments and those of the Kabaka's Government. At this conference Buganda's reluctance to co-operate was overcome by allowing the Lukiiko to elect indirectly the twenty-one representatives from Buganda to the National Assembly and also by allowing Buganda a greater measure of control in her internal affairs such as schools, justice and hospitals. Ankole, Bunyoro, and Toro were also given some control over their internal affairs but of a more limited nature.

On the members' return from London, the Kabaka's Lukiiko of Mengo formed a political party known as Kabaka Yekka (King alone) (KY). Its duty was to protect the Buganda monarchy in an independent Uganda and also to protect the political interests of Buganda. The knowledge that the KY had the support of the Kabaka, Sir Edward Muteesa, made many people in Buganda join and support it with almost fanatic enthusiasm which was baffling for a non-Muganda to understand. April 1962 had been set for another election and KY allied with UPC and together they won. When independence was achieved on 9th October 1962, it was A. M. Obote who became the Prime Minister of Uganda.

Political Developments after Independence

In 1963 Sir Edward Muteesa, the then Kabaka of the Buganda kingdom, became non-executive President. Disagreements soon arose between him and Dr. Obote. In such circumstances Obote saw no way of building a united Uganda and towards the end of 1965 Sir Edward Muteesa was removed from the presidency. In September 1967 Uganda had a new constitution with an executive President. Dr. Obote ceased to be Prime Minister and became the President and the four kingdoms of Buganda, Bunyoro, Toro and Ankole were abolished.

The most notable political problem that faced independent Uganda on the 9th October 1962 was to create a spirit of belonging to one country among about fifteen different ethnic groups of people. The constitution that ushered Uganda into independence had left each ethnic group of people with a sort of traditional ruler and a semi-federal relationship to the Uganda Government. Such a situation could not be said to help the creation of developing a spirit of belonging to one country. This meant fragmentation of power and each group of people focusing its attention on the traditional ruler and on his political headquarters, rather than on the sole ruler of the whole of Uganda and on the National Assembly of the country. Indeed it was the creation of this atmosphere of unity which Sir Andrew Cohen from 1952 to 1956 had struggled to achieve but without success, though through no fault of his. The independent Government fortunately adopted the wise stand that it must create at any costs this spirit of belonging to one country among its different ethnic groups. The decision of 1967 which abolished the traditional rulers all over Uganda created a favourable situation for achieving this end.

On 25th January 1971 Milton Obote was dramatically deposed by the Uganda armed forces under the leadership of Major General Idi Amin Dada. The coup took the world by surprise, for Obote had seemed to be fully in control, but the majority of Ugandans enthusiastically supported the new régime because they felt that Obote's government was repressive and no longer capable of running the country. The armed forces pledged themselves first to restore order and then to hand over power to civilians. Political activities were proscribed for a period of two years.

The armed forces justified their action by an 18-point indictment of the former ruler. Among the reasons given were increasing lawlessness in the country and a failure to bring criminals to justice. The proposal for compulsory two-year national service for all citizens had caused unease and resentment. Political dissatisfactions included the failure to call a meeting of the Defence Council for two years and a growing alienation from the rest of the East African Community as a result of refusing to allow workers from Kenya and Tanzania to remain in Uganda and forbidding imports from their countries. Economic prosperity had decreased, with high taxes and the rising cost of living. Commodity prices fell, particularly for coffee and cotton, affecting the livelihood of many people. The mood was one of disillusion with one-party government, all other parties having been banned in 1969 and constitutional elections postponed. There also seemed to be a contradiction between the declared policy of socialism and the self-interest of some politicians.

Since the take-over of the government by the armed forces several developments of a far-reaching nature were initiated in Uganda. In August 1972 General Idi Amin declared an 'economic war'. This was the beginning of the policy of 'Ugandanization' and the transfer of business and commerce to indigenous Ugandans. For many years the business world had been dominated by Asians. The Government now asked Britain to repatriate all Asians holding British passports by the end of November 1972. A similar request was made to the governments of India, Pakistan and Bangladesh. Through the co-operation of the various governments all 50 000 Asians had left the country when the deadline was reached. Their businesses were allocated free of charge to indigenous Africans. The Government made arrangements for the compensation of the previous owners. The administration of large enterprises and industrial concerns presented a difficult challenge to Ugandans, who lacked training and whose success could only be judged after several years' experience.

A second result of the take-over was the attempt to achieve an efficient form of administration. In 1973 the Ministry of Provincial Administration was set up. The country was divided into nine provinces, each with a governor. Large counties and sub-counties dating from colonial days were sub-divided into smaller units. This arrangement simplified the mobilization of people for development schemes.

The third remarkable change introduced by the new administration concerned land tenure. A restrictive system of private land ownership had grown up since the 1900 Buganda Agreement between Britain and the Kingdom of Buganda. Before that time land had been communally held by each tribe. From 1900 there was a division into crown land, belonging to the government, and private land owned by the 4000 leading Buganda families. The private land became an increasingly valuable asset and source of social status. By the 1940's the system existed in several parts of Uganda such as Busoga, Bunyoro, Toro and Ankole and seemed likely to spread to the rest of the country. It presented a twofold problem. First, land was now concentrated in the hands of a few wealthy owners. Frequently it was left undeveloped and commanded such a high price that ordinary people wishing to obtain land for their own use could not afford it. The system was felt to be contrary to the traditional use of land whereby it had once been freely available to all. Secondly, the government had to pay large amounts of taxpayers' money to private owners each time it wished to purchase land for development. In 1975, therefore, a Land Decree abolished private land ownership and instituted a scheme for 99-year leases, an approach to land utilization which opened a new chapter in Uganda's economic and social history.

Economic Development

After the Second World War there was a heavy demand for primary products in America and in Europe. As a result of this, Uganda's cotton and coffee enjoyed rising prices. By 1950 coffee had become so much a favourite with Uganda growers because of rising prices, that cotton slipped into second place. Besides these two export products, smaller crops were developed for the internal and external markets. Maize became very popular, owing to the ease with which it could be grown.

Of importance in economic development was the deliberate planning by the Government for industrialization and the greater involvement of Africans in trade. In 1947 the Government had begun to build the Owen Falls Dam at Jinja, with the intention of providing an adequate supply of electric power for both Kenya and Uganda and so helping to industrialize Uganda.

Following this the Protectorate Government set up the Uganda Development Corporation (UDC), a para-statal body to spearhead industrial and agricultural development. The Corporation set up industries all over the country. It started a Cement and Asbestos producing scheme at Tororo in Eastern Uganda. It set up a Textile Industry at Jinja and it built a chain of hotels in those parts of the country most attractive to tourists. It also started agricultural enterprises in tea and tobacco in different parts of the country. In 1953 the UDC, in co-operation with a Canadian firm, started to exploit the copper of the Kilembe mines at the foot of the Ruwenzori in the Western Region.

To assist this industrial and agricultural development, the building of Uganda's roads was speeded up all over the country and today Uganda's roads are some of the best in Africa as a result of the road construction carried on during this period. Between 1951 and 1956 the Government extended the railway from Kampala westwards to the foot of the Ruwenzori Mountains; thus the Uganda Railway, begun in 1896 to open up Uganda, reached the other side of the country 60 years later. This line was intended to transport agricultural products from the Western Region and also to transport the copper from the Kilembe Mines to Jinja for smelting.

Another policy for helping Africans by the Protectorate Government was to assist them process cotton and coffee. The Government started to lend co-operatives three-quarters of the money needed to buy a cotton ginnery or a coffee curing factory. Even individual Africans were assisted to purchase small coffee pulpers. The Government also helped Africans participate more in retail trade by building shops for them in towns at lower rates. Then, as now, the problem of the African traders was how to obtain sufficient capital to start trading and how to manage funds once obtained. The Government set up the Credit and Savings Bank, to lend money to African businessmen. Yet often lack of property as security acceptable to the banks prevented many would-be businessmen securing a large enough amount of money to open large businesses, as only those who owned land could borrow.

However, the period from 1952 to 1962 was a time of great economic development of the country's resources and the provision of social services. On his arrival in Uganda Sir Andrew Cohen appointed a committee, under the chairmanship of B. de Bunsen, then Principal of Makerere University College, to survey the country's educational needs. It recommended the reorganization of the teacher training colleges to raise standards and revision of the secondary school course, so that the junior secondary school course would last for two years instead of three and the senior secondary course would last for four years. Also the Government actively began to build secondary schools, a field it had left chiefly to the missionary bodies. Makerere College in 1949 achieved a special relationship with the University of London. From 1950 it offered courses leading to the London B.A. and to B.Sc. degrees; the first students graduated in 1953.

35 Kenya 1939-75

The Political Situation

When war broke out in August 1939, the Kenya Government feared that the Italians from Somaliland would invade Kenya and took precautions to prevent this, at the same time banning the Kenya Central Association and its sister associations and detaining their leaders at Kapenguria so as not to disrupt Government war efforts.

As during the First World War, the European settlers used the British preoccupation with the war to pass laws favourable to themselves in the Legislative Council. For example, they restricted Asian immigration and residence to certain areas and they introduced forced labour for Africans on European farms at wages ranging between eight and twelve shillings per month. Under the settlement scheme of 1943 white settlement was speeded up. Immediately after the war they introduced a system of appointed members holding portfolios. The first ministerial posts given to the settlers were those of agriculture and of local government. It was these ministries that mainly concerned the Africans and the settlers who ran them did all they could to keep the Africans in what was considered 'their place'.

In the early 1940's the settlers realized that Africans could not be kept out of national politics entirely. So in October 1944 E. W. Mathu was nominated to the Legislative Council and he was soon followed by F. W. Odede in 1946.

After the war, the ex-servicemen who made up twenty per cent of the adult population were restless. They were joined by the leaders of KCA and other allied association members of the Ukamba and the Taita Hills Associations – who were now freed from Kapenguria. Besides these, there were many secret associations operating in various parts of Kenya, including breakaway Christian and traditionalist religious groups. Many of these Africans felt that the grip of the settlers on Kenya could only be broken by violence.

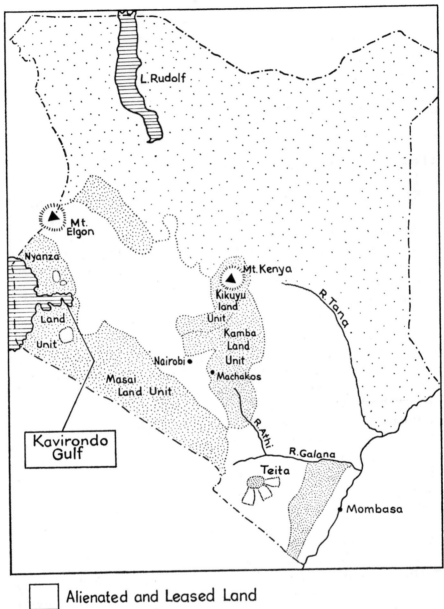

Alienated and Leased Land

African Land

Crown Land which could be given to the settlers at any time.

The state of land division in Kenya by 1939

Violence erupted through the Mau Mau Movement, which began slowly in early 1950 when both Africans and settlers took the law into their own hands, with the Africans hoping to change a system of economic and social injustice. On 20th October 1952 the Mau Mau Movement was banned, a state of emergency declared and British troops were brought in to control the situation. The emergency was not lifted until 1960. Before the Mau Mau revolt the settlers had been convinced that, if given independence, they could hold the Africans of Kenya in perpetual subordinancy. Given the large number of British troops required to suppress the revolt, it became obvious to all that they could never maintain Kenya as an independent white country. Thus the Mau Mau Movement caused a complete re-thinking of the settler position. It was the Mau Mau incident more than any other event which prevented Kenya from becoming another Southern Rhodesia.

Constitutional Development

In 1945 a ministerial system had begun and by 1946 there were two African members – Mathu and Odede – on the Legislative Council. During the same year Mathu formed the Kenya African Union (KAU) to focus African opinion. At the same time Jomo Kenyatta returned from abroad, where he had been since 1931. He became chairman of the Kenya African Union and began reorganizing the Kikuyu educational movement, which, in the 1930's, had been responsible for educating people politically. KAU grew stronger and went outside Kikuyuland to other parts of Kenya and Kenyatta was looked upon as the leader of nationalism in the whole country.

In 1948 Africans were given a total of four seats on the Legislative Council. This did not satisfy the political leaders and in 1951 KAU demanded more seats, equal representation with other races and elections on a common roll.* At the same time the settlers were demanding a majority in the Legislative Council and they threatened to take matters in their own hands if the Government of Kenya did not grant them this. Soon after, Kenyatta was arrested as a suspected leader of the Mau Mau Movement and all political

*Fearing the Africans might dominate the Legislative Council, the Europeans had a very large number of seats which they contested among themselves, the Asians had the next largest number and the Africans the smallest number.

associations were banned and their leaders detained. Kenyatta was imprisoned in 1953 for seven years. Political activities were permitted again only in mid-1955, except in Central Province which was dominated by the Kikuyu. Up to 1960 when the emergency was lifted, it was only the Kenya Federation of Labour led by Tom Mboya that operated throughout Kenya, very much as a political movement.

In 1954 the Lyttelton Constitution attempted to foster multi-racialism. Moderate settlers led by Michael Blundell accepted the principle of partnership between Europeans and Africans in government. Extremist settlers led by Group Captain Briggs still thought in terms of white domination and they brought forward their veteran leader, Cavendish-Bentinck, who had succeeded Lord Delamere on his death in 1931, to lead them again.

A limited franchise was allowed in March 1957 and seven Africans were elected to the Legislative Council. In October of the same year the subsequent Colonial Secretary Lennox-Boyd proclaimed the Lennox-Boyd constitution to replace that of Lyttelton. This gave Africans six more seats and a second ministry. Africans were now equal to the non-elected whites in the Legislative Council.

Some African members of the Legislative Council disliked the partnership between Africans and Europeans in government as they wanted Africans to run the Government themselves. To foster the idea of multi-racialism, the Government assisted Michael Blundell, in 1954, to form a multi-racial party called the Kenya National Party. A number of Africans in the Legislative Council were persuaded to join it but Oginga Odinga and Tom Mboya, supported by the rest of the African members in the Legislative Council, formed the Kenya Independence Movement with its membership restricted to Africans only. Oginga Odinga was its president and Mboya its secretary.

In a further bid to attract Africans to Blundell, the Government in October 1959 announced the removal of barriers to African settlement in the White Highlands. This infuriated the majority of the settlers and they denounced Michael Blundell and his fellow European followers as traitors. Their cup of bitterness was filled in January 1960 after the Lancaster Constitutional Conference in London. Under the new constitution, Africans received four ministerial posts, the settlers three and Asians two. Africans also secured the majority of non-elected members in the Legislative Council. In utter disappointment at the crushing of their hopes built up over sixty years as the owners of the country, the settlers began to ask

Britain for compensation for their land holdings so that they might pack up and leave Kenya as soon as possible.

Following the Lancaster Conference new African political parties developed. Gichuru, Oginga Odinga and Mboya formed the Kenya African National Union (KANU), which appeared to be town-centred and dominated by the Kikuyu and Luo, the largest ethnic groups of Kenya. Minority peoples began to fear domination and, under the leadership of R. Ngala, Muliro and Moi, they formed the Kenya African Democratic Union (KADU) to press for a federal constitution to safeguard minority rights. In the 1961 election KANU won nineteen seats, KADU eleven, Blundell's party one and Cavendish-Bentinck's party none.

Since KANU refused to form the Government unless Kenyatta was released from prison, Blundell's party and KADU formed a Coalition Government. In August 1961 Kenyatta was released from prison and was at once elected to the Legislative Council. He tried to bring KANU and KADU together but failed and in October 1962 became President of KANU.

A second Lancaster Constitutional Conference was held in February 1962. In order to bring about a compromise between KANU and KADU, a strong Central Government was set up with a federal constitution. The elections, held in May 1963, were won by KANU with an overall majority and, on 12th December 1963, Kenya became independent, with Jomo Kenyatta as its Prime Minister.

Within the first year of its independence Kenya became a one-party state since KADU voluntarily dissolved. A new constitution made Kenya a republic. It provided for an executive president and abolished the regional governments. In this way it brought about centralization which had not been provided for in the constitution that led Kenya into independence. Then on 12th December 1964 the Republican Constitution came into force and the Prime Minister, Jomo Kenyatta, became the first President.

36 Tanganyika 1939-75

Constitutional Development Before TANU

After the Second World War it seemed Tanganyika would progress slowly to independence. By mid-1955 Government officials and political thinkers were putting the time of independence twenty years ahead. The Government, however, with a view to handing over responsibility to the Tanganyika people, began to train them in the management of local government. The British officials considered indirect rule out of date and, by a Local Government Ordinance in 1953, they gradually removed traditional chiefs from local administration.

At the Central Government level two Africans were nominated to the Legislative Council in 1945 and in the following year the number was raised to three. By 1951 four Africans were on the 15-strong Legislative Council and one African was a member of the 8-strong Executive Council. In 1953 the Governor ceased presiding over the Legislative Council and a Speaker was appointed to do so. In the following year three Africans from outside Government employment were appointed to the Executive Council together with two Europeans and two Asians.

The Nationalist Movement

By the late 1930's there were a number of associations; the Tanganyika Territory African Civil Service Association, the Tanganyika African Association and numerous ethnic associations in different districts of Tanganyika. But none of these associations was nationalist and none had mass support; they were concerned either with the welfare of an ethnic group or that of particular groups of people sharing a similar social background. In 1954 a nationalist movement was formed by a process of integration.

In 1953 Julius Nyerere became the president of the Tanganyika African Association. He reorganized it into an effective organ of nationalist politics. In July 1954, the association changed its name to Tanganyika African National Union (TANU). It aimed at uniting all the people of the country so that they should think of themselves as members of one cohesive country. It also worked for independence and economic and social opportunities for Africans. Under the presidencies of Julius Nyerere and Oscar Kambona, TANU spread all over the country. Nyerere was careful to restrain a number of members who were prepared for violence.

By the 1950's the United Nations Organization was pressing for independence for all colonies and especially those which had come under its responsibility after the First World War as a result of Germany's defeat. Tanganyika was one of these. In 1954 the U.N. sent a mission to Tanganyika to examine the progress of the territory. TANU gave evidence to the mission, which was seen as responsible and thoughtful. The mission recommended that the British administration set up a time-table for planned progress towards full independence. It also advised the Protectorate administration to listen to the views of the African politicians and to be sympathetic to them. From this time onward there was close contact between TANU and the United Nations headquarters in America.

Meanwhile in 1956 another party under the name of the United Tanganyika Party was formed. It was opposed to TANU's programme of achieving independence under African rule alone. It fostered a multi-racial government whereby seats would be proportionally reserved for Africans, Asians and Europeans. This new party was backed by the Government and it introduced a good deal of bitterness into politics.

Both TANU and UTP contested the 1958 elections. TANU won all the seats and the UTP in dismay disbanded immediately. During the same year Sir Richard Turnbull became Governor of Tanganyika, with instructions from the British Colonial Office not to retard the constitutional progress of the country. He was also determined not to raise consistent and widespread discontent among Africans by refusing to accelerate the advance towards independence. He soon won the confidence of the African politicians and Julius Nyerere became one of the persons with whom he constantly discussed Government problems.

Soon after the arrival of Turnbull, a committee, under the chairmanship of Sir Richard Ramage, was set up to consider the future shape of the Legislative Council and the Executive Council. It recommended a majority of African elected members to the Legislative Council, with some seats reserved for the Europeans and Asians. The Executive Council was to be replaced by a council of ministers most of whom would be elected. This council of ministers was formed and five TANU members became ministers.

In 1960 a general election for seventy-one members was held. Ten of these seats were for Europeans and eleven were for Asians. TANU contested all the seats, even some Europeans and Asians standing as TANU members. A party under the name of the African Congress led by Tumbo was hastily organized to contest the elections. Three of its candidates plus a few independents stood for election. TANU won seventy seats and, on 1st May 1961, Nyerere became Prime Minister with a cabinet. The Legislative Council assumed the name of the National Assembly and, on 9th December, Tanganyika became independent.

One year after independence Tanganyika became a one-party state, opting for a republican constitution and an executive President. Nyerere became the first President.

On 22nd April 1964 Tanganyika and Zanzibar formed a political union under the name of Tanzania with Nyerere as President and Abeid Karume of Zanzibar as the first Vice-President of the Republic of Tanzania.

An important landmark after the formation of the union between Tanganyika and Zanzibar came with the Arusha Declaration of 6th February 1967. This declaration prepared the path, based on self-help, which socialist Tanzania is following now.

37 Independence and Economic Development in East Africa

Historical Background to East African Co-operation

From the beginning of the colonial era in East Africa, Lugard and Johnston, both of whom worked in Uganda, and Eliot, Commissioner of Kenya from 1900 to 1904, all championed the idea of administering East Africa as one unit. After the First World War Tanganyika came under the administration of Britain and the idea of administering East Africa as one unit appeared even more practical.

In 1924 L. S. Amery, the British Colonial Under-Secretary, set up a commission to examine the possibility of forming East Africa into a federation. However, the Governments of Uganda and Tanganyika opposed federation for fear of domination by Kenya settlers. After the commission's report, an arrangement was made for the Governors of Kenya, Uganda and Tanganyika and the Resident of Zanzibar to meet annually and discuss common affairs.

In 1927 another commission from London, led by Sir Hilton Young, came to East Africa to examine further the possibility of an East African federation. Another commission came in 1929 to do the same. Both commissions reported that federation was not yet possible as most Africans opposed the move. Yet the three Governors and the Resident of Zanzibar continued to meet and discuss policies on postal facilities, communication systems and customs services. During World War II a Joint Economic Council was created for East Africa, Malawi and Zambia to co-ordinate their war efforts and economies. The Economic Council was abandoned after the war.

The idea of economic co-operation in East Africa continued with the formation of the East African High Commission in 1948. This body was responsible for operating communications, customs, taxes, postal services, meteorology, statistics, higher education, research and currency. It had a Central Legislative Council in Nairobi on which all races were represented, though the Europeans were in the majority.

Tanganyika's independence in 1961 made it necessary to redefine the role of the East African High Commission and its name was changed to the East African Common Services Organization. When Kenya, the last territory to gain independence, became free from colonial rule in 1963, discussions on both economic and political federation were continued, but since that time the idea of a political federation has been dropped. Only economic co-operation has been maintained.

The East African Community

As there was a feeling that the profits from economic co-operation were not being shared evenly among the three East African countries, the Philip Commission was set up in 1965 to look into the matter. Its task was to review the economic relationships between the three countries. Its report formed the basis of the Treaty for East African Co-operation in June 1967. The treaty recommended the setting up of an East African Development Bank to promote an equitable distribution of industry in the three countries. A number of councils were set up to assist the working of the common services. The treaty also established a common market for East Africa to ensure free movement of goods, capital and labour among the East African countries. This would also help to create a common tariff barrier to prevent foreign imports that could ruin the development of local industries.

Although during the colonial days East Africa possessed a common currency, in 1965 the three countries agreed to have separate currencies and separate central banks.

Neighbouring countries such as Zambia, Burundi, Somalia and Ethiopia have applied for membership of the community. Botswana, Lesotho, Malawi and the Sudan have expressed interest in joining, but no firm decision has yet been taken.

Economic Plans

In each Government of East Africa there is a Ministry of Planning, which draws up development plans in blocks of five-yearly periods. These plans aim at increasing economic growth and, secondly, aim at changing the structure of the economy by increasing industrial activities which were less important during the colonial era.

In agriculture they are trying to convert subsistence peasants into progressive farmers. They plan to do this by increasing the range of crops for domestic and overseas markets and improving methods of agricultural production. By this method it is hoped to help the development of rural areas, which are being shunned by young people in favour of towns at the moment.

The three Governments have been encouraging Africans, through co-operatives, to process, market and distribute their agricultural produce. At the national level, new marketing boards have been set up and the old ones strengthened so that the Governments can control the marketing of agricultural products to ensure that farmers are not exploited.

In commerce and industry the three Governments are seeking to help Africans to own commercial and industrial enterprises. In Uganda, African Business Promotion Ltd. helps African businessmen to acquire commercial know-how, to subsidize rentals on shops for them and to give them cheap and easy credit. In Kenya, the Industrial and Commercial Development Corporation of the Kenya Government does the same; while in Tanzania the International Trading and Credit Company of Tanganyika Ltd. and the Co-operative Supply Association of Tanganyika do this work. All three Governments have set up Government-owned trading organizations to trade directly with the producers and also to supply African wholesalers and retailers. Tanzania employs the two bodies already mentioned while Uganda and Kenya use National Trading Corporations.

Education is very much bound up with the progress of the economy. During the 1960's educational resources were greatly concentrated on secondary and higher education for manpower needs. Since independence there has been a rapid increase of students in this educational sector and much money has been spent on it. This has happened because, at independence, Africans with the required skills in many occupational spheres were very few. The Protectorate Governments had relied mainly on expatriates for these skills, and many left before or soon after independence.

Primary education did not expand at the same rate as secondary and higher education. By 1960 43% of primary age pupils were being enrolled every year. From the purely economic point of view primary education is less important than secondary and higher education, which produces badly-needed skilled personnel at a more advanced level.

With the expansion of secondary education, emphasis has tended to shift to technical and science subjects. More students now take science courses and the farm schools, technical and vocational colleges have been expanded.

At a higher level, the University of East Africa was set up in June 1963, comprising the three colleges of Makerere, Nairobi and Dar es Salaam. The number of students taking courses for diplomas, degrees and post-graduate studies has been rising steadily, reaching about 6,000 in the three colleges by 1970, in which year the University of East Africa ceased to exist. In its place East Africa from June 1970 got three independent universities, one at Dar es Salaam, another at Makerere-Kampala and the third at Nairobi. But academic co-operation for all East Africa continued in such matters as the preparation of secondary and university syllabuses and exams.

By increasing production of high level personnel it was hoped to free East Africa from depending so heavily on expatriates. This dependence is most evident at the moment in the teaching staff of the secondary schools and at the three universities.

38 Ethiopia

Geographical Position and the People

Geographically Ethiopia shares the north-eastern horn of Africa with Somalia and is part of East Africa regionally, covering 1 183 624 square km. The western plateau, forty per cent of Ethiopia, was known in Biblical days as Abyssinia, a name sometimes incorrectly applied to the whole of Ethiopia.

The population of Ethiopia is over 23 million, made up of many different ethnic groups. The Galla, who invaded the empire during the seventeenth century, make up the largest group of 9 million. Likewise there are many languages, Semitic, Cushitic and Nilotic. Amharic is the official national language, derived from the ancient language of South Arabia but much modified by local Cushitic influence. Religions practised include Christianity, Islam and traditional African religions.

The Growth of the Empire

The first important stage in Ethiopia's history began at Axum when Semitic people from Yemen in Southern Arabia arrived in the seventh century B.C. Axum, later to become a kingdom, was a trading centre where ivory from Kenya and Uganda was brought and then shipped to Southern Arabia, Egypt and parts of Asia. The new settlers intermarried with the indigenous Hamitic people, producing a language and culture known as Ethiopic. Gradually their influence spread to Amhara, Shoa and Tigré. The aboriginal people of these places came under their rule and absorbed the Ethiopic language and culture. This was the area called Abyssinia in the Bible.

Gradually the areas became three separate kingdoms ruled over by separate royal dynasties but paying allegiance to Axum. In A.D. 333 Frumentius from Syria came to King Ezana's court at Axum and converted him to Christianity. The king subsequently ordered all his subjects to become Christians. From then on the Christian way of life became integrated with Ethiopian culture. The kings of Axum continued to enlarge their empire by conquering neighbouring peoples, forcing subject rulers to pay tribute. The most important result of their conquests was the absorption into Ethiopic culture of various outside elements.

It is often claimed that the emperors of Ethiopia are connected with the Jewish dynasty of King Solomon. The Emperor of Ethiopia in fact was known as the Lion of Judah, King of Kings. But the claim has been disputed by historians. The Jews believed in one God, but the people of Ethiopia worshipped a number of gods borrowed from South Arabia, only being converted to Christianity in A.D. 333.

In the tenth century the Falasha dynasty, claiming descent from Solomon, was driven from power by a Judaized tribe known as the Agaw. A later Agaw dynasty known as the Zagwe who became Christians, also claimed descent from Solomon to enhance its authority. These rival claims continued to be made, from Roha in Lasta province where the Zagwe continued to rule, and from Shoa by the Falasha.

During Zagwe rule, many churches were cut out of rocks, evidence of the growth of a Christian culture.

In the thirteenth century the pressure of Muslim attacks on the empire forced the Zagwe to abdicate their throne to the old rulers who gradually asserted their claim to the Solomon connection. Zara Yaqob (1434 to 1468) is remembered as a strong Christian emperor who fought successfully against the Muslim states of Adel, Ifat, Dawaro, Sidamo and Fatijar on the eastern coast of Ethiopia. All these states were brought into the empire.

During this period the empire had under its hegemony the kingdoms of Gojjam, Amhara, Tigré and Shoa, together with the conquered territories along the Red Sea and Sidamo. From the thirteenth century onwards emperors for many years came only from Shoa. Later, however, emperors came from Tigré, Amhara or Shoa.

One of the darkest periods in Ethiopian history occurred in the sixteenth century when the youthful Lebna Dengel was emperor. The Muslims of Adal under the leadership of Ahmed Gran joined forces with the Ottoman Turks, declaring a 'jihad' in 1531 against Ethiopia which they intended to conquer for Islam. In four years they took Dawaro and Shoa, Lasta and Tigré. Many chiefs deserted to the Muslims; Lebna Dengel fled to the mountains in the north-west where he died in 1540. Ninety per cent of the Ethiopian population was now converted to Islam.

Support for the Christians came when Portuguese soldiers landed at Massawa in 1541 to help the new emperor Claudius. Tigré and Bakr Nagash rallied to Claudius. Fighting was fierce between Muslims and loyal Ethiopians and their Portuguese allies. Ahmed Gran, the Muslim leader, was killed in battle in 1543. Claudius re-occupied much of the empire though the Turks still kept Massawa and remained until dislodged by the Italians in 1888.

Portuguese involvement in Ethiopia meant greater European contact. Europeans knew only of the Queen of Sheba and the legends of Prester John, the rich and powerful African king, believed to be Abyssinian. By the end of the fifteenth century Italian and other European traders had reached Ethiopia. The emperors retained them at court for their technical skills and refused to allow them to return home. Consequently news of Ethiopia rarely reached Europe from travellers.

In 1557 and 1603 Jesuits entered the country and were forced to stay as technical teachers. Emperor Susenyos (1607 to 1632) was a Roman Catholic convert who decreed that his subjects should also be Christians. When the old Ethiopian Orthodox Church revolted, Susenyos was forced to abdicate, while the Jesuits were expelled.

At this time the Galla, who had invaded Ethiopia from the south, were a threat to the empire. They had seized and occupied the fertile regions along the eastern borders and also the southern and western parts of Shoa. By the end of the sixteenth century they had more than one third of the empire. The Galla now intervened in Ethiopian politics, identifying themselves with the Amhara royal house. Through them, Susenyos returned to the imperial throne and married a Galla princess of the Amhara royal dynasty.

The reign of Fasilidas, son of Susenyos, was the last great period of Ethiopian history until 1855. He moved his capital from Lasta in Shoa to Gondar, north of Lake Tana in Amhara. Gondar remained the imperial capital for more than a century, the centre of a new culture expressed in literature, architecture and painting.

After the death of Fasilidas in 1667, central government was weakened. Galla influence increased through numerous marriage alliances with the house of Amhara, whose power and that of the Galla nobles grew at the expense of the emperor.

By 1753 the empire was on the verge of disintegration. Gallinya, rather than Amharic, was spoken at court. Galla nobles vied with those of Amhara and Tigré for the imperial throne. Between 1769 and 1855 central government almost disappeared, with five nobles simultaneously claiming the throne. Power devolved on the nobles in the kingdoms and provinces; imperial power fell into abeyance. Local rulers made their positions hereditary and appointed area governors. Thus from the late eighteenth to the mid-nineteenth century, the Ethiopian empire ceased to exist.

Nineteenth Century Developments

With the weakening of central government, bandits called 'shifta' came into the central highlands plateau. Their leaders were usually connected with various ruling houses but rivalry between these houses and the bandit leaders led to open war. One shifta leader, Kassa, defeated the local King of Gojjam and of Begemder, then planned attacks on the kings of Tigré and Shoa. In 1855 he became the Emperor Theodore III.

The new emperor set up his capital at Magdala, a fortified city. He fought Shoa and took prisoner its young King Menelik, whom he treated kindly and kept at his court. To strengthen his régime, Theodore won over the church with land, money and power. He put down all opposition, particularly among the Galla. He traced a connection with the Solomonic lineage, which gained increased respect for his leadership. Crowned in the historic church of Axum, he established himself beyond doubt as the Lion of Judah, King of Kings.

Theodore III planned to re-organize the administration by replacing local rulers as governors and appointing his own nominees without local ties or interests. These officials would be answerable to him alone and he could transfer or dismiss them at will. But the nobles resisted the plan and Theodore had to rely on the support of his army to overcome them.

Theodore welcomed European traders and missionaries, especially those from Germany. They were employed in making armaments and were trusted advisers. He made a commercial treaty with Britain to increase the supply of arms and ammunition for his army. The long isolation of Ethiopia from Europe was ended, but the change did not come without repercussions.

Meanwhile at the court some of the Europeans incurred the

emperor's displeasure and were put in prison at Magdala in 1864. Queen Victoria sent Hormuzd Rassam as envoy, requesting Theodore to release them. But negotiations failed and Rassam was imprisoned also. Britain sent Sir Robert Napier in July 1867 to lead a military expedition. Consequently a force of 32 000 men under Napier sailed from India and landed at Zula, arriving within striking distance of Magdala at the end of March, 1868. Fighting broke out between Ethiopian soldiers and Napier's men. Theodore, realizing the odds were against him, with his soldiers deserting, tried to make peace. But Napier refused and the war continued until the Ethiopian army was utterly defeated. Theodore committed suicide rather than be taken by the British. Magdala fell, the British released the prisoners and left for Massawa. It has never been clear why Britain did not at this point take over Ethiopia in accordance with her traditional colonial policy.

Theodore was one of the greatest figures in Ethiopian history. At a time of disunity and civil war he endeavoured to unite the empire and re-shape its political institutions. He was also a great warrior and leader of men, but ruthless to those who defied him. The seeds of his downfall lay mainly in the opposition he had stimulated among the nobles. They eagerly welcomed the British. The church too had been dissatisfied, though it supported him at first. When Theodore took away its land and gave it to his supporters, the church campaigned for his overthrow.

Rivalry between Shoa and Tigré

After the death of Theodore and the departure of the British came civil war and chaos. In 1871 Kassai, a prince from Tigré, ousted all other claimants and was crowned Emperor Johannes IV. He pursued Theodore's policy of restricting the power of the nobles. He was bitterly opposed and further had to contend with the combined resistance of the Europeans and the Sudanese Muslims. His greatest rival was King Menelik of Shoa, who had returned to his kingdom after Theodore's death. Like Johannes, Menelik claimed descent from Solomon and he had a large group of followers. Johannes arranged a marriage between his own son and Menelik's daughter and also made Menelik successor to the imperial throne. With this alliance the royal houses of Tigré and Shoa were reconciled.

During the long reign of Johannes, the Italians established their

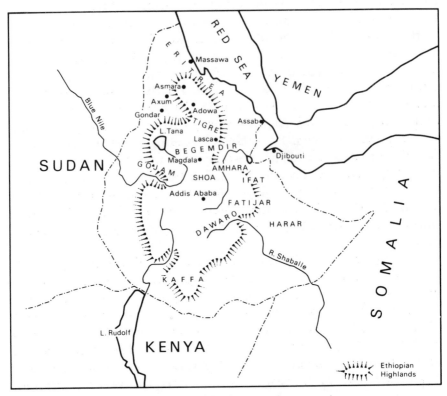

Expansion of Ethiopia over the centuries

hold on the Red Sea coast at Assab. In 1888 they occupied the port of Massawa, formerly held by Turkish and Egyptian soldiers, then extended to the borders of Tigré. Here Johannes's general, Prince Alula, stopped their advance into the fertile highlands around his provincial capital of Asmara. He routed the Italians at Dogali in 1887. An African victory of this magnitude was a setback to European imperialism and a signal encouragement to Ethiopians to fight for independence.

Having failed militarily, the Italians tried to exploit the rivalry between Shoa and Tigré. By means of a treaty to sell arms to Menelik they hoped to provoke hostilities between him and the emperor. Menelik might then become a tool in their hands. Meanwhile, from 1881 to 1890, in the Sudan the Mahdists were fighting the Egyptians. Menelik took the opportunity to seize Harar and the greater part of the eastern highlands in 1887, thereby nearly doubling the area of Shoa. Johannes also led his armies westwards to acquire Sudanese land, slaves and gold. He was killed at Metemma in an encounter with the Mahdists. Menelik then acceded to the throne.

The Reign of the Emperor Menelik

Menelik immediately concluded the Treaty of Uccialli with Italy. A European ally would strengthen his hand against the son of Johannes and other rivals. The Italian version of the treaty implied that Ethiopia was under Italian protection. All treaties signed by Europeans at this time with African rulers were deemed to give this right. But the Amharic version of the document made no such stipulation. Italy warned off all other Europeans and let it be known that Ethiopia was hers. Menelik, alarmed and affronted at the presumption of the Italians, was still in a weak position, with insufficient weapons and an empire in disarray.

Menelik modernized the army with French arms and tactical training and all princes, kings and provincial governors were forced to obey him. Thus the kingdoms of Gojjam, Begemder, Amhara, Tigré and Shoa were all securely under his control. His armies occupied part of the Somali country within 180 miles of the Indian Ocean. The kingdoms of Kaffa, Sidama and the Galla Boran were all conquered. Only Eritrea, taken over by the Italians, remained outside modern Ethiopia. He made Addis Ababa his capital. He also made a treaty with the British, agreeing not to interfere in the affairs of the Sudan, where the Mahdist war was in progress.

Having put down all subversive elements in Ethiopia, he was now able to deal with the Italians. He declared war and defeated them at Adowa, 1st March 1896, using the very weapons bought from them earlier. This, the second Italian defeat by the Ethiopians, was profoundly disturbing to Italian morale. While other European powers readily overcame African armies and acquired vast empires, Italy failed to make headway in her colonial aspirations. A British newspaper correspondent commented: 'It is to be feared that our Italian friends have got a wolf by the ears in their African colony.' After Adowa, all European powers recognized the independence of Ethiopia.

Menelik was aware that independence meant keeping abreast of modern technology. With European assistance he brought his army up to date and improved communications and the efficiency of government departments. He granted a concession to the French to construct a railway from Djibouti to Addis Ababa. The power of the princes was weakened by appointing some to administrative posts. He gained Galla support by marrying a Galla fourth wife, Empress Taitu. A cousin was married to a prince of Lasta, ensuring loyalty from that province. Prince Tafari Makonnen, also a cousin, was appointed to control Harar and the Ogaden; another, Prince Wolde Giorgis, controlled Gondar. One of Menelik's daughters married Prince Mikael of Wollo. Such alliances helped to promote harmony and loyalty throughout the empire.

By 1906 Menelik had created a new and different type of government machinery. His bureaucracy was administered by a trained élite instead of the traditional feudal lords. From that year, however, his health began to fail, his rule weakened and old rivalries reappeared in the form of court intrigues, attempted coups and disputes among regional leaders. All that Menelik had striven to build up began to crumble. The power he had succeeded in removing from kings and provincial rulers began to return to them.

The Emergence of Haile Selassie

After Menelik's death in 1913 Lidj Iasu came to the throne. Europeans believed that without the strong hand of Menelik Ethiopia would disintegrate. Germans and Turks sought the goodwill of Iasu. The British consul advised Britain to extend her influence in Ethiopia. The French hoped for economic advantage. Italy, still nursing hurt pride over her defeat at Adowa, saw a fresh chance to establish a protectorate.

In 1916 Lidj Iasu dramatically announced his conversion to Islam. This was a shock for Christian Ethiopia. Hostility to Islam was shared by the nobles, the army and the church, who disowned Lidj Iasu. They chose Menelik's daughter, Zauditu, in his place with Prince Tafari Makonnen of Harar as regent; Wolde Giorgis, another popular noble and cousin of Menelik, became war minister. These two were the real rulers of Ethiopia. But intrigues and rivalry soon occurred. Tafari Makonnen managed, however, to maintain his position. Wolde Giorgis died in 1926 and Zauditu died in 1930. Tafari Makonnen became Emperor, taking the name of Haile Selassie, which means 'Power of the Trinity'.

As regent, Haile Selassie had continued the modernization started by Menelik. He had founded schools to educate the future civil service. He had sent his army officers to study at the French military academy at Saint Cyr. In 1924 he had visited Europe and come back with ideas for reorganizing government institutions. Many Europeans had come as technical advisers. After he became emperor in 1930, the rate of progress towards a modern state increased tremendously.

Since their victory at Adowa, Ethiopians still feared that the Italians in nearby Somalia and Eritrea would strike again. From 1930 onwards Haile Selassie imported arms. At the same time he set up the first constitution with a ministerial government. This development, however, was cut short by the Italian invasion of Ethiopia from 1934 to 1935. Using aeroplanes and poison gas, they avenged the defeat of forty years earlier. Haile Selassie fled and lived as an exile in England from 1936 to 1940.

Ethiopia Under Italy

Though some princes came to the aid of the Italians, a large group of loyalists resisted resolutely. Organized guerrillas harassed the Italians, who retaliated by assassinating a number of leading Ethiopians. But Italians went in fear of their lives and Addis Ababa was guarded by a strong military garrison.

From 1937 Italy, under Mussolini, began feverishly developing Ethiopia as her colony. She built a network of roads all over the country. She wanted Ethiopia to produce grain, food and raw materials for Italy and become a settlement for Italians. Yet despite the Italians' colossal expenditure on development, the Ethiopians were never reconciled to them. They obstructed the foreigners at every point and the Italians got little for their pains. The minerals which were discovered were insufficient to be commercially viable; taxes were hard to collect in face of general opposition. The majority of the people still retained their loyalty to Haile Selassie.

Effects of the Second World War

In June 1940, Italy declared war on Britain during the Second World War. Britain feared an Italian invasion of the Sudan from Ethiopia. So in January 1941, British and Sudanese forces, together with exiled Ethiopians trained by Britain, invaded Ethiopia and captured Addis Ababa. Early in May, Haile Selassie re-entered Addis Ababa and the Italians were driven out.

Britain assumed that Ethiopia would remain an occupied territory under her. Ethiopians, however, insisted that Ethiopia was a liberated allied country. They demanded that the British should leave Addis Ababa as soon as possible and allow Haile Selassie to rule once more over his empire. On 31st January 1942, Britain recognized Ethiopia as a sovereign state, though she kept troops there until 1945. To lessen dependence on Britain, Ethiopia now turned to the U.S.A., Yugoslavia, India and Israel for economic aid.

Post-war Developments

After the war, Haile Selassie continued the work of modernization, furthering education and finding replacements for the highly qualified administrators who had been victims of the Italian terror. Eventually central government was successfully re-established. His post-war policy produced a large group of élite, among whom unrest developed, causing the crisis of December 1960. While Haile Selassie was on a state visit to Brazil, the imperial bodyguard staged an abortive coup, which was, however, swiftly put down by the army. Generally speaking, Haile Selassie's modernization programme had the effect of bringing education and new political awareness to many Ethiopians. This was especially true of the armed forces, where the seeds of discontent were now sown.

After the defeat of Italy by the Allied Forces during the Second World War, Ethiopia was determined to bring Eritrea into the empire. She applied to the United Nations in 1947 to recognize it as part of Ethiopia. The United Nations finally decided that Eritrea should form a federation with Ethiopia. Eritrea, however, was too small for such a relationship, and in consequence Ethiopia put Eritrea on a provincial footing, before formally annexing it in 1962 as the thirteenth province of the empire.

Ethiopia's role since the Second World War has been remarkable in African and international politics. She has shown a deep concern for African affairs and has been opposed to colonization. She has built a remarkable assembly hall where numerous conferences of African states take place. In 1963 Addis Ababa was chosen as the seat of the permanent Secretariat of the Organization of African Unity, in recognition of Ethiopia's role in championing the African cause.

Political Unrest

From the late 1960's Ethiopia gradually saw a new social revolution. In spite of his efforts at modernization, the rule of Haile Selassie had been largely authoritarian, relying on an aristocratic governing élite. Many newly-independent African countries had a system of democracy, if not altogether resembling a European parliament, at least embodying the freedom for political parties to represent the will of the people. The paternal and feudal system of the Lion of Judah began to crack when the educated, articulate and politically conscious demanded far-reaching changes.

Student demonstrations and riots took place in Addis Ababa early in 1967 and the university was closed after disturbances in December 1969. In May 1971 a newly-formed students' union was declared illegal and all secondary schools closed for an indefinite period. An army conspiracy led to the execution of a general in 1970. The army was, in fact, to be the main vehicle of protest, since it contained a number of well-educated, dissident young Ethiopians whose dissatisfaction with their pay and conditions led to a general strike in October 1973. The emperor promised constitutional reform in the face of mounting tension and further strikes. At this point reports of a widespread famine in Ethiopia released by the Food and Agriculture Organization and foreign missions astonished the outside world. Devastating figures told of many thousands starving in the months of April and May 1973.

Overthrow of Haile Selassie

The suppression of news of the famine added further to the mood of disquiet. Serious unrest resulted in the armed forces taking effective control of the country in June 1974. A ruling committee was appointed and it issued a manifesto, rounded up a number of the country's prominent figures and put the emperor under close arrest.

Eventually on 11th September 1974, the armed forces deposed the 82-year-old emperor after forty-four years' rule. They invited his 57-year-old son to be crowned in his place. Crown Prince Asfa Wossen, known as a reformist, was in Switzerland at the time, recuperating from a stroke. He was to be a figurehead, however, with no authority in the country's administration and politics. He did not respond to the invitation. There had, moreover, been two previous attempts to establish him as a puppet ruler, in 1936 at the time of the Italian invasion and again during the coup of 1960. On the first occasion he escaped with his father to exile. On the second he was actually proclaimed head of the new government, but the insurgents were swiftly crushed and from then on distrust existed between emperor and son, although Haile Selassie appointed the Crown Prince governor of Wollo Province. Accordingly, in April 1974 the emperor named his grandson, Prince Zera Yacob Asfa Wossen, direct successor to the 3,000-year-old throne. But circumstances dictated otherwise. In March 1975 the monarchy was abolished by proclamation. Haile Selassie, who stripped of his former power became an anachronism when the progressive government took over, died in a mud hut in an army barracks in Addis Ababa in August 1975, his once brilliant reputation sadly tarnished.

Without doubt, 1974 was a year of traumatic and far-reaching changes in Ethiopia. Its events brought to an end the ancient feudal system which had long given enlightened Ethiopians cause for uneasiness.

39 The Sudan

Location, Size and Inhabitants

The Sudan is the largest country in Africa, comprising two-and-a-half million square km. Its position and those of the surrounding countries can be seen on the sketchmap.

Though large, the Sudan has a sizeable portion of desert. Its population is sparse, only thirteen million or so and about half is concentrated in the central part which is about fourteen per cent of the total area.

Two distinct kinds of people live in the Sudan. In the north are about nine million Muslim Arabs. In the south are negroes, some Christian, some Muslim and some of various African religions.

The word Sudan is of Arabic origin and means 'the country of the blacks'. If used literally the word would apply only to the south of present-day Sudan.

Although the Africans are divided among many tribes, the following are the largest. The Shilluk, Dinka and Nuer people are classed as Nilotic and are cattle-keepers. The Bari, Didinga, Turkana and a few others are Nilo-Hamitic and are predominantly growers of crops living in the Lake Plateau. To these one must add the Azano in the Bahr el Ghazal, who migrated from Zaire during the nineteenth century. The south comprises three provinces – Equatoria, Upper Nile and Bahr el Ghazal – and these contain all the tribes, apart from a few who go north in search of work.

Though the black people are divided into tribes, the differences between them are as nothing compared with the division between them and the Arabs. This is made worse by the traditional hostility between the Arab north and the African south. The inhabitants of the north for centuries invaded the south and carried off people to be their slaves or to be exported to Egypt and Saudi Arabia. This has left a legacy of bitterness and mistrust that only time and a change of attitude can eradicate.

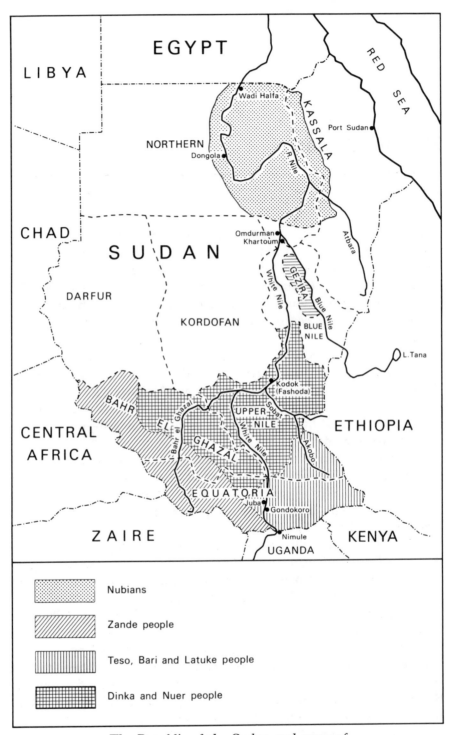

*The Republic of the Sudan and areas of
origin of some of its peoples*

Early History

From 2000 B.C. the northern Sudan was under Egypt. Arabs from Arabia had moved into the area as far as Khartoum, conquering the negroes who had preceded them. The negroes consequently moved further south to central Sudan but even there they were not free of the Egyptians, who made frequent raids on them. This was the start of the typical attitude adopted by Egyptians and Arabs towards all negroes, from early times to the second half of the nineteenth century. Trade took place, however, and the Egyptians obtained gold, gum, oils, ebony, ivory and monkeys from some of the negroes in return for iron tools.

In the Dongola region a Sudanese royal family arose in 1085 B.C. Its members were descendants of Kush and had been influenced by Egyptian culture. During the eighth century B.C. they became so powerful that under King Piankhi their people conquered all Egypt. Piankhi built his capital at Napata near Barkal. His successors, however, were driven from Egypt with the aid of the Assyrians in 663 B.C., but retained their capital of Napata. They were eventually expelled from this city by the Romans in 23 B.C.

The story of the Sudan becomes clearer from 630 A.D. when the Islamic Arabs conquered Syria and Egypt. Their armies moved on to Dongola in 641 A.D. The rulers of the northern Sudan then began to pay annual tribute to the Muslim rulers of upper Egypt, such as those of Thebes. During the ninth century the numerous slaves in Egypt, known as 'Mamelukes', found a leader and defeated the Muslim rulers of Egypt. The Arabs there moved into the northern Sudan because of discontent at being governed by former slaves, intermarried with the negroes and introduced Islam.

By the tenth century Arabs were migrating in large numbers from Arabia into the north and central Sudan via the Red Sea, occupying all this area by the sixteenth century. They left Arabia on account of religious and political disagreements and also in quest of arable and pasture land. Christianity, which had been the predominant religion in the northern Sudan, gave way to Islam and Arabic became the language of daily use and foreign trade. Regular raids were carried out on the southern negroes for slaves for domestic and export purposes.

In 1504 a Fung Sultan of Bornu extraction, Amara Dunkas, founded the Sennar kingdom of the Blue Nile. His family had been converted to Islam and he established cordial relations with the Arabs. The zenith of this empire was between the sixteenth and eighteenth centuries. It controlled a large area from Dongola in the north to Fazugli in the south, Ethiopia in the east and the Blue Nile in the west. Under these African rulers Islam spread throughout the territory.

Early Nineteenth Century Developments

The whole picture of the Sudan was drastically changed from 1800. In that year an Albanian under the sovereignty of Turkey, Muhammad Ali, seized power in Egypt. Wanting gold to finance his schemes and men for his armies, he turned to the Sudan. The south was traditionally the area for raiding and the northern Arabs now descended on it in full force.

Muhammad Ali had two objects in view. He wished to rout the former Egyptian rulers who had taken refuge in Dongola and he was also curious to discover where the river Nile, so important to Egypt, had its source. At that time the mystery of where the Nile rises was as yet unresolved. The truth was known only to the people of Uganda.

He sent one army under his son Ismail to defeat the Fung rulers of Sennar and a second army under his son-in-law to occupy Kordofan. Both accomplished their missions successfully. But Ismail was assassinated in 1822 at Shendi. His death was avenged by his brother-in-law who carried out mass murders in Shendi.

After putting down all opposition in the Sudan, Muhammad Ali divided northern Sudan into provinces and districts over which he set Turkish officers to levy taxes for his treasury in Cairo. High taxes were imposed on the people of the north, part being sent to Cairo and the remainder being diverted to the pockets of the Turkish officers. Regrettably, hardly any of this revenue was used to develop the northern district, so that its people remained impoverished and embittered. The south, meanwhile, continued to suffer the depredations of raiders seeking slaves and conscripts for the Egyptian armies.

Muhammad Ali, pursuing his enquiries into the source of the Nile, employed European scientists, explorers, travellers and various adventurers who offered theories on how this riddle could be solved. In the course of their travels in the south of the Sudan, they revealed the deplorable nature of the slave trade carried out by Turks, Egyptians and North Sudanese Arabs.

Said Pasha, who succeeded Muhammad Ali, went to the Sudan and was profoundly shocked at what he saw, in terms of misery arising out of excessive taxes in the north and the slave trade in the south. He ordered a drastic reduction in taxes and an end to the slave trade. But the Egyptian and Turkish officials were profiteering so handsomely and the Arabs growing so rich on the slave trade that the decree was ignored and the situation remained as before.

In 1863 Ismail Pasha, a grandson of Muhammad Ali, became Khedive or ruler of Egypt, in succession to Said. He tried to make effective reforms in the Sudan, improving communications, promoting education and introducing measures to reduce the slave trade. He appointed Europeans as provincial governors in place of the corrupt Egyptian and Turkish officials. Even so, the Arab slave traders managed to outwit them, and taxation continued to oppress the people of the north.

Sir Samuel Baker becomes Governor

In 1869 Ismail appointed Sir Samuel Baker governor of all the Sudan. He was charged with two missions – to extend the power of Egypt further south from Gondokoro which is between Nimule and Juba and to stop the slave trade. Thus territorial aggrandizement could be disguised as a purely philanthropic venture.

Baker annexed parts of present-day West Nile and Acholi in Uganda in May 1871. He next marched to Bunyoro and claimed it for Egypt. Bunyoro then was ruled by Omukama Kabarega. He had instilled in his people a longing for the grandeur of the old Bunyoro-Kitara empire, which had included much of Uganda also. He had a well-organized regular army of the Abarusura. On hearing of Baker's presumption, Kabarega ordered his Abarusura to teach the Egyptian forces a lesson they would not forget. The Bunyoro army defeated Baker's men who hurried across the Nile and took refuge in Acholi at Patiko near Gulu. Baker never tried again to annex Bunyoro nor did he ever dare to proceed further south to Buganda, where Kabaka Muteesa I was ruling.

He concentrated on trying to stop the Arab slavers in Acholi and in the West Nile. He built strategically placed forts manned by Egyptian soldiers. On his resignation from the Egyptian service in 1873, he left them to keep law and order in this area. But once his restraining hand had gone, they collaborated with the Arab slavers from motives of greed and the slave traffic increased.

The Acholi resented the presence of the forts and harassed the garrisons by interfering with their freedom of movement and preventing their going out for food supplies.

The Sudan under Gordon

Colonel Charles Gordon succeeded Baker in 1874. Again, his mission was the southward extension of the Egyptian empire and the ending of the slave trade. He wished to acquire power over Bunyoro and Buganda, the latter being seen as a stepping stone to gain all the rest of East Africa up to Zanzibar. But neither Omukama Kabarega nor Kabaka Muteesa I would agree to a diplomatic understanding. Muteesa's holding for a week of Nuehr Aga, Gordon's emissary, and his group of sixty men was a warning to Gordon not to presume too far.

By 1876 he had not enlarged the empire of Egypt nor had he managed to reduce the volume of the slave trade. In the following year he was made Governor-General of all the Sudan. By this time there was so much unrest in northern Sudan under the corrupt Egyptian rule that Gordon had to travel from one area to another putting down rebellions. Consequently the administration suffered. He resigned in 1880 and left for Europe. In 1885 he returned to Khartoum under British auspices, only to meet his death at the hands of the Sudanese.

Emin Pasha

Ismail's next representative in southern Sudan, in 1878, was a German doctor, Eduard Schnitzer, who became better known as Emin Pasha. He was based near Juba at Gondokoro and the north east end of Lake Mobutu (Lake Albert) was then Egypt's southern boundary. He was a good manager of men, won great respect from his soldiers in the south and brought some measure of order to the area with a campaign against the slave trade.

The Rise of the Mahdi

Still excessive taxation, corruption and inefficiency persisted in the north. In this state of confusion Muhammad Ahmed, an Arab from Dongola, in his early thirties rose up in 1881 to lead his people against Egyptian oppression. He proclaimed himself at Abba Island on the White Nile the 'Mahdi', or long awaited saviour, ordained by Allah to guide his people to salvation.

The total breakdown of government under the Egyptian and Turkish administration in the Sudan and the intolerable taxation, easily won him followers in the north who rallied behind his banner and began to attack Egyptian garrisons. Wherever they went they triumphed against the Egyptian armies and a general revolt followed in the entire north Sudan.

Meanwhile the Egyptian government was also under pressure in Cairo. It had borrowed a great deal of money from both Britain and France to carry out economic projects. One of these was the construction of the Suez Canal, opened in 1869. But the Egyptian government by 1880 was bankrupt and unable to pay back the loan. It was even finding it difficult to pay the army which consequently became harder and harder to control. Arabi Pasha, one of the officers, mutinied and in June 1882 a massacre of French and British was carried out by his men at Alexandria. Britain and France intervened and overthrew Arabi Pasha. Eventually Britain outmanoeuvred France, gained control in Egypt, reorganized the army and re-established law and order.

In the midst of all these events, it was not surprising that when Muhammad Ahmed declared himself the Mahdi in northern Sudan, the Cairo government could take no action against him.

When Britain took control of Egypt she concentrated on consolidating her position and took little heed of events in the northern Sudan. Towards the end of 1882 the capital, Khartoum, was on the point of falling to the Mahdi and his men who planned to march to Cairo afterwards.

The Fall of Khartoum

In January 1884 the British government sent Colonel Charles Gordon to Khartoum to evacuate the Egyptian garrison and leave the Sudanese to rule themselves as best they could. On his arrival

Gordon abolished the taxes and declared an end to Egyptian rule there. Power was to pass to the indigenous people. He also promised that they would retain ownership of their black African slaves. But the Mahdi was not impressed by Gordon's promises. He refused to co-operate in the removal of the Egyptian garrison from Khartoum and continued to fight against Egyptian soldiers wherever they held on. By August 1884, the Mahdi controlled the whole of the Sudan except in the extreme north and the south, on the Red Sea coast and inside the walls of Khartoum where Gordon found himself surrounded and in great danger. In October Britain sent a relief expedition under Colonel Stewart who unfortunately arrived too late. On 25th January, 1885 he and his men reached Khartoum, only to find that Gordon and his officers had been murdered two days earlier and the city had fallen to the forces of the Mahdi.

The Relief of Emin Pasha

Britain, unwilling to incur further expense for dubious gains in the Sudan, decided to leave it for the time being and concentrate on Cairo. They told Emin Pasha, who was still established in the south, to leave because his life was in danger, but he refused. He and his soldiers were successfully maintaining law and order there and the activities of the Mahdi did not affect his southern part. As a result, however, the northern Arabs had made fewer raids for slaves in the south, a benefit which was attributed to Emin Pasha.

Yet after the murder of Gordon in Khartoum it was rumoured that Emin Pasha was also in peril and should be rescued before he was murdered by the forces of the Mahdi. A relief expedition, it was thought, would win widespread acclaim. But there were ulterior motives, in the form of imperialist schemes for acquiring more territory. The country responsible for the relief of Emin Pasha would be in a position to claim that part of the Sudan. A race developed between the German, Carl Peters, and H. M. Stanley, a naturalized American but English by birth, who was acting on behalf of Britain.

Stanley won the race in 1887. But he was disappointed to find Emin Pasha unconcerned about his safety and reluctant to leave the province. After much persuasion, Emin Pasha went with Stanley to Zanzibar. On arrival there he joined his fellow Germans and obtained an administrative post in Tanganyika, which Germany had taken over in 1886.

The End of the Mahdi Revolt

The Mahdi had died on 22nd June 1885. He was succeeded by his nominee Khalifa Abdullah who was more military than religious. Religious reform had little appeal to him and he sought only to conquer more territory.

The Khalifa decided to conquer Egypt and Ethiopia. Egypt was only saved by the resistance put up by the Egyptian and Sudanese army, commanded by British officers, and the Mahdi soldiers were stopped at the frontiers. In June 1887 the Khalifa inflicted a crushing defeat on the Ethiopian army at Gondar and the Ethiopians retreated to the mountains. King Johannes met his death at the battle of Metemma in 1889.

In their turn the Khalifa's armies were decisively defeated in August 1889 at Toski under the command of General Grenfell. The Khalifa's famous general, Wad el Negussi, was killed. This ended the menace of the invasion of Egypt by the Mahdist forces. But throughout the northern Sudan there was a collapse of law and order resulting in anarchy, famine and disease. These last two took a heavy toll of lives. Revolts broke out in Kordofan, Darfur and the Upper Nile.

At this juncture two events occurred which forced Britain to stop the Mahdi's troops once and for all. In 1896 the Ethiopians defeated the Italians at Adowa. The Italians seemed likely to suffer another defeat, this time by the Mahdi in Eritrea. Britain was asked for help which she readily gave, not wishing to see her ally and fellow European power humiliated again at the hands of African armies. Britain therefore sent Sir Herbert Kitchener to the aid of the Italians. Moreover since she held Egypt, Britain wanted to retain control of the Nile valley, for the river was Egypt's lifeline and had to be safeguarded.

Kitchener and his British troops occupied Dongola and in September, 1896 he retook Khartoum from the Mahdi. The Khalifa and his troops were defeated at Kerreri (Omdurman) in 1898. Although the Khalifa fled he was later captured and shot by an Egyptian force under Sir F. R. Wingate in November 1889, and so the Mahdi revolt, which had lasted for fifteen years, came to an end. The whole of the Sudan passed to Britain and Egypt by right of conquest.

Immediately after Kitchener had beaten the Mahdi forces at Khartoum, Major Marchand appeared about 650 km away at Fashoda, now renamed Kodok. He had been sent by France to assess where the effective limits of British power lay between the Sudan and Uganda. If any gap existed between these two British possessions, France meant to occupy it and thus link her West African possessions with her East African territories in French Somaliland. Kitchener came to Kodok in great haste with a larger force of men. The meeting, however, proved peaceful and the two military leaders referred the matter to their governments at home. An agreement was reached whereby France received more land in the west and in return abandoned her interests in the Sudan.

Establishment of the Anglo-Egyptian Administration

On the defeat of the Mahdi forces there was a need for strong government in the Sudan. Britain agreed to administer the territory jointly with Egypt, to avoid international complications. Officially the Sudan was under Egypt which had taken it over during the days of Muhammad Ali. Britain was in Egypt only to try to recover the money lent to Egypt. If Britain alone had taken over the Sudan there would have been an uproar from France, Russia and other European powers accusing Britain of imperialistic intentions. Yet to leave the government of the Sudan solely to Egypt would have been irresponsible because her record of government there had shown shocking abuses and inefficiency between 1821 and 1885. In fact Britain was the sole ruler of the Sudan from 1899 until it regained its independence in January 1956. This arrangement came to be called the Condominium, a Latin term meaning 'joint administration'. The interests of Britain were looked after by a governor-general residing in Khartoum. Under him he had several British governors, each with a British deputy governor and numerous British officials of all ranks.

The first governor-general was Sir Herbert Kitchener. But on the outbreak of the Boer War in 1899 he was succeeded by Sir Reginald Wingate and Kitchener went as a general to join the British forces fighting the Boers in South Africa.

Stable government was established in the Sudan and resistance in all quarters crushed. Confidence was restored by fixing low taxes; land reforms were carried out and titles of land were registered. Schools and communications were established and by 1914 firm boundaries of the Sudan with Uganda, Kenya, Ethiopia and Zaire were agreed.

Administration 1900-1946

It was remarkable that from 1900 to 1946 the north was administered separately from the south. The Muslim and Arab north had its own system, as did the British-controlled south. This, added to the long historical and cultural separation of the two areas of the Sudan, helped to draw them even further apart. In 1910 the governor-general set up a Legislative Council, in which his senior civil servants featured prominently, to help him debate and pass laws and also debate the budget.

In 1944 an Advisory Council for the northern Sudan – intended to become a representative legislative council in the years ahead – was inaugurated with eighteen members. The south was not represented and members were not expected to debate southern affairs.

The south was divided from 1900 into three provinces: Upper Nile, Bahr el Ghazal and Equatoria. After all resistance to British rule had been quelled, particularly amongst the Nuer tribe which was the last to submit, administration by indirect rule was established. The British government furthermore encouraged missionaries to work in the south (and also in the north, on certain conditions). As a result many Italian Verona Fathers came to the south. These were joined by the Anglican Missionary Society, the American United Missions and the Australian and New Zealand United Missions. From the outset, relations between Christianity and Islam were strained by the missionaries' efforts to make the south Christian and to make converts from Islam. English was taught and eventually became the medium of secondary and further education because of the multiplicity of African languages. It was also destined to become the language of the south, as Arabic was the language of the north.

Naturally, Arabic in a simplified form was widely understood in the south. But the missionaries and the British officials wanted to restrict its use and also the spread of Islam.

In 1918 English was declared the official language in the south and Sunday became the weekly holiday. (In the north Arabic was spoken and Friday was the holiday.) In addition to English, Dinka, Bari, Nuer, Latuke, Shilluk and Zande were to be used in southern schools.

From 1924 official government policy was separate development for north and south. Lugard's principle of the Dual Mandate was followed. It encouraged the preservation of native traditions and life and the protection of tribes from disruptive outside influences. The policy was to protect the south from undue Arabic and Islam influence coming from the north. This policy was welcomed by the southern Sudanese themselves, by the missionaries and by the British administrators.

Towards Unification

Two ideas were formulated in the 1920's. One was that the south should form an independent country. The second was that it should be linked with Uganda or Kenya. From 1921 the three southern governors were no longer required to attend the annual governors' meetings in Khartoum. They met independently and were encouraged to keep in touch with the governors of Uganda and Kenya. But neither country was anxious to be attached to the southern Sudan in view of its unproductive character. From 1942 politically aware northerners saw the danger of this policy and demanded an end to it. They asked for a unification of syllabuses in northern and southern schools and greater freedom of movement in southern Sudan for the northern people. From that time onwards, senior British administrators began to favour the amalgamation of the two parts of the Sudan.

When a new Legislative Assembly was established in 1948, politicians from the north demanded that the south should also be represented and thirteen southern delegates were sent.

Communications were now developed to improve the links between south and north. Development schemes financed by the north were set up in the south. A typical example was the £1 000 000 Azande scheme which encouraged the growing and processing of cotton. Experienced workers from the north were allowed to take jobs in the south. From 1945 the Khartoum government began to treat both parts as belonging to one political entity, bound together by geography and economics. Arabic became the medium of instruction in southern schools also and a common syllabus was introduced. In 1948 Arabic became the national language of the Sudan.

Some British officials and also the missionaries had misgivings, however. They felt that it was merely the accident of western imperialism which had brought together peoples completely different in race, culture and religion to form one nation and that there was something incongruous in the result.

The Coming of Self-Rule

In 1953 Sudanese self rule was declared. Yet no political parties existed in the south, where allegiance was to the tribe rather than to the Sudanese nation.

From the beginning the south was an uneasy partner. It was afraid of being subordinated to the north and soon these fears were realized. Northern politicians often ignored southern leaders and excluded them in vital political discussions on independence. The southerners, fearing domination by the north, were reluctant to accept full independence for the Sudan before they felt the time was ripe. But the northerners wished to go ahead at once.

After 1953 election campaigns began. The north had two major parties, the UMMA Party, derived from the Mahdists, and the Union Nationalist Party. In the south the Southern Liberal Party was formed. The UMMA Party did not campaign in the south, but the Union Nationalist Party was active there, claiming that if its rivals, the UMMA Party, won the election, its members, being sons of former slave-dealers, would enslave the southerners once more.

In 1954 an intensive policy was set in motion so that the Sudanese took over all administrative posts throughout the country before independence. Unfortunately nearly all the senior appointments vacated by the British went to northerners, by virtue of their qualifications and experience. To southerners it seemed that the many civil servants from the north in their midst were simply another set of imperialists replacing the former set. Southern politicians believed their interests would be better served if the south were separated from the north. But this was no longer acceptable either to the British or the politicians of the north.

Meanwhile after 1948 the remaining British officials in the south and the missionaries saw the failure of all their efforts to keep the south and north apart and to resist the advance of Arabic and Islam. Accordingly they advised the southerners to insist on separation from the north. In August 1955, the Equatoria Corps (formed in 1900 with soldiers from the south) mutinied. They resented the mismanagement of affairs in the south by northern politicians and civil servants. The mutiny was put down by Arab soldiers from the north. Many Equatoria Corps soldiers took to the forest, only to return in the 1960's as the Anya-Nya guerrilla fighters.

To appease the south, northern politicians in 1955 agreed to consider a federal arrangement for the Sudan after independence. The southern representatives in the Legislative Assembly then agreed to the Declaration of Independence on 1st January, 1956.

From February 1957, the government took over all the schools run by missionaries in the south. The Roman Catholic Verona Fathers presented a thirteen-point petition expressing opposition to the government action. Their demands, if accepted, would have meant a continuation of the previous policy. Naturally they were turned down. There was a general feeling, however, that the north was dictating to the south. When the south introduced the proposal of federation, already agreed as a preliminary to independence, it was turned down by the north.

The year 1958 saw the start of the Southern Federal Party. Its objectives were to see Christianity recognized as the established religion in the south on a par with Islam, and English as a state language on a par with Arabic. It also asked for a federal organization and a different education system from that of the north.

When elections were held in 1958 the Southern Federal Party won forty seats out of forty-six in the south. It refused to accept a proposed new Sudanese constitution that did not provide for a federation.

The Years of Military Dictatorship

Meanwhile there was widespread dissatisfaction in the whole country because of the worsening economic and political situation. The army, under General Ibrahim Abboud, was invited by Prime Minister Abdulla Khalil to take over the government on 17th November, 1958. Clearly, the politicians had failed to unify the people and to lead them effectively.

During the next four years Abboud concentrated on quelling opposition throughout the Sudan. He stepped up efforts to spread Arabic and Islam in the south and Koran schools were established at an astonishing rate. Schools of all grades were established in the south to teach Arabic culture. Southerners who did not accept this policy fled to Uganda, Kenya, Ethiopia, the Central African Republic, Zaire and Brazzaville in the Congo. They included most of the intellectuals and by 1965 over 100 000 refugees had left the south. Finally, on 27th February, 1962, Christian missionaries, accused of being against the unity of the Sudan, were expelled from the southern Sudan; but missionaries in the north were allowed to remain.

The exiled intelligentsia led by J. O. Oduho, continued to resist, first with headquarters in Brazzaville and later in Kampala. They appealed to UNO and OAU for separate independence for southern Sudan. But both organizations stated that the problem was an internal one and must be resolved by the Sudanese themselves.

In 1963 the Anya-Nya terrorists appeared in the southern Sudan. These ex-soldiers of the Equatoria Corps were joined by ex-prisoners freed by the military government and others who were adventurers. They wanted to force a solution to the southern problem and began guerrilla warfare, attacking not only northern officials and soldiers but also southern collaborators. The northern army in its drive to stamp out the guerrillas killed innocent people, as happens inevitably in time of war. The war proved expensive to the north and damaging to the economy.

Revolution and a New Régime

In October 1964 the military dictatorship of General Ibrahim Abboud was overthrown by the October Revolution. The southern leaders in exile welcomed the revolution and immediately made contact with the new leaders under Prime Minister Sir El Khatim Al Khalifa. The new government stated that its aims were peace and negotiation. On 10th December, 1964, it declared a general pardon for all southern political refugees and called on them to return to the Sudan. Two ministers were sent to Kampala to negotiate with their leaders. But the situation was complicated by a split among the leaders, one group led by J. O. Oduho wanting separation from the Sudan and the other led by William Odeng wanting federation.

After much hesitation and negotiation, a round table conference was eventually arranged in Khartoum from 16th-19th March, 1965. It was attended by observers from Uganda, Kenya, Tanzania, Ghana, Nigeria, Algeria and the United Arab Republic.

The northern politicians refused both a federal arrangement and a separation but proposed a regional organization. This arrangement would establish safeguards as to the number of places in parliament and civil service posts to be reserved for southerners. It would also allocate certain powers to the south which could not be overridden by the parliament in Khartoum.

However, the majority of the southern representatives insisted on separation and independence. A deadlock was reached and discussions broke down. A committee was appointed to continue the talks but that too achieved nothing.

Between April and May 1968 there were general elections and a party known as the Southern Front was formed. It won seats in the south and together with the Union Democratic Party of the north, formed a government in Khartoum under Premier Mahgoub. This government, with considerable assistance from the United Nations Organization, began to arrange the rehabilitation of refugees. Southern Sudanese refugees now returned. They had been promised pardon, employment and the restoration of their war-torn and devastated homeland.

40 The Development of Education

Education, in the sense of the handing down of a culture, had existed in Africa long before the coming of formal schooling. Society at large, and parents in particular, undertook the transmission of a whole complex of knowledge, skills, institutions, manners, customs, laws, beliefs and values. Each individual was equipped to lead a life useful both to himself and the society to which he belonged. The characteristics of this type of 'education' were threefold: it was universal, it ensured the continuing pattern of that society – maintaining the established norms and standards by the safeguards of taboos – and it was essentially practical and directly related to actual situations. When, for example, a child was taught to distil salt, his new skill was of benefit to the family. At the same time this education, for all its merits, was demonstrably not adequate for the needs of a modern society.

Origins of the Present Education System

The first schools were established by missionaries in the mid-nineteenth century on the east coast. Among the pioneers were Dr. Ludwig Krapf, J. Erhardt and the Rev. J. Rebmann who started a school at Rabai, near Mombasa. Africans reacted with coolness and indifference and saw little purpose in the venture, accustomed as they were to their own methods of education. Similarly there was little initial success among the Arab and Swahili communities, for these Muslim peoples had their own system of schools based on the teachings of the Koran and pupils learned to read and write in Arabic.

The missionaries achieved better results among the displaced peoples on the coast who had been brought from the interior by Arab and Swahili slave traders and then freed by a British naval patrol. The mission posts in Mombasa, Zanzibar and on the mainland of Tanzania offered them the chance to learn skills so that they could support themselves. They were also taught reading, writing and simple arithmetic and the rudiments of Christianity. They settled in villages, one of the most famous being Bagamoyo, which was established by the Holy Ghost Fathers. The language of literacy was naturally the lingua franca of all the East African territories, namely Kiswahili.

In the interior, missionary activity closely followed in the wake of the travellers and traders and posts were set up to aid the spread of literacy and to instruct Africans in Christian doctrine. Education was seen as a powerful medium for influencing local peoples and an excellent example can be found in Tanganyika when it was declared a German 'sphere of influence'. The German government and missionaries together built up an extensive network of schools which at the outbreak of the First World War included primary and secondary schools and also agricultural, technical and teacher training colleges, with an overall total of 40 000 students. The scheme was of great benefit to the German administrators, whose task of government was made easier by the use of Kiswahili throughout the area and by a certain amount of indoctrination of the German point of view. There were, however, undoubted benefits to the Africans also, both socially and economically. Unfortunately, the war disrupted the school system. Fighting took place in the territory and when Britain took over the administration of Tanganyika in 1919 she had to re-establish the educational structure.

Uganda in its turn gained a system of schools, thanks largely to the efforts of the Church Missionary Society, the White Fathers, the Mill Hill Fathers and the Verona Fathers, who came from Italy to join them in 1909. The government of the protectorate encouraged the missionaries to concentrate on educating the sons and daughters of chiefs. The success of the administration depended on having educated leaders among the people and a supply of clerks as civil servants. Unfortunately there was little financial assistance for the missions in their work.

Kenya, too, by 1900 had a system of missionary schools devoted mainly to technical and agricultural subjects. But the arrival of large numbers of settlers in 1903 created a demand for European-type schools. The government decided on a policy of academic education for Asians and Europeans and vocational training for Africans – with the implication that Africans were expected to play a subordinate role. In 1911 a government education department was set up and it established technical schools for Africans at Machakos, Narok and Kabete. It also informed the missionary schools that to qualify for financial assistance they must give vocational training to Africans.

In Zanzibar political power had passed to the British by 1900. The Koran-based teaching of the Arab schools was no longer appropriate to social and economic conditions and a wider western-type curriculum was needed. Accordingly in 1907 a department of education was set up to provide schools for the Muslim population. In spite of this the missionary schools with their Christian teaching still survived to serve the needs of descendants of freed slaves and Christians arriving from the mainland.

In East Africa generally the missionaries played a large part in the expansion of education in the first two decades of the twentieth century. Chiefs helped with gifts of land and labour and supported the schools by sending their own sons there. Financial help was given to mission schools by some of the European traders.

New Developments in Education from 1925

From 1925 a change took place in East African education as government involvement increased. Two main factors lay behind this. The first was the desire to promote better social welfare and services, coupled with the fact that the colonies were becoming financially self-supporting and money was available. The second was the American-sponsored Phelps Stokes Commission of 1924-5, set up to look into the development of education in South, Central and East Africa, which urged that responsibility for it should not rest entirely with the missionaries. As a result Uganda and Tanganyika were now provided with departments of education under the direction of Eric Hussey and Stanley Rivers-Smith respectively.

With government backing, reorganization and improvement of education began. Better schools were built, teacher training and grading systems were introduced and the missionary schools also received assistance through grants. Yet many elementary schools continued without government aid, still deriving their finances from missionaries and Africans.

African Schools

Some Africans were now beginning to look critically at the education system because it took no account of earlier culture and traditions.

There was a tendency to question the basis of colonial methods of education and the implications they held for African society and political development. Resistance grew up, particularly towards the mission schools and African schools were started in Nyanza and Kikuyu. Of the two the Kikuyu took a stronger line against mission and government-run education. They felt that Africans themselves were the guardians of their historic culture and better equipped than outsiders to teach their fellow countrymen. Between 1920 and the 1950s two groups of such schools made headway. One was the Kikuyu Independent Schools Association (KISA) and the other was the Kikuyu Karinga Education Association (KKEA), with a supply of trained teachers provided by the college at Githunguri in Kiambu which was established in 1939. Their activities led to a growth of nationalist feeling in Kenya and in 1952 the majority of these schools were banned because of a suspected connection with the Mau Mau movement. The rest of them were saved by being made over to local native councils.

The 1920s also saw the rise of private schools in Uganda, sponsored by the Rev. Spartas Sebbanja Mukasa of the African Greek Orthodox Church and by Dr. B. Kalibbala. Their motive was not so much a disagreement with the character and views of missionary teaching, as a feeling that it put Africans into an inferior position. They wished to prove that they could offer an equally good education to their fellow countrymen. Despite opposition from the missionaries, on the grounds that the education was not as good as theirs and not entirely based on Christian principles, the new school system went from strength to strength. By 1960 it was drawing secondary school pupils from the whole of East Africa, Malawi, Zambia, South West Africa and the Sudan.

Opposition to Government Policy

Kenyans were strongly opposed to the government policy of giving a mainly vocational education to Africans, which condemned them to a minor and subservient place in their country's affairs. The settlers' children, on the other hand, received a type of schooling that would enable them to be the future administrators. By 1939 the battle had been won. Although the systems for African and European schools were not exactly the same, and the African schools had fewer amenities, it was now possible for the African child to receive both an academic and a vocational training.

Another subject which provoked heated debate was agricultural and technical education. One view held that not enough was provided. Yet this type of training had been offered from the colonial days throughout East Africa at primary and secondary level and in 1956 higher courses were started at the Royal Technical College of Nairobi (now the University). The trouble lay in the fact that many students of agriculture and technical subjects were faced, at the end of their training, with a shortage of suitable jobs. Some went into clerical work. Others drifted back to the land, but made such poor use of any knowledge they might have acquired that the schools were considered a failure. This was, perhaps, hardly a fair comment, since schools alone cannot bring about a revolution in agricultural methods. The problem must be tackled by society as a whole. What is more, the desire of young people in modern times to leave the land and settle in towns can be seen not only in East Africa, but in many other parts of the world.

Growth in Student Numbers after 1940

From 1940 to independence, education attracted more and more pupils at all levels, primary, secondary, teacher training colleges, agricultural and technical schools. Parents realized that education was the key to success in later life and were determined that their children should not miss the chance of schooling. Primary schools, on the whole, could cope with the increased numbers, but there were not enough secondary schools. This was one reason for the larger numbers of children who flocked to the private secondary schools in Uganda. It had not originally been thought necessary to educate East Africans to secondary and higher levels. The manpower for middle and top management would, it was assumed, come from Britain. Britain, however, had not expected the strong desire for independence after the Second World War, and plans for granting it had to be accelerated. It was then that the deficiencies of African education became clear. Very few Africans had adequate training for the task of running the country, in all its complicated political, social and economic aspects. The short-term solution was to give crash courses in Britain to those Africans who would hold essential posts in the new administration. Even so, when independence came and the Europeans left, there were few Africans with the necessary qualifications to take over.

Education after Independence

Independence brought further expansion in education. Money was borrowed from the U.S.A., Britain and the World Bank for the building of more secondary schools. Private secondary schools increased in Uganda, so that by 1970 there were over 300. Kenya also built Harambee (secondary) schools with self-help projects. Sponsorship schemes for students enabled many to attend universities overseas, so that they could return as qualified graduates to take up government posts. And the three universities of East Africa increased their numbers of students.

Syllabuses were now felt to be in need of reshaping to make them more relevant to East Africa and less Europe-oriented. The move towards this continued, though beset with the difficulties of retraining primary teachers and the lack of suitable text books, which had to be written.

The new government decided to end outside influence in education by taking schools out of the hands of missionaries and other bodies. Denominational schools were abolished, as were separate schools for Europeans, Asians and Arabs. All schools were opened to all children, whatever their race or faith. Tanzania achieved this by the Education Ordinance of 1962 and Uganda and Kenya by the Education Acts of 1963 and 1965 respectively.

Aims and Purposes of Education

As numbers of pupils in East African schools rose – in Uganda, for instance, 600 secondary pupils in 1962 had become 2000 in 1970 – a shortage of suitable jobs became apparent. The desperate need for manpower at the time of independence was now over, and posts were filled. It was seen that the fault lay in having taken over an educational system from the colonial power without relating it to the actual needs of the country. The main aim had been to produce 'white collar' workers. But a challenge was made to these accepted ideas. In 1967 Mwalimu J. K. Nyerere put forward his philosophy of 'education for self reliance'. He wished to change the whole educational system in Tanzania and give it new aims and values. 'Each school,' he said, 'should have, as an integral part of it, a farm or workshop which provides the food eaten by the community, and makes some contribution to the total national income. This is not a suggestion that a school farm or workshop should be attached to every school for training purposes. It is a suggestion that every school should be a farm and that the school community should consist of people who are both teachers and farmers and pupils and farmers.'

Dr. Milton Obote of Uganda also questioned the view that education should be merely the pathway to paid employment. Members of the Ugandan parliament felt that primary education should teach the basic skills of the three R's – in other words it should be broadly based and not a specific training for jobs. The debate on the aims and functions of education in East Africa was not easily resolved. The tendency already mentioned for school-leavers to turn away from work on the land alarmed some leaders. Various suggestions were made and in Kenya 'self-help' projects were started, using schools of technology where primary school leavers continued their studies and received practical training in rural development. The aim was to equip them to be self-employed workers in country areas.

Primary Education for All

In 1961 African Ministers of Education passed a resolution that by 1980 every child in every African country should receive primary schooling. In the following years great progress was made, despite difficulties in allocating sufficient funds to the project. Kenya and Tanzania both achieved free primary education in 1973.

University Education

The first foundation for higher education in East Africa was Makerere in Uganda, established in 1922 by the colonial government. Courses included medicine, agriculture and technical subjects. Students could also be trained as teachers and others enrolled for Cambridge School Certificate courses. In 1929 the college began to accept students from Kenya, Zanzibar and Tanganyika.

The Colonial Office's De la Warr Commission in 1937, set up to report on the needs for higher education in East Africa as a whole, gave Makerere its own administrative council and it no longer came under the Ugandan Department of Education. The result was a general upgrading of secondary schools in East Africa, from which the Makerere students came. In 1949 Makerere established links with

London University and from 1950 offered courses leading to London degrees.

Two other colleges were established – the Royal Technical College of Nairobi, founded in 1956, achieved university college status (again linked to London University) in 1959. The year 1961 saw the creation of the University College of Dar es Salaam on a similar footing. From 1964 to 1970 the three colleges jointly constituted the University of East Africa, now quite independent of London. Then, owing to the need for expanded facilities and separate institutions for each country, the three colleges became separate universities in their own right. There followed a period of great development with a dramatic rise in student numbers. In 1973 Makerere had 4500 students (compared with 850 at the time of independence), Dar es Salaam had 3500 and Nairobi 4300. As the student numbers rose the number of faculties and courses increased also, offering a wide choice of subjects and leading to the highest academic qualifications.

41 Railways in Kenya and Uganda

Construction of the Uganda Railway 1897-1901

The economic prospects of a railway that has over the years had tremendous impact on the economy and society of Kenya and Uganda were not clear to the British Parliament. After a long debate it passed the Bill on 1st August, 1896 to authorize the construction of the Uganda Railway. The cost ultimately proved to be £7 909 294. The statesmen who were persistent advocates of the project justified it on the grounds that in building the railway Britain would be honouring the agreement reached at an international conference held in 1890 at Brussels, which obliged colonial powers to build communications in order to suppress the slave trade in East Africa. To this, of course, must be added the political and strategic aspects of the imperialist policies of Britain in the last quarter of the nineteenth century. Sir Edward Grigg, Governor of Kenya from 1925 to 1930, when speaking at a dinner of the African Society in London on 15th March, 1927, threw light on this point. He said that the railway was built to provide the easiest route to Uganda, where the British aim was to establish a base in the Congo and secure control of the source of the Nile and thus, in time, the Sudan and Egypt. The railway also created the Crown Colony of Kenya.

Difficulties Encountered

The laying of the track commenced on the mainland just opposite Mombasa in 1897. For strategic reasons, it was intended to build the railway with the utmost speed. Hence under the supervision of a handful of British engineers, no fewer than 35 000 indentured Indians were put to work, building bridges and embankments and laying the rails. Despite the employment of this formidable labour force, work was slow and costly owing to the nature of the country the line had to traverse.

Lieutenant Colonel J. H. Patterson, D.S.O., an engineer on the railway, in his book the *Man-eaters of Tsavo*, vividly described instances of the demoralizing odds the railway builders had to contend with. Patterson records that two man-eating lions in the Tsavo area become such a menace that in December 1898 work was brought to a complete standstill. The lions had carried away and eaten a number of labourers with the result that the terrified workmen believed they were devils in the shape of lions. Lions also killed some engineers, including Mr. O'Hara in March 1899 at a point twelve miles from Voi, and Mr. C. H. Ryall, Superintendent of the Railway Police, in June 1900 at Kima. The railway authorities even offered a 200-rupee reward for every grown lion shot within the railway area.

By 1898 only a third of the line had been completed, and in consequence the Uganda Railway Committee in London sent out Sir Guildford Molesworth to report on progress. In his report, he stressed the difficulties railway constructors had to face. The route included steep gradients; detours had to be made to avoid prohibitive expense. He informed the committee that it was useless to expect the work to be completed in a short time. He also reported that the part of the railway which had been completed was being used by traders and travellers and that trading centres were beginning to grow up around the stations, quoting as an example the station at Voi which already had a thriving market place.

But Sir Guildford omitted to mention two subjects of complaint. The first was the unsupervised and ill-administered coolie camps. F. D. Jackson, Deputy Commissioner of Uganda, protested about the squalor, indiscipline, overcrowding and apparent vice in coolie camps. The Nandi and Lumbwa leaders often complained about the irresponsible behaviour of inmates of the labour camps and were rightly critical of the officers in charge of them.

Secondly, there was a lack of co-operation between the railway authority and the civil administration. In fact Sir Charles Eliot, Commissioner of the East Africa Protectorate 1901-1904, maintained in his book *East Africa Protectorate*, that this had been responsible for the slow progress of the construction. The Uganda Railway committee arranged that matters such as the policing, sanitation and administration of the railway zone of 1·6 km on either side of the line should be the responsibility of the railway authority. This was placing too much on the shoulders of the authority, which was heavily burdened with the problems of construction.

The Use of the Railway

Even before completion, the railway was in use, as Sir Guildford had noted. The Railway Committee too, in 1898, reported something like 28 799 passengers, while 1241 transport animals and 2468 tonnes of stores were carried by the railway.

UGANDA RAILWAY: Passengers and Goods 1898			
	Passengers		Tonnes
Military personnel and porters	25 529	Goods carried (largely imports)	5945
Ordinary passengers			
1st Class	70		
2nd Class	200		
3rd Class	3 000		
	28 799		

As the rails advanced so did imports, but the Mombasa-bound traffic still remained disappointing. For example, in 1899 the railway carried from Mombasa 91 235 tonnes of goods as against 470 tonnes carried to Mombasa. Ivory, hides, skins and horns were still the major items of export, but now their volume far exceeded what had previously been carried by porters.

From Nairobi to Kisumu 1899-1901

On 30th May, 1899, the line reached Nairobi where a base-camp was built for the materials to be used when building the stretch to Lake Victoria. There was no indication then that this frog-infested swamp, although at a height of 1524 m above sea-level, would in future be the site of the largest city in East Africa. Building the line from Nairobi was no light task. The work involved making the line descend on to the Nandi plateau, and finally descend to the low-lying Nyanza Province where its terminus was to be.

It was on this last lap of the line that the railway builders met with the first serious opposition on the part of Kenyans to the building of the railway through their homeland. In 1900 the Nandi are reported to have made a number of raids on stores and the railway line. Three punitive expeditions were sent by the railway authority. The first two were on a minor scale and as they had no effect a third and major expedition was organized to go and discipline the Nandi once and for all. In July 1900, Colonel Evatt, commanding a company of Indian troops, advanced from Kisumu to Nandi country. The young Nandi warriors evaded the Indian troops and instead launched an attack on a patrol of Sudanese infantry at Fort Ternan, killing nine of them. Near Eldama Ravine they ambushed and killed twenty Sudanese soldiers who had been escorting Uganda mail to the railway. The Indian troops captured Nandi cattle, which they hoped would pay for the damage done to the property of the railway authority, but in a determined night attack the Nandi warriors not only recovered their cattle but inflicted severe casualties on the troops who fled back to base. For several years the Nandi continued to harass the railway builders until they were eventually subdued.

In December 1901, the first train arrived in Kisumu from Mombasa. Although the railway was destined to reach Uganda, it stopped at Kisumu in Kenya and for many years from 1902 it was connected to that part of Uganda west of Jinja by steamer services on Lake Victoria. A number of steamers on Lake Victoria of capacities varying between 150 and 525 tonnes were introduced. The boats called at Entebbe, Port Bell, Kibanga, Jinja and several ports which were afterwards established.

More Railway Lines Built before 1931

In Kenya, railway lines were built to serve newly settled areas:

Nairobi to Thika 1913
Nakuru across the Gishu Plateau to Eldoret
Eldoret to Uganda and branches to Solai and Kitale 1926
Branch to Thomson Falls.

In Uganda a short line of six miles was built and completed in 1913 to connect the rapidly-growing town of Kampala with Port Bell, while the Jinja to Namasagali line was open to trains in 1914; in those days a number of short distance lines were recommended, although not built. When at last the Nile was bridged at Jinja in 1931, the long-awaited Mombasa to Kampala railway was complete.

More Railways built in Uganda after 1931: Western and Northern Extensions

In 1951 work started on the line from Kampala to Kasese, a distance of 345 km. It had always been the desire of the Government to have a link joining Kampala and the Congo borders, but money was never readily available. Lengthy discussions took place as to what route the line should take, but finally the Katonga route was approved. The line was opened for traffic in 1956. Since then the line has provided transport facilities for the Kilembe mines, whose copper contributes to the economy. A northern extension to serve the district of Lango, Acholi and West Nile was built after independence.

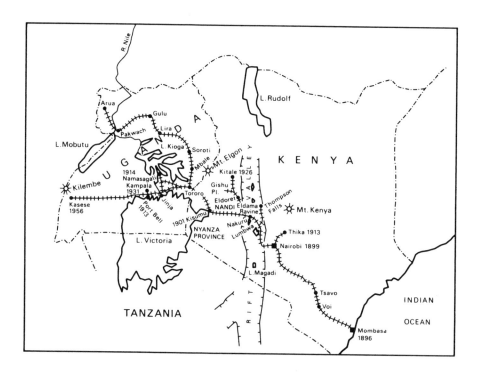

Development of Uganda and Kenya Railway System

The Economic Significance of the Uganda Railway and Later Railways

The Uganda railway considerably reduced transport costs and linked Kenya and Uganda with world trade. Before 1902, exports and imports alike had to be carried by porters to and from Mombasa and the cost, low as the rates were then, exceeded 600/- per tonne. With the railway in operation it cost 48/- to transport a tonne from Kisumu to Mombasa, and the journey, instead of taking three months, took about six days. Apart from providing easy and cheap transport of goods the railway also offered passenger facilities so that traders and administrators could reach a number of places in Kenya and Uganda in a short time, and mail could be despatched on the line with a speed hitherto unheard of in East Africa. The figures in the table given below illustrate the magnitude of the development of export trade in the first eleven years of the line's existence.

Year	1902	1907	1913
Value of Exports	£29 450	£178 608	£607 253

It should be noted that cotton contributed largely to this rise.

The Uganda Railway, built without a thorough survey, had cost the British Government a lot of money and in the attempt to make it pay its way administrators like Sir Charles Eliot and game-hunters like Lord Delamere, publicized the opportunities for farming in Kenya. Consequently, from 1903 there was an influx of settlers from England and South Africa who occupied the richest land in the country. While it is true that white settlement caused discontent among African Kenyans, the fact is that settlers transformed the face of the country and in less than twenty-five years established an economy which in many ways contributed to the prosperity of Kenya.

The Uganda Railway was important as the biggest employer of regular paid labour, particularly in Kenya and to some extent in Uganda. But for many years Africans could only get unskilled manual jobs. When construction was started the skilled and clerical labour – and surprisingly most of the unskilled labour – was brought from India. Even after the railway had been completed the practice of employing Indian staff continued. Recruits from India filled all artisan and clerical posts as well as the positions of locomotive drivers, station masters and traffic managers.

It is surprising that the railway authority who were well aware that the railway brought no quick return of money should have let this expensive arrangement continue. For example, Indian artisans were paid from 80-350 florins a month, were given rations, housing accommodation (or an allowance in lieu) ranging from 25 florins for a bachelor to 45 florins for a married man, plus free passages for the man and his family to and from the place of recruitment. The railway authority also paid one-sixteenth of a man's pay into a provident fund and gave him three-months' leave with full pay. The railway authority also paid heavy charges to the recruiting agents in India.

It is even more surprising that the railway authority should have been blind to the economic and political danger of drawing the bulk of their staff from a different country. It seems odd that little, if any, interest and initiative was shown in training East Africans. Railway authorities used to explain that there were two main obstacles.

In the first place, East Africans had a habit of returning and retiring to their villages when they had earned enough to keep them for some months or to get a wife and settle down. This was understandable, because often the East African was provided with indifferent housing. Employees were lodged in large barracks. The standard of accommodation, it seems, prevented the African employee from wishing to stay in his job permanently. The other difficulty was that the East African worker returned periodically to his village for festivals and harvest purposes. This again was not really a valid reason for not employing him, for the periodic visits could have been covered by leave regulations.

For many years, therefore, the African railway worker remained in the category of porter and Africans holding posts of station masters or clerks appeared on the scene only after many years.

Lastly, as far as Uganda was concerned, the railway resulted in a drive to grow more cotton and by the year the railway reached Kampala, cotton was picked from over a million acres and expansion was still going on. Again, for nearly thirty years a number of Ugandan ports on Lake Victoria assumed importance as they handled greater quantities of exports and imports. Furthermore, the railway encouraged greater efforts to improve the road network of Uganda so that roads could serve as feeders to the Lake Victoria Services which were linked with the railway. Even after the wide use of road transport, the original railway and those constructed later have continued to play a major role in the economy of Kenya and Uganda. Heavy goods, for example cotton and coffee exports, have over the years continued to be carried by the railway. The bulk of imports, for instance cars and heavy industrial equipment, are brought up country by the railway.

The Impact of Railways upon Society in Kenya and Uganda

Since the construction of Mombasa to Kisumu line, East Africans have enjoyed a mobility previously not available to them. When Kampala was linked to Mombasa by railway in 1931 the volume of traffic changed as shown in the following table:

Year	Passengers	Goods Tonnage
1926	991 753	193 849
1927	1 065 225	168 094
1928	1 102 110	152 002
1929	1 161 770	188 611
1930	1 106 106	148 596
1931	768 224	93 226
1932	558 492	71 611
1933	524 771	766 365
1934	493 818	728 706
1935	487 419	849 795

Passenger traffic decreased in the 1930's because of the slump and because fast road transport was developing, but freight increased.

Railways have made possible the distribution of newspapers. Ugandans and Kenyans have over many years been able to exchange newspapers and the facilities offered by the railways for the despatch of mail have only recently been superseded by an air mail service.

With the establishment of the East Africa Community the railway systems of Kenya, Uganda and Tanzania (see next chapter) were jointly administered by the East African Railways Corporation.

42 Railways in Tanganyika 1900-63

Construction of the Railway System

In 1887, persuaded by of Dr. Carl Peters, the German East African Company asked for a surveyor, Von Hacke, to find out whether a railway could be built to connect Dar es Salaam and Morogoro. In 1891, a meeting of well-known African explorers under the chairmanship of Wilhelm Oechelhauser, a director of the German East Africa Company, strongly recommended that when constructed this railway should be extended to Lakes Tanganyika and Victoria. Construction was delayed for some time while the advantages and disadvantages of colonial railways were debated.

After the Uganda Railway had reached Kisumu, practically all the trade to and from the German part of the Lake region was being fast diverted to Mombasa. It was only then that the Germans stopped quibbling and considered linking ports on the Indian Ocean coast to their enormous hinterland by railway. The primary purpose was not to build strategical railways, as has been suggested by some writers, but to promote peaceful and quick penetration into the territory. The Germans wanted to build three railways:

1. A railway from Tanga to the foot of Kilimanjaro and from there to Meru. This was started in 1891 with private capital.
2. From the capital Dar es Salaam to Lake Tanganyika – but with Morogoro as the terminus in the first phase.
3. A line to link Kilwa with Lake Malawi. This project was finally abandoned.

Construction of the Tanga to Moshi Line

In 1891 it was decided by German authorities to build a metre-gauge line from Tanga to Muheza as a first stage and extend it later to Korogwe. It was part of the plan to continue the line to Tabora and then to a terminal on the shores of Lake Victoria, but there was no indication of the route to be taken. Although construction started in 1893, progress was so slow, because of labour problems and lack of adequate funds, that it was not until 1895 that the line reached Muheza – about 40 km from Tanga. For three years after this, there was no further progress and the line reached Korogwe in 1902 and Moshi in 1911.

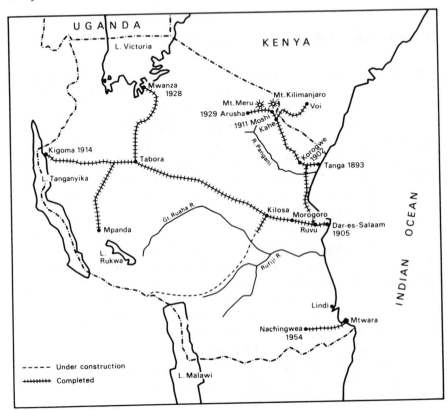

Development of Tanganyika Railway System

The Tanga line which had taken about eighteen years to build at great cost, was seriously damaged and its bridges destroyed by the Germans themselves during the First World War in 1916.

Construction of the Central Line, Dar es Salaam to Kigoma

After Dar es Salaam had been made the capital of the German

Protectorate, and after lengthy discussion and administrative delays, a private company with a capital of one million pounds was given permission to construct a metre-gauge line from Dar es Salaam to Morogoro in the first instance, and later on to Lake Tanganyika. The German government in Berlin guaranteed interest on the company's capital and conferred powers and rights on the contracting company for prospecting and mining in the area adjacent to the proposed line. The company was told it could be expected to take an active part in providing large hotels at Dar es Salaam, Tabora and Kigoma and encouraging tourists. Further, the provision of electric light, power and marine services on Lake Tanganyika was part of the project.

Construction began in 1905 and after many difficulties Morogoro was reached in 1907. With the experience gained so far it was possible in only seven years to undertake and complete the extension to Kigoma. In 1914 it was thus possible to travel by railway all the way from Dar es Salaam to Kigoma.

German railway planners thought of constructing a line from Tabora to the southern shores of Lake Victoria and if possible to Rwanda and Burundi, which then were part of the German Protectorate. The other idea was to build a line from Kilosa to Iringa and eventually have it extended to Rhodesia through Mbeya. The war of 1914 prevented the Germans from carrying out these plans, since after it they ceased to control Tanganyika.

Tanganyika Railways 1919–1939

During the 1914-18 war, the Germans destroyed most of their work. All the bridges between Dar es Salaam and Kigoma were blown up. Army engineers repaired the damaged parts, however, and the Central line was in use during certain periods of the war.

After the war, the control of Tanganyika Railways and Ports Services was assigned to the British civil administration which had to look after:

1. The Tanga to Moshi 352 km metre-gauge line.
2. The Central line, Dar es Salaam to Tabora 840 km of metre-gauge. (The Tabora to Kigoma section of 360 km, captured by the Belgians in 1916, remained in their hands until 1921.)
3. The Sigi branch, 23 km of 75-cm gauge.
4. The Lindi Tramway, 95 km 60-cm gauge (hardly usable for some time.)

5. The Voi line, 151 km, most of it in Kenya.
6. The ports of Dar es Salaam and Tanga.

The British civil administration had a difficult time. As a result of the war, there was a considerable amount of confusion to clear up, and organization needed to make the services usable for peacetime conditions. Although in the first year of their operation under the British civil administration the railways carried 248 000 passengers and 44 000 tonnes of goods, the working expenditure of £285 000 was more than double the total revenue of £108 000.

In short, the railways were being operated at a disturbingly great loss. It is possible to suggest some reasons for this. First of all, after the 1914-18 war Tanganyika Railways, previously a commercial concern supported by loans from the German Protectorate, now became the responsibility of a government department. The resulting large increase in staff, particularly in the clerical and accountancy sections, and the consequent rise in the wages bill meant that working expenses were now much higher.

Secondly, although the Germans had hoped to use the Central line to Kigoma to capture some of the mineral traffic of the Katanga District (then partly Belgian Congo), this was never realized while they administered Tanganyika nor was it achieved when the British took over. The Central line continued to have an alarmingly low traffic density as it passed through undeveloped country most of the way.

Thirdly, although by 1933 new lines had been pushed into potential producing areas (for example, the Tabora-Mwanza line to the Lake province completed in 1928 and Moshi-Arusha completed in 1929) this did not improve the revenue position. The bulk of the trade of the two most productive parts of Tanganyika was captured by Uganda-Kenya Railways and Steamer services because good coffee-curing factories had been established at Nairobi and Mombasa. Moreover Uganda-Kenya Railways had better freight-handling facilities than Tanganyika Railways. Consequently the products of the Kilimanjaro and Meru plantations were drawn into Kenya by the Voi-Kahe link. In addition the Uganda-Kenya steamer services were better organized than the Tanganyika launch services and therefore handled the African produced coffee in the Bukoba area around Lake Victoria. The Tabora-Mwanza line and the Mwanza port itself therefore became less and less used. The Uganda-Mwanza Railways administration seems to have foreseen this and had protested against the construction of the Tabora-Mwanza line, arguing that the services the administration had established were capable of handling all traffic in the provinces around Lake Victoria.

From 1930-31 there were signs of moderate improvement. For instance, whereas in 1922 goods traffic had been 60 000 tonnes in 1930-1 it rose to 320 000 tonnes. The depression of 1932-33, however, hit Tanganyika Railways severely. It became necessary to curtail expenses by dismissing many workers of all races. Of the 316 European employees only 174 were retained. Asian numbers dropped from 1140 to 495, and African from 11 400 to 7070. The administration borrowed money for essential re-equipment and closed down branches that were not of metre-gauge.

When the Railway Advisory Council was set up in 1932 the Tanganyika Railway system had been cut down to four lines:
1. Central line, Dar es Salaam to Kigoma 1248 km (728 miles)
2. Tabora–Mwanza line 378 km (236 miles)
3. Manyoni–Kinyangiri 151 km (93 miles) – closed 1947
4. Tanga–Arusha 435·2 km (272 miles)

Before the Second World War of 1939-45, with strict economies and efficient management the railways could just maintain themselves in a satisfactory financial position and that was all.

Amalgamation with Kenya and Uganda Railways

Tanganyika Railways and Port Services and Kenya and Uganda Railways and Harbours were generally amalgamated under the East African High Commission from 1948 to 1950 under an Act made by 'the High Commission with the Assent of the Assembly'. The two transport systems became 'East African Railways and Harbours.' As Kenya and Uganda Railways were financially in a stronger position, projects in Tanganyika could now be taken up with vigour.

Railways Built After 1945
The Mpanda Branch

As the map indicates, this short line runs for about 210 km in a south-westward direction from the Central line. It started operating in 1950. The purpose was to carry lead ore from the mine at Mpanda. After nine years of operation of the lead mine at Mpanda it was unfortunately established that the original estimate of the deposit of some two million tonnes had been incorrect. Although the lead traffic had risen from 1600 tonnes in 1951 to 14 248 tonnes in 1960, it was then discovered that the supply of profitable workable ore had been exhausted. The railway was used to carry away mining equipment from Mpanda in 1961 when the mine was closed.

The railway remained after the closure of the mine but in the period under review there was little evidence to indicate its impact on the economic activity of the area. During the mine's peak output there was a thriving retail trade but many traders left when it closed. The main activity around Mpanda remained subsistence agriculture.

Southern Province Railway

At the inception of the abortive government groundnuts scheme a railway was constructed from the port of Mtwara to Nachingwea, about 211 km away, to carry groundnuts. The advocates of the scheme thought the crop would be produced in thousands of tonnes a year. When the grandiose groundnut scheme collapsed in 1949 the construction of the railway continued, however. The line was opened in 1954.

The expectation in official circles that this southern railway would be followed by considerable economic development proved false. Development in the province from 1951 to 1957 was at a slower rate than in most other parts of the territory. In the period under review, the production of cashew nuts, the main crop in the area, providing a regular traffic for the railway, was no more impressive than agricultural production in areas which lacked railways. As most of the sisal estates are far from the railway, the line handled very little of the sisal exported from the area. In the southern province, which is relatively well populated and suited to agriculture, it is surprising that the railway did not give rise to agricultural development as would have been expected.

With the gradual improvement of road services after 1950 and relatively cheap lorry transport, the railway did not benefit the province. While it is true that passenger traffic yielded about £15 000 a year, this was insignificant compared with the losses of between £210 000 and £250 000 each year in the period 1955-61.

DATE CHART OF IMPORTANT EVENTS IN EAST AFRICAN HISTORY

A.D.

1st Century	Migrating Bantu peoples settled on East African coast
	The Periplus of the Erythrean Sea was written
	The Geography of Ptolemy was written
7th Century	Arabs from Oman and Shiraz settled in Pemba and Zanzibar
	Settlers arrived in Ethiopia from the Yemen
	Arab conquest of Egypt and Syria
8th Century	740 Zaidiyah Arabs arrived on East African coast
9th Century	850 Revolt of African slaves in Mesopotamia
	869 Revolt of African slaves in Persia
12th Century	Establishment of Shirazi dynasties on East African coast
13th Century	Batembuzi rule in Bunyoro-Kitara
14th Century	Bachwezi rule in Bunyoro-Kitara.
15th Century	1498 Vasco da Gama reached the East African coast
	Beginning of Portuguese influence
16th Century	1557 First Jesuit teachers entered Ethiopia
17th Century	1600 Moru-Madi migration to West Nile began
	1650 Start of Hinda dynasty in Ankole
	1680 Lugbara expansion in West Nile began
	1698 Fall of Mombasa to Oman.
	End of Portuguese rule in East Africa
18th Century	Large increase in slave trade
	1798 British treaty with Oman
19th Century	1806 Seyyid Said became ruler of Oman
	1822 Moresby Treaty between Britain and Zanzibar

257

19th Century
(*continued*)

1830 Kingdom of Toro founded by Prince Kaboyo

1840 Seyyid Said settled in Zanzibar

1844 Dr. Ludwig Krapf opened CMS Mission at Rabai

1845 Hammerton Treaty against slavery

1855 Emperor Theodore came to the throne in Ethiopia

1856 Sultan Majid succeeded Seyyid Said
Burton and Speke expedition to seek source of Nile

1862 Anglo-French Agreement on Zanzibar

1863 Ismail became Khedive of Egypt

1866 Livingstone's expedition to seek source of Nile

1867 Napier's military force entered Ethiopia

1868 Holy Ghost Fathers set up station in Bagamoyo

1870 Omukama Kabarega succeeded to throne of Bunyoro
Sultan Barghash came to throne of Zanzibar

1871 Meeting of Stanley and Livingstone at Ujiji

1873 End of slave trade in Zanzibar

1877 CMS group arrived in Kampala

1881 Rise of the Mahdi

1884 Berlin Conference

1885 Death of Gordon at Khartoum

1886 Anglo-German Agreement

1887 Imperial British East Africa Company formed

1888 Abushiri Revolt in Tanganyika

1890 Anglo-German Agreement, Brussels

1890 Zanzibar became British Protectorate

1894 Uganda became British Protectorate

1895 Kenya became British Protectorate

1896 Fashoda Incident
Defeat of Italians at Adowa

1897 African Hut Tax Imposed in Tanganyika

20th Century

1900 Buganda Agreement

1902 Village Headmen Ordinance

1903 Conquest of Burundi by the Germans

1905 Maji Maji Rebellion in Tanganyika

1910 King Mumia of the Wanga made Paramount Chief of N. Kavirondo

1914 Dar es Salaam–Kigoma Railway completed

1914-1918 First World War

1919 Tanganyika became British controlled mandated territory

Tanganyika African Association founded (later TANU)

1921 First session of Uganda Legislative Council

1924-5 Phelps Stokes Commission on Education

1924 Kikuyu Central Association founded

1925 Local Native Councils set up in Kenya

1929 Native Land Trust Bill

1930 Haile Selassie became Emperor of Ethiopia

1936 Italian conquest of Ethiopia

1939-1945 Second World War

1941 Ethiopia regained independence

1946 Jomo Kenyatta became President of Kenya African Union

1948 East Africa High Commission

1950 Outbreak of Mau Mau revolt in Kenya

1953 Self rule declared for Sudan

Muteesa II of Buganda deposed and deported to Britain

1955 Buganda Agreement

1961 9th December Tanganyika became independent

1962 9th October Uganda became independent

1963 12th December Kenya became independent, Kenyatta President

1963 University of East Africa set up

1964 Overthrow of military dictatorship in Sudan

20th Century
(continued)

1964 Zanzibar became a republic

1964 Formation of Tanzania

1967 June, Treaty for East African Co-operation

1970 Universities of Dar es Salaam, Makerere-Kampala and Nairobi set up

1971 25th January Army take-over in Uganda under Maj. Gen. Idi Amin Dada

1974 Army take-over in Ethiopia

1975 TanZam railway opened

Some of the most useful books consulted in the preparation of this text

R. Oliver	*The Missionary Factor in East Africa* (Longman).
Editors: B. A. Ogot & J. A. Kieran	*Zamani – A Survey of East African History* (EAPH/ Longmans).
J. J. Mbotela	*The Freeing of the Slaves in East Africa* (Evans Brothers Ltd, London).
B. A. Ogot	*A History of the Southern Luo*, Vols. I & II (The East African Publishing House).
Merick Posnansky	*Prelude to East African History* (Oxford University Press).
Charles Richards & James Place	*East African Explorers* (Oxford University Press).
E. R. Vere-Hodge & P. Collister	*Pioneers of East Africa* (African Literature Bureau).
E. R. Vere-Hodge	*Imperial British East Africa Co.* (East African Literature Bureau).
J. Wild	*The Uganda Mutiny 1897* (E. A. Literature Bureau).
F. H. Goldsmith	*John Ainsworth – Pioneer Kenya Administrator* (E. A. Literature Bureau).
Editor: A. Roberts,	*Tanzania before 1900* (East African Publishing House).
Boxer & Azevedo	*Fort Jesus and the Portuguese in Mombasa* (Hollis & Carter).
Elspeth Huxley	*Settlers of Kenya* (Longman).
John Osogo	*The Baluyia* (Oxford University Press E. A.).
John Middleton & J. Campbell	*Zanzibar – Its Society and Its Politics* (Oxford University Press).
R. Coupland	*East Africa and Its Invaders*, Vols. I & II (Oxford University Press).
J. N. Kimambo & J. I. Temu	*A History of Tanzania* (East African Publishing House).
A. Roberts (Editor)	*Tanzania Before 1900* (East African Publishing House).
C. Seligman	*Races of Africa* (third edition) (Oxford University Press).

Sir John Gray	*Early Portuguese Missionaries in East Africa* (East African Literature Bureau).
James Frederick	*Elton and the East African Coast Slave-Trade* (East African Literature Bureau).
J. A. Hunter & Dan Mannix	*African Bush Adventures* (Hamish Hamilton).
L. W. Hollingsworth	*The Asians of East Africa* (Macmillan).
L. W. Hollingsworth	*A Short History of the East Coast of Africa* (Macmillan).
K. Ingham	*A History of East Africa* (Longman).
K. Ingham	*The Making of Modern Uganda* (Longman).
Zoe Marsh	*East Africa Through Contemporary Records* (Cambridge University Press).
Editors: R. Oliver & G. Mathew	*History of East Africa*, Vol. I (Oxford University Press).
Editors: V. Harlow, E. M. Chilvers, & Alison Smith	*History of East Africa*, Vol. II (Oxford University Press).
J. C. Taylor	*The Political Development of Tanzania* (Oxford University Press).
G. S. Were & D. A. Wilson	*East Africa Through 1000 Years* (Evans).
M. S. M. Kiwanuka	*Muteesa of Uganda* (East African Literature Bureau).
A. R. Dunbar	*A History of Bunyoro Kitara* (Oxford University Press).
K. M. Stahl	*History of the Chagga People of Kilimanjaro* (Mouton & Co.).
Editor: Robert I. Rotberg	*Travels, Researches and Missionary Labours in East Africa* (Frank Cass & Co.).
G. S. T. Freeman-Grenville	*East African Coast – selected documents* (Oxford University Press).
Elspeth Huxley & Margery Perham	*Peace and Politics in Kenya* (Faber).
Government of Kenya	*Kenya Land Commission – Evidence*, Vols. I, II and III.
A. F. Calvert	*German East Africa* (T. Werner Laurie Ltd).
Judith Listowell	*The Making of Modern Tanganyika* (Chatto & Windus).
J. Gray	*History of Zanzibar from the Middle Ages to 1856* (Oxford University Press).
J. Strander	*The Portuguese Period in East Africa* (East African Literature Bureau).

G. S. Were   *Western Kenya – Historical Texts* (East African Literature Bureau).

D. Apter   *The Political Kingdom in Uganda* (Princeton University Press).

H. Brode   *Tippoo Tib* (Edward Arnold).

C. H. Stigand   *The Land of Zinj* (Frank Cass & Co.).

Editors: J. C. Anene & G. Brown   *Africa in the Nineteenth and Twentieth Centuries.*

The Survey Dept. of Kenya   *Atlas of Kenya*, First Edition.

Dept. of Lands and Survey – Tanzania   *Atlas of Tanganyika*, Third Edition.

Dept. of Lands and Survey – Uganda   *Atlas of Uganda*, Third Edition.

Sir Harold Macmichael   *The Sudan* (Ernest Benn Ltd.).

Sir Samuel W. Baker   *Ismailia* (Macmillan and Co.).

John Hyslop   *Sudan Story* (Naldrett Press).

K. D. D. Henderson   *The Making of the Modern Sudan* (Faber and Faber).

David Thomson   *Europe Since Napoleon* (Longman).

J. Gunther   *Inside Africa* (Hamish Hamilton).

Lord Hailey   *African Survey* (Oxford University Press).

E. B. Cromer   *Modern Egypt* (Macmillan and Co.).

R. Oliver & J. D. Fage   *A Short History of Africa* (Penguin Books).

Mohammad Omer Beshir   *The Southern Sudan, Background to Conflict* (C. Hurst and Co.).

Bashir Mohammad Said   *The Sudan – Crossroads of Africa* (The Bodley Head).

Oliver Albino   *The Sudan – A Southern Viewpoint* (Oxford University Press).

N.B. These questions are meant to test the initiative of students, rather than to call upon them to reproduce exactly what they have read in each chapter.

One – Geography and its Influence on East African History

1. Choose any climatic area in East Africa and show how the climate has conditioned the kind of politics and occupation of the different peoples.
2. How much did East African lakes and rivers in the past help the contact of peoples of different areas in East Africa?

Two – The Peoples of East Africa

Attempt to trace how and when the different linguistic groups of people started to inhabit their present areas in East Africa.

Three – The Kingdoms of Lake Victoria (or the Interlacustrine Kingdoms) 1250-1650

1. What was the significance of mythology in the interlacustrine Kingdoms?
2. What was the impact of the Luo on the empire of Bunyoro-Kitara?
3. The royal drums were some of the important regalia in the interlacustrine kingdoms. Try to find out about other regalia in these kingdoms.
4. How did the Hinda Kingdoms in Tanzania lose their power during the German Colonial days?

Four – The West Nile

1. Trace the migrations of the Lugbara from the Juba region to what is today Lugbaraland.
2. Describe the economic and military way of life of the Lugbara.
3. Account for the ascendancy of the Alur in their rivalry with the Lugbara.

Five – City States on the East African Coast up to 1497

1. Why was it so easy for the East African Coast to be in contact with India and Arabia?

2. Account for the rise of Swahili culture on the East Coast from the ninth century.

3. Account for the rise and fall of the City States on the East Coast.

4. Why did the Coast have little contact with the interior before 1840?

Six – The Eastern Bantu Peoples of Kenya and Tanzania

Try to find out from old people how each tribe came into existence and finally started to occupy its present area.

Seven – Kalenjin Peoples

1. How did the Nandi rise over the other Kalenjin during this period?

2. What part did the laibon play in the social and political life of the Masai?

3. Ask old people about the early relationship between the Karamojong and the Iteso and account for the reasons why these two peoples with the same ancestry have become so different over the years.

Eight – The Luo-Speaking Peoples in East Africa

Try to find out from old people how each group of the Luo cluster came into existence and started to occupy the area it occupies now.

Nine – The Interlacustrine Kingdoms 1650-1900

1. Account for the rise of Buganda from the second half of the seventeenth century to the beginning of the nineteenth century.

2. How did the British destroy the enthusiasm of the Banyoro and yet encourage that of the Baganda from 1890 to 1900?

3. How did the Bagabe of Ankole enlarge their kingdom from the eighteenth century to 1900?

4. How did the Kingdom of Toro manage to keep its independence from 1830 to 1900?

Ten – The Portuguese in East Africa North of the Ruvuma

1. Relate the events which led to the rule of Portugal being established on the East African coast by 1508.

2. Why were the Portuguese less successful as traders than the Arabs and Africans?

3. What was the result of the rivalry between the Sultans of Mombasa and Malindi?

4. Give reasons for the decline of Portuguese power after 1635.

Eleven – The Struggle Between the Mazrui Family and the Busaidi Dynasty of Oman on the East African Coast

1. Name the territories under the rule of Oman and those under the rule of Mazrui by 1810.

2. How did Seyyid Said build up his commercial empire based on Zanzibar?

3. What were the trading activities of the Americans and Germans?

Twelve – the Slave and Ivory Trade

1. Why did the volume of slave trade grow between the mid-seventeenth century and 1840?

2. How far did the supply routes of the ivory and slave trade go from the coast into the interior of East and Central Africa and what was the effect of this trade in East Africa from the very beginning to 1875?

Thirteen – The Suppression of the Slave Trade

1. Imagine you are somebody captured from West Africa, then taken to the West Indies and finally to England as a domestic servant. Write a letter about your life.

2. What efforts did Britain make to stop the slave trade?

3. What steps did Britain take to limit the slave trade in East Africa and how far were these steps successful?

4. How did the suppression of the slave trade in East Africa affect the political, social and economic situation of the Sultan of Zanzibar and his subjects?

Fourteen – The Impact of the Ngoni Invasion on East Africa

What circumstances helped Mirambo to create and maintain an empire?

Fifteen – The Empire of Mirambo

1. Try to find out the military tactics of the Zulus and how much they differed from those of other Africans in Central and East Africa.

2. How did the coming of the Ngoni into East Africa affect the history of Southern and Western Tanzania?

Sixteen – European Travellers in the Interior of East Africa

1. What was the purpose of Europeans in visiting the interior of East Africa during this period? Was there some benefit in the growth of scientific knowledge?

2. Try to find out the local names for Lake Victoria.

3. What was the effect of Livingstone's journeys?

Seventeen – Christian Missionaries

1. Why was it necessary for the missionaries to give shelter to the freed slaves during this period and how did the missionaries treat them?

2. What kind of treatment did the missionaries usually receive at the hands of the African chiefs and Arabs?

Eighteen – European Traders

1. Why was it difficult for European traders to establish themselves in the interior before the Europeans set up their governments there?

2. What led European countries to take over the administration of East Africa in the late nineteenth century?

Nineteen – The Scramble for Colonies

1. Give reasons why the European powers attempted to secure colonies in Africa in the second half of the nineteenth century.
2. What were Leopold's aims in Africa?
3. What were the provisions of the Berlin Conference?

Twenty – The Egyptian Scramble for East Africa

1. Estimate the relative success and failure of Sir Samuel Baker's work as Governor of the Equatorial Provinces and as explorer and envoy for the Egyptian Khedive.
2. What were the abortive negotiations between Gordon and Muteesa I?
3. What events finally led to the withdrawal of Egyptian expansionism?

Twenty-one – European Colonization of East Africa

1. What was the importance of Fashoda in the rivalry between France and Britain in the Nile valley?
2. What were the provisions of the Anglo-German Agreement of 1886?
3. Outline the final partition of East Africa agreed at the Anglo-German Conference in Brussels in 1890.

Twenty-two – European Teachers Come to Uganda

1. What was the result of Stanley's meeting with King Muteesa I?
2. Describe the achievements and difficulties encountered by Mackay in his Christian and educational work in Uganda.
3. Why did Christianity come to be distrusted at the Uganda court?

Twenty-three – Uganda Becomes a Protectorate

1. Outline the difficulties which faced Lugard after his return from the north to Kampala in 1890.
2. Why was the Imperial British East Africa Company replaced by the British government in the administration of Uganda?

Twenty-four – Uganda 1894–1920

1. How did the British defeat Omukama Kabarega, Kabaka Mwanga II and Awich of Acholi?
2. What kind of help did Kakungula give to the British?
3. How did the Sudanese soldiers come to Uganda and what part did they play in the early history of the Uganda Protectorate?
4. How did each part of Uganda come under the Protectorate?
5. How did the educational and economic life of Uganda develop from 1900?

Twenty-five – Kenya 1895–1920

1. Describe the strategy used by the British in subduing the Kenya tribes.

2. Why was the system of British administration through local chiefs and councils of elders unpopular among the Kenya Africans?
3. What was the effect of white settlement on the Masai?
4. How was European settlement consolidated after World War I?

Twenty-six – Kenya 1920-40

1. How did the British administration exploit tribal rivalries to consolidate its power?
2. To what extent was the land question a source of grievance among the Kenya Africans?
3. Describe the activities of the Kikuyu Central Association in its opposition to the colonial system.

Twenty-seven – Tanganyika under the Germans

1. What was the reason for the Abushiri revolt and how was it crushed?
2. Describe the administrative problems of the German governor appointed in 1891.
3. Outline the resistance encountered by the Germans between 1891 and 1894.

Twenty-eight – The Maji Maji Rebellion

1. What were the causes of the Maji Maji rebellion?
2. Give reasons for the failure of the rebellion.

Twenty-nine – After Maji Maji

1. How did von Rechenberg's policy conflict with the views of the German settlers?
2. In what ways was Tanganyika prosperous between the years 1906 and 1914?
3. What was the effect of the First World War on Tanganyika?

Thirty – Uganda 1920-39

1. How did the Legislative Council originate in Uganda and why did the Africans react to it as they did?
2. How did some Baganda and the Buganda Provincial Officers react to the terms of the 1900 Buganda Agreement?
3. The Kingdom of Bunyoro was the oldest and had dominated most of Uganda's political affairs for a long time before the seventeenth century. Account for its apparent apathy during the colonial period.
4. Why was there less agitation against the political administration outside Buganda during this period?
5. What prevented Uganda from becoming a planters' country?
6. Discuss the economic situation of Uganda during this period.
7. How did the Government's greater participation in education from 1925 affect the education system in Uganda?

Thirty-one – Tanganyika 1920-39

1. How did Sir Donald Cameron organize Tanganyika from 1925 to 1930?
2. How did indirect rule work in Tanganyika and what complaints were made against it by the Africans?
3. Trace the origins of nationalist movements in Tanganyika.
4. Why did the economy of Tanganyika not revive quickly enough after the First World War?

Thirty-two – Zanzibar 1890-1964

1. Why did the British Resident in Zanzibar take over control of the political administration from the Arabs in 1891?
2. Why did Africans start to feel that the opportunities in Zanzibar were mainly for the Arabs?
3. Why did the Arabs think of an Arab nationalist movement rather than a nationalist movement of all citizens of Zanzibar from the 1940's?

Thirty-three – Islam in East Africa

1. What were Muhammad ibn Abdullah ibn Battuta's observations on Mombasa in the fourteenth century?
2. Account for the increase in prosperity on the coast resulting from the invasion of the Omani rulers?
3. Why did education develop more slowly among the Muslim people in East Africa than in the Christian communities?
4. Account for the conversion of so many people in East Africa to the Islamic faith.

Thirty-four – Uganda 1939-75

1. How did the riots of 1945 and 1949 reflect the economic and political dissatisfaction of the people of Uganda?
2. What was the impact of Sir Andrew Cohen's administration economically and politically?
3. Trace from 1958 to 1962 the political developments in Uganda.
4. What did the Uganda Revolution of 1966 achieve?
5. Trace the economic development of Uganda from 1945 to 1962 and show how it prepared the people of Uganda for independence.

Thirty-five – Kenya 1939-75

1. Why did the Mau Mau movement erupt when it did and what factors did this movement reveal?
2. How did the government attempt to reconcile the demands of the white settlers with the political aspirations of the Africans?
3. Try to examine the reaction of the settlers to the fact that Kenya was going to be ruled by the Africans after all.

4. Why did Kenya become independent with a federal constitution and why was this constitution changed soon afterwards?

Thirty-six – Tanganyika 1939-75

1. Trace the constitutional developments in Tanganyika from 1945 to 1953.
2. How did TANU originate and how did it develop as a mass movement?
3. Trace the political developments in Tanganyika from 1954 to 1961.

Thirty-seven – Independence and Economic Development in East Africa

1. Why did the idea of an East African Federation fail to be implemented?
2. Trace the co-operation of the East African states from 1924 to 1963.
3. Examine how the East African Common Market is working.
4. What efforts have been made by each East African Government to promote rural development and commercial enterprises for the Africans?

Thirty-eight – Ethiopia

1. Why did Axum play such an important part in the early history of Ethiopia?
2. Describe the various attempts made by the Italians to extend their influence in Ethiopia.
3. Account for the gradual decline of the central government from the seventeenth century to the mid-nineteenth century.
4. What were the effects of the Second World War on Ethiopian history?

Thirty-nine – The Sudan

1. What were the aims of Muhammad Ali in the Sudan?
2. What attempts were made to suppress the slave trade in the Sudan in the nineteenth century?
3. Account for the success of the Mahdi's rising against the British and Egyptian forces.
4. Give reasons for the historical and cultural separation of the north and south in Sudanese history.

Forty – The Development of Education

1. Describe the contribution to education made by the missionaries in the nineteenth century.
2. What were the main reasons for the growth of secondary education in Kenya and Uganda?
3. Explain the philosophy of 'education for self reliance'.

Forty-one – Railways in Kenya and Uganda

1. Describe the main difficulties encountered in the building of the railway from Mombasa to Nairobi.

2. To what extent does Nairobi owe its existence to the railway?

3. Why did the authorities use indentured Indian labour in the construction of the railway?

4. What were the major consequences in Kenya and Uganda following the building of the railway?

Forty-two – Railways in Tanganyika 1900-63

1. What were the three railways planned by the German East African Company?

2. Give reasons for the railways operating at a loss after the First World War.

3. What economic factors influenced the construction of railways in the years after the Second World War?

Index